891106

DATE DUE

AUG 1 0 1990			

DEMCO NO. 38-298

Contemporary Political Culture

Contemporary Political Culture

Politics in a Postmodern Age

edited by
John R. Gibbins

SAGE Modern Politics Series Volume 23
Sponsored by the European Consortium for
Political Research/ECPR

S SAGE Publications
London · Newbury Park · New Delhi

First published 1989

SAGE Publications Ltd
28 Banner Street
London EC1Y 8QE

SAGE Publications Inc
2111 West Hillcrest Drive
Newbury Park, California 91320

SAGE Publications India Pvt Ltd
32, M-Block Market
Greater Kailash – I
New Delhi 110 048

British Library Cataloguing in Publication Data

Contemporary political culture: politics in a
  postmodern age. – (Sage modern politics series; 23).
  1. Politics
  I. Gibbins, John R., *1945*–
  320

  ISBN 0-8039-8176-7
  ISBN 0-8039-8177-5 Pbk

Library of Congress catalog card number 88-64171

Typeset by AKM Associates (UK) Ltd, Southall, London
Printed in Great Britain by J.W. Arrowsmith Ltd, Bristol

Contents

Preface

Genuine conversation is the ideal breeding ground for academic research and the workshop on politics and culture which took place in Amsterdam in 1987, under the auspices of the European Consortium for Political Research, proved to be both stimulating and fertile. All of the contributions below, with the exception of Bryan S. Turner's paper on Daniel Bell, were presented and hotly debated over a week. All have undergone review and revision in preparation for this book and are presented jointly as an effort to re-open a debate on the contours and directions of change in contemporary political culture.

Unfortunately, space for all the contributions to the work-shop could not be found here, but elements of at least three can be found in contemporary journals (Bianchini, 1987a,b; Knudsen, 1987; Leite-Viegas, 1987). However, thanks are due to all of the contributors to the workshop whose ideas are in evidence here. Special thanks are due to Philip Daniels from the University of Newcastle upon Tyne for his paper, his encouragement and chairmanship while acting as co-director for the workshop, to Bryan S. Turner and to Ronald Inglehart for their valuable contributions under pressure. Thanks are due to Michael Laver for valued comments on the manuscript, to Graham Land, to Teesside Polytechnic and especially the Data Preparation Section for their help with a manuscript and the conference organization.

Finally, thanks must be given to my family and friends without whom the opportunity and energy to produce this book would not have been available.

1

Contemporary Political Culture: an Introduction

John R. Gibbins

Contemporary Political Culture is written to tackle several issues at the heart of recent political thought and experience. What changes, if any, have occurred in the political cultures of modern industrial states in the last thirty years? Is there any uniform direction or pattern in the changes that are occurring? Are the changes identified explicable within established cultures and paradigms, or do they signify a break with the past and a new beginning? Does a 'new politics' accompany the new political cultures? While neither agreeing on the answers to these questions nor advocating a common method, theory or paradigm, the authors of these essays are agreed that major changes in political culture have taken place on a scale and of a character that demand this reappraisal of both contemporary political culture and political cultural literature.

New ideas and sometimes new concepts have entered contemporary political science which indicate the transformations in the political culture and behaviour of industrial societies in the last three decades. Terms such as dealignment, realignment, volatility, incivism, decline, crisis and especially legitimation crisis, discontinuity, incongruity, dissonance, cleavage, fragmentation, dissensus and overload reflect the type of changes that have made the terrain of contemporary politics seem unfamiliar and very definitely new. These changes include alterations in party support and voting behaviour; the decline of consensus politics and the re-emergence of conviction politics; the decline of trust, of pluralism and along with it the marginalization of pressure groups; the emergence of new social movements such as feminism, environmentalism and sexual politics; the re-emergence of ideological politics and especially of the new right; the rise of terrorism, political violence, rising crime accompanied by declining levels of interest and participation in politics; increasing exposure of citizens to political information via the new media, the computer and videotex industries; the politicization of new areas of life and the depoliticization of many others, the decline of old style and the emergence of new style politics. Faced with such changes and the subsequent challenges to political science the authors brought together below have addressed the four questions above and have provided new critical, analytic and interpretative answers.

This introduction tackles these points above by first reviewing the dominant literature that informed political culture in the 1960s and 1970s and by reviewing the key changes taking place in contemporary politics and culture and the theoretical attempts to understand them. It ends with a review of the contributions to this collection and draws some tentative conclusions as to the character of contemporary political culture. However, the most original contribution of this introduction and collection to the contemporary debate is the application and testing of postmodernistic theory and the postmodern paradigm to contemporary political culture. We aim to introduce political scientists to the idea of postmodern politics and of a postmodern political culture.

History and definitions

During the 1960s, at a highpoint in confidence in political science, the place of the study of political culture appeared secure. Several individualist theories, such as existentialism, and various rational action and games theories, found no place for the holistic notion of a culture but approaches as diverse as Parsonian pattern variable analysis, Dahl and Easton's systems theory, Almond's functionalism, Oakeshottian idealism, Winchian anthropology and several varieties of Marxism were supportive. To Marxists political culture was a dependent variable but to all others it was taken seriously as an independent or at least an interdependent variable. To systems theorists and functionalists culture was a part of the political environment of a society, while to idealists and Winch, a culture or a form of life was a constituent of and a precondition for understanding and engaging in a political practice. Today, as ever, an agreement to use the language and methods of political cultural study and to attach explanatory significance to political culture, signifies little more than that. There is little or no agreement on the definition and theories of, methods for and paradigms of political culture. Indeed the concept of political culture has many members to its family, few of which share much more than a common name.

The study of political culture underwent first of all stagnation and then a gradual retreat during the 1970s. First order research and contributions adopting the concepts and methods of political culture research became rare, and a dull consensus emerged around the research paradigm of Almond and Verba, transported variously to Britain, Germany, and to the rest of the Western world (1963). There were several reasons for this demise most of which are analysed in the timely and influential survey of the state of the field by Max Kaase in 1982.

At the heart of the problem for political cultural studies lay three problems, (a) definition, (b) paradigm conflict, and (c) operationalization. The problem of plurality and incommensurability in conceptual definition has been highlighted by several commentators (Kaase, 1982; Kavanagh, 1983: 19; Patrick, 1984). Definitions seem to fall into four categories according to Kavanagh:

1　Psychological accounts which stress the individual's orientation to political objects (Parsons and Shils, 1951; Almond and Verba, 1963).

2　Comprehensive sociological accounts which include both individual orientations and behaviour which carries orientations (Fagan, 1969; Tucker, 1973; Geertz, 1983).

3　Objective definitions which define culture in terms of the consensual or dominant values and norms embedded in society (Durkheim, 1933).

4　Heuristic definitions, those that provide hypothetical or ideal type constructs employed to explain partial phenomena, such as authoritarian or cynical beliefs and behaviour (Weber, 1968; Bell, 1964; Lipset, 1960: Ch. 4).

But we may add other categories since political culture has also been defined as:

5　Linguistic, a discourse of meanings for a group (Winch, 1958; Pekonen, this volume).

This last category has many merits, fitting as it does within the wider consensus concerning the fundamental place of language, discourse and semantics in the human and social worlds.

A final category would perhaps satisfy W.J.M. Mackenzie if we called it:

6　Equivocations, a multiplicity of definitions, which only shift the burden of defining a political culture to such ideas as national culture, political identity and dominant ideology (Mackenzie, 1967, 1978).

All of these accounts of political culture have undergone ruthless critical examination. One new and illuminating contribution to the debate is provided by Richard Topf (this volume), for whom a political culture is 'the form of the moral order' of a society.

Paradigms of political culture

The multiplicity and incommensurability of paradigms of political culture echoes the definitional problems. We may benefit from a short review of paradigms popular before the emergence of Ronald Inglehart's *Silent Revolution* (1977b). Functionalist and pattern variable analysis of political culture attributes to value conformity and conflict a central determining role in explaining political behaviour (Durkheim, 1933; Parsons, 1966). To Durkheim and Parsons values and norms are a species of social facts, the glue or cement of a society. The failure of a society to create and maintain an agreed culture, however consensual or pluralist, would produce behavioural and structural problems and changes that could threaten the social body. In the hands of Gabriel Almond and Sidney Verba, as well as of Richard Rose in Britain, the paradigm required that a natural set of norms and values be discovered and that both research and practical politics explore the cultural preconditions for stable and effective government in a variety of states. Such a view was premised not only upon questionable sociological assumptions, such as the correlation of value dissensus and political stability, but it rested on several ideological assumptions, namely that it was the job of governments and political science to maintain stability and organize gradual change. With the *civic culture* thesis there was also the prejudgement of the moral superiority of democracy, and in 'convergence theory' the assumption that all cultural roads would lead to a civic culture.

Systems theory, which arose in the 1960s, tried hard to remove these contestable political assumptions, by judging each polity as a system whose survival depended upon supplying the outputs that the particular system needed (Easton, 1965). Two major problems appeared: one, that questionable sociological and biological assumptions came to replace the political, and secondly, that political culture was allocated to the political environment away from the centre of political activity and behaviour. From here on the problem arose as to how values (context) influenced behaviour (text) and how the output of systems behaviour fed back into the environment. Again assumptions about the undesirable and asystemic nature of certain values and behaviour abounded and political cultural research became marginalized within political science.

Marxism provided the third major paradigm approach to political culture, and this too seemed to relegate the study of political culture to a secondary role. Traditionally, Marxists conceived political culture to be a part of the superstructure of society, an epiphenomenon, a reflection of economic relations. Cultural norms and values were determined by the economic and social base in society. As the economic and social base was fractured into classes, so was culture, which took on the picture of a war between the dominant culture of the ruling class and a variety of class subcultures. Such a picture was crudely reductionist and overdetermined, it oversimplified the variety and character of cultures within a society and underestimated massively the role and significance of culture in creating and maintaining a hegemonous order in society. Amendments were originally provided by Antonio Gramsci, and subsequently Lukacs, Korsch, Bloch, Adorno, Benjamin, Mandel, Leclau and today Stuart Hall have exploited his model (Hall, 1988a; Gramsci, 1971).

Hegemony theory argued that values of all sorts may play a central role in creating and maintaining a culture. Ideas and values are products of popular consent and hence any party or government needs success in constructing, selling and defending a legitimating set of ideas. A culture is not immediately natural nor determined by the economy or social class, but is a response to 'current relations of force' and is the effect of political power conflicts. A society always witnesses a plurality of conflicting hegemonies seeking, but rarely achieving, dominance. The study of political culture is then the historical account of their emergence, a critical analysis of the political and economic forces they represent, a study of their internal character and a rigorous critique or negation of their logic and effect. In practice, Gramsci insists on the practical need for groups regularly to construct anew their political cultures and to delegitimate those of their opponents. Once a prerogative of socialist political scientists, hegemony has gained converts from other positions on the political spectrum, and as we shall see, Hall and others consider its most conspicuous success to be the creation of a hegemonic authoritarian culture by contemporary conservatives (Hall, 1988a; Brown, 1984). This paradigm can be subjected to criticisms, for its overreliance on voluntary consent and instrumentality, downplaying, as it appears to, evidence of continuity and the unconscious reproduction of political culture witnessed by Durkheim, Almond and Verba and Rose. More recently, Bryan Turner and others, have argued that the 'dominant ideology' paradigm was both misconceived and unnecessary. Political harmony and order could best be guaranteed not by hegemony but by dissensus, not by consensus but by a plurality of cross-cutting cleavages and pure pragmatism (Turner et al., 1980; Lipset, 1960: 33–4; Mann, 1970, 1973; Held, 1987: 182).

Wittgenstein, Oakeshott and Winch seem an unlikely group to found a paradigm of political culture, and their avoidance of the phrase confirms our discomfort. However, all three argued, in one language or another, that what holds a society together, what makes actions possible and meaningful was a tradition of beliefs and practices, a language game and an accompanying practice or form of life. A society is a moral community joined by a common subscription to a language, to some rules of life, some techniques of discourse and debate, and a practice or 'going on'. Within a society a plurality of languages, conversations or cultures may practise alongside each other, politics being the public activity by which citizens negotiate, within the language, about these rules and practices. Political culture is the largely unself-conscious attitudes, beliefs and norms of political association within and between subcultures, and their embodiment in practices and institutions. Elusive in character, eschewing operationalization and implicitly conservative, this account has found few friends, though the work of Alasdair MacIntyre (1984, 1988) has suggested its heuristic value (Rengger, this volume).

Methodology

Whether the defects of these paradigms can be overcome or the paradigms made synchronic can be discussed later, after note has been taken of the methodological problems within traditional political cultural theories. As already noted, political culture is a holistic concept which has required macrolevel theory and analysis to make it operational. First, this has posed problems at the intersection between macro- and microlevel studies and has left research somewhat stranded as the social sciences have warmed to more individualistic methods of analysis. Secondly, methodological problems have dogged efforts to identify, measure and correlate cultural phenomena. Difficult at the local level, they have become formidable at the comparative level. How can we categorize and measure cultural orientations, how can we claim to know the minds of others, and identify normative factors? Once these questions are answered do we adopt mass survey or in-depth interviews, content analysis, or projective experimental techniques? What are the relations between culture and political culture, how can we determine the relationships between structure, behaviour and culture, can all hypotheses be tested and how? These and many other problems concerning the explanatory potential of political culture had surfaced by the late 1970s and a silent retreat from its once central position within political science resulted. Richard Topf, Detlef Jahn, Rüdiger Schmitt and Michael Minkenberg have tackled these questions and provide stimulating answers in this volume.

The civic culture

Through the 1970s the results of various national and international research efforts emerged, but until the new database and paradigm of postmaterialism was introduced by Ronald Inglehart, the dominant model of Western political culture was that made famous in *The Civic Culture* (Almond and Verba, 1963, 1980), and in Seymour Lipset's *Political Man* (1960: Ch. 3). To its adherents, political culture was defined as 'a particular distribution of political attitudes, feelings, information and skills', or as, 'political orientations – attitudes toward the political system . . .' (Almond and Powell, 1984: 37; Almond and Verba, 1963: 13). Orientations may be of three sorts, cognitive (knowledge), affective (feelings) and evaluative (values). Holistic assumptions were made about the character and function of a political system, and to allow for empirical testing four ideal types of political culture blending the cognitive, affective and evaluative orientations in various patterns were created. After conducting five national surveys, using stratified, multistage, probability samples, the authors were able to confirm distributions of three types: the parochial or traditional culture; the participant or rational activist culture, and the subject or deferential culture. While all political cultures are somewhat mixed, only the 'civic culture' blends and balances the elements in such a way that a stable and effective democracy can be maintained – the blend appropriate here being a mix of subject-participant cultures combining trust and a strong deference to authority with a positive attitude to the goods of active participation. The five-nation survey discovered that only in Britain, and to a lesser extent in the United States, was the civic culture blend present alongside the structures of an effective and legitimate democracy.

With minor exceptions such an explanation of British political culture became the everyday norm of Western political scientists (Christoph, 1965; Parkin, 1972; Miliband, 1973; Kavanagh, 1971, 1972; Pateman, 1973; Rose, 1965). The civic ideal paradigm of the British as feeling competent about and trustful towards politics, knowing and doing just enough, and knowing when to defer to authority or wisdom, was used to explain Britain's non-revolutionary road to modernism, the effectiveness of its structures and processes, and the consensual and non-combative nature of its party and group conflicts (Kavanagh, 1974). Only on the peripheries of society (Lipset and Rokkan, 1967) and amongst working-class authoritarians (Lipset, 1960; Almond, 1954) did civic culture theorists see challenges and sources of change. Why then did this model come to lose its appeal? We should look for defects in the original research programme; at advances in theoretical perspective, and at actual changes in political culture itself.

Internal critiques of the civic culture are readily available within *The Civic Culture Revisited* and are best exemplified in the essay by Carol Pateman (Almond and Verba, 1980). To Pateman the main thesis of civic culture is premised upon an ethnocentric, Anglo-American confidence in liberal democracy; indeed, it is little more than this plus a 'celebration of the role of political apathy and disinterest' (Pateman, 1980: 58). Secondly, the thesis is never properly grounded, indeed Pateman argues that:

> Despite the claims of empirical theorists, they have not produced a convincing account of the relationship between the pattern of attitudes and activity revealed in their findings and the political structure of the liberal democracies. (1980: 58)

Other critics note that the evidence provided could suggest either that democratic structures cause civic culture or vice versa. But these critics were followed by researchers who, either using the original database or updates, using similar methods and assumptions, began to draw different conclusions, which either suggested defects in the original data analysis or that change was taking place in Western societies. Originally finding only new and more persistent cleavages (Christoph, 1965; Mann, 1970; Held, 1984, 1987), later reviewers began to discover weakening in orientations and allegiances, culminating in the recent thesis of the 'decline' of civic culture (Goldthorpe et al., 1968; Kavanagh, 1980, 1985; Marsh, 1977; Beer, 1982). Today, once confident adherents of the civic culture hypothesis are amongst those speaking of a 'crisis' in British, and indeed Western, political culture (Kavanagh, 1985; Beer, 1982; Norton, 1985). Characterized by a decline in deference, cynicism towards politics, a rise in instrumental rationality, a collapse of traditional attitudes and allegiances with a concomitant rise of new attitudes and allegiances, this crisis in culture was related to class and party dealignment, at first a weakening of allegiances (Goldthorpe et al., 1968), then volatility, and finally, the prospect of cultural or legitimation crisis (Butler and Stokes, 1971; Crewe et al., 1977; Harrop and Miller, 1987; Held, 1984, 1987). So, by the late 1970s, political culture, especially for British political scientists, had become problematic because traditional concepts, methods, theories and paradigms no longer seemed to have the same level of explanatory value and support.

Inglehart and postmaterialism

Apart from neo-Marxist critiques and reappraisals the only serious attempt to reconstruct a paradigm of political culture came from Ronald Inglehart. While the former updated and reapplied the notion of hegemony introduced by Gramsci, which suggested that new cultures were ebbing and flowing, being recreated primarily by new elements in the ruling classes (Miliband, 1973, 1983; Parkin, 1972;

Hall, 1976, 1988a), Inglehart considered that a fundamental shift had taken place in the water level of culture. While Parkin analysed conflicts between 'radical', 'subordinate' and 'dominant' cultures, and Hall began to explain how deviant cultures were created and controlled, Inglehart tested his novel hypothesis of postmaterialism.

Sponsored by the European Community Inglehart's six-nation study stimulated the production of a new database on political values. In addition he had a new motive; he not only intuitively recognized value change, especially amongst the young in the West, but he also noticed serious changes in the political behaviour and support for political parties. Most obviously he noticed the decline of class alignments in political party choice, the emergence of new political movements like feminism, and the growth of lifestyle and consumer issues in modern politics. The aim of the project was to test whether the sustained experience of economic growth and relative world peace since 1945 was connected with new forms of expressive political activity and new political movements through the development of postmaterialist values and attitudes. Building on generational models of political cultural change (Butler and Stokes, 1971), he argues that the unique socialization and experience of the postwar period, where basic needs had generally been met, had produced needs of a higher kind, for self-realization, self-esteem, affection, a better quality of life and improved social relationships. While older generations, socialized in periods of material need, retained materialistic and acquisitive values, preferring a higher standard of living and security, the new generations developed postbourgeois or postmaterialist needs and values. In like manner those most exposed to affluence and education, the middle class, were more likely to develop new values than the working classes, and those societies experiencing higher levels of economic affluence and peace would score most highly in terms of postmaterial orientation.

Not only did it appear that Inglehart's hypothesis was confirmed by his research, but his predictions that new forms of political expression would emerge, involving new and somewhat unconventional political groupings, came to fruition in the form of alliances around ethnicity, environmentalism and peace; new movements such as feminism and new trade unions. Indeed new symbolic and lifestyle politics emerged in the form of Green politics and in the concentration upon images and optional lifestyles in conventional party performance and literature. These developments have in turn supported the claim that there was a gradual move from 'old' to 'new' politics in Western Europe, with the new politics being an expression of postmaterialistic values (Barnes and Kaase, 1979; Baker et al., 1981; Habermas, 1983, 1984; Müller–Rommel, 1989). The politics of lifestyle had arrived but so had the politics of the life cycle. From now on, values and orientations, allegiances, alignments and political groupings would be fluid, the shock of the new would be a permanent feature of the new world as one generation replaced another and as 'period' effects were absorbed (Braungart and Braungart, 1986).

Additional survey work in 1973, 1976, 1979, and subsequent analysis have produced some modifications in the original model. In 1977 Inglehart moved to concentrate upon 'the need to understand and measure subjective well-being' as he sought to explain why in the affluent West reported levels of happiness were at a low ebb (1977a: 430). Working from the notion of 'relative deprivation' it was discovered that reported satisfaction levels between materialists and postmaterialists showed little variation. Only the recently prosperous recorded a short-term sense of gratification. Amongst postmaterialists only short-term improvements in lifestyle and quality of life induced reported increases in satisfaction. Rapidly consumed, these changes gave way to further needs to consume and higher levels of dissatisfaction, and on this basis Inglehart predicted increasing levels of protest potential amongst the middle classes (1977a: 456). Following the oil crisis and recession in the late 1970s a new question was asked, 'have the economic uncertainty and the deterioration of East–West detente in recent years produced a sharp decline in Post-Materialism? As yet we see, the answer is No' (Inglehart, 1981: 880). However, a sharpening in the political cleavage between materialists and postmaterialists was detected, correlating with preferences for rearmament, reindustrialization on the one hand and arms limitation, a welfare society and postindustrial solutions on the other (1981: 898). However, subsequent surveys have revealed that young people socialized since the mid-seventies show a decline in the ratio of postmaterialists to materialists compensated for by increases in the older cohorts, thus confirming the generational nature of the attitudinal change. The most recent development of the postmaterial thesis is offered in this volume by Michael Minkenberg (one of Inglehart's research students and with his approval); it explains new political cleavages and the rise of the new right in the Western world as reactions to the rise of postmaterialism and postmaterialistic political alliances.

Reception of Inglehart's work has been slow and fairly restricted to the field of political science. Though praised by Jürgen Habermas the postmaterialist theory of contemporary culture has not been widely analyzed by psychologists and sociologists in Europe. Criticisms have also been muted within political science, with only a few requiring Inglehart to make any defence or modification of his claims (Flanagan, 1980; Inglehart, 1982, 1985; Inglehart and Flanagan, 1987). One debate refers to the dichotomy of value preferences. Flanagan prefers to add an authoritarian/libertarian component to the scheme; and he adds new methods of measurement. Flanagan then argues that Inglehart's data on optional value preferences all support his own hypothesis. Finally, he claims that the presence of a postmaterialistic culture does not necessarily lead to changed behaviour patterns. In Japan, intergenerational value change was not accompanied by the emergence of postmaterialist lifestyles, political movements and alliances. Worse still, Suhonen (1985) argues that value change had gone in an opposite direction to that which Inglehart had predicted, with the 15–24 age group in the late 1970s showing more materialistic concerns than its predecessors in the early 1970s. Adding weight to the methodological argument Milton Rokeach has produced an alternative 18-item questionnaire which he considered would cover a wider scale of social values (Rokeach, 1973, 1979). Both Rokeach and Suhonen have discovered in their surveys that the most popular combinations of value preferences were for the satisfaction of the more physiological needs, health and peace, and that generational change and value revolution had been overstated. While departing from Inglehart on interpretation, Bo Reimer has confirmed Inglehart's research findings on this question in a contemporary Swedish survey (Reimer, this volume).

Contemporary theories: hegemony and consumer culture

At the turn of this decade sporadic and spasmodic evidence of a revival in interest in political culture began to appear with little sign of convergence on methods or interpretation (Welch, 1987; Wildavsky, 1985, 1987) with one major exception, the field of Communist Studies. Emerging from Oxford University and from Professor Archie Brown in particular, and based on the journal *Studies in Comparative Communism*, a major debate emerged on the methods and efficiency of the attempt to impose a hegemonic culture of socialist man upon traditional cultures in communist Eastern Europe (Brown, 1984; Brown and Gray, 1979; White, 1979; Jancar, 1984; Symposium on Political Culture, 1983; Krisch, 1986; Almond, 1983):

> Communist revolutions can readily be interpreted as self-conscious efforts on the part of Leninist revolutionary elites to impose a universal way of life (Soviet plus electrification) on all humanity. This is in every case a *new* way of life, so that communist revolutions aim for the replacement of one *culture* by another. Communist revolutions thus are wars between cultures. (Meyer, 1983: 6)

Relatively unread outside Soviet Studies specialists, the debate has produced new methods for tapping both the cultural ideals and methods of elites and the value responses of citizens. Exploring the ability of groups to manufacture a political culture it works from non-Marxist assumptions and, not surprisingly, finds that the results of socialist experiments had generally been poor (Jancar, 1984: 71).

In academic fields outside mainstream political science, research of great significance to cultural studies was surfacing (Featherstone, 1983, 1985, 1987; Hebdige, 1979; Leiss, 1983; McKendrick et al., 1982; Bourdieu, 1985; Robertson, 1985; Elias, 1978, 1982, 1983; Lyotard, 1984; Baudrillard, 1984). One major area concerned the cultural imperatives of capitalism and late capitalism and the tensions and crises that were in evidence during the change (Bell, 1976; Habermas, 1976, 1983, 1984; Offe, 1985; Held, 1987; Lash and Urry, 1987). In this area, discussed by Bryan Turner in this volume, an argument emerges that in late 'disorganized' stages of capitalist development culture becomes the scene of radical change. Because of changes in work practices, production, new technologies and the mass media, and because of exposure to the new consumer society, conflict had emerged between modern culture and the economic and social structure of bourgeois society. In postindustrial society these writers also observe a rise of more hedonistic, narcissistic and expressivist cultures that undermined bourgeois culture and subsequently bourgeois society and economy. To Habermas the crisis extended not only to value attitudes but into the level of motives, and with Offe he argues that the new economy and state are incompatible and contradictory. In this view modern states which sought to solve the economic crisis of unemployment and inflation did so by overextending and overloading themselves and by encouraging citizens to widen their needs and expectations (Brittan, 1975, 1977, 1988). The social democracy, welfare and consumerist society that followed created problems of unmet political demand and this produced a political crisis over the ability of parties and the state to deliver, which in turn resulted in motivational and legitimation crisis. Offe and Habermas were confident that any attempt by the state to divest its role as manager of the economy, provider of welfare and opportunities for consumption, would be rejected.

Yet this strategy of 'rolling back the state' has, with the astute creation and management of social and political culture, had great success in Britain, the United States and other Western countries (Brittan, 1975, 1977, 1988; Daniels, 1987; Hall, 1988a). By constantly recreating human needs, by providing a bewildering array of 'options' and 'distinctions' by which the successful self can realize its goals; by creating a repressive sphere for the dependent, the poor, the lazy; and by propagating a culture of independence, freedom and enterprise, both the market and the welfare state in Britain and the United States have sought to avoid disenchantment. At what expense and with what effects will be for future generations to discover.

However, this resurgence of interest in culture has been disappointing for political science research. First, no new consensus on how to overcome the problems of conceptualizing political culture has emerged and little advance has taken place in fields of political theory and macropolitical analysis. Secondly, few successful efforts have been made to construct a research methodology that would show the efficacy of political culture as a research frame. Worse still, there are few good examples of the production of first-order research in political culture.

Three responses to this situation have been explored, the first being the abandonment of the concept as a centre for political science research. This has been both explicitly advanced and implicitly followed by some researchers. The second response has been to advance actively the merits of eclecticism in the hope that piecemeal research will achieve what larger research efforts had failed to obtain (Kaase, 1982: 32). A third involves an attempt to reconstitute and reconstruct the theory and methods of political culture.

At present, despite the efforts of the Birmingham Centre for Contemporary Cultural Studies and other such centres[1] to develop the third route, the greatest hope appears to lie with pluralism and eclecticism. Material for and the possibility of synthesis are available despite the fact that:

> There is no single definition of culture on which everyone would agree. There are no universally accepted classifactory categories which everyone would accept as the most useful; and the various causal relationships provided as explanations of cultural phenomenon may be plausible, but remain unverifiable; and too many of them have plausibility. (Meyer, 1983: 8)

It was at this juncture that a workshop on 'Politics and Culture' was convened at Amsterdam in 1987 under the auspices of the European Consortium for Political Research with three general aims. The first aim was to draw together European academics researching in the fields of culture, and, by concentrating their efforts and utilizing their methods and knowledge, to chart the correct state of political cultural research and to endeavour to give new impetus to contemporary research. The second aim was to ask whether there had been a major shift in the orientation of citizens towards politics and political institutions in the modern world. A number of questions were on the agenda: How, if at all, had political culture changed in the past three decades? What were the main determinants of this change? Did the rise of expressivist and consumerist culture affect political activity and how? Did the new styles of political participation, new political movements, match the new political culture or must we expect a deepening crisis in both political practice and culture? How, if traditional political cultures are being eroded, can obedience and order be maintained? Are the cultures associated with new exclusivist movements such as feminism, the peace movement and terrorism, compatible with a market culture? Finally, in a more ambitious vein, the workshop sought to explore a hypothesis of cultural change already made popular outside political science, the theory of post-modernism and of a postmodern culture (Lyotard, 1984; Vattimo, 1988; MacIntyre, 1984; Berman, 1983; Jameson, 1984; Hassan, 1985; Jencks, 1977).

Postmodernism and political culture

Postmodernism is a relatively new theory which seeks to explain the cultural conditions and effects of the economic, social and political changes which have been elaborated earlier. Without either an agreed testable hypothesis, or agreed definitions, descriptions or a narrative of recent historical events, postmodernism is as yet little more than a macrotheoretical paradigm. However, the heuristic appeal and the potential explanatory value of postmodernism have attracted a wide range of scholars from a wide range of disciplines, several of whom have contributed to this collection of essays.

Originally coined to label an architectural movement that countered the modernist movement associated with Le Corbusier, deconstructing it with an eclectic usage of old and new styles involving pastiche, nostalgia and an awareness of citizens' real needs (Jencks, 1977; Rose, 1988), the term has developed numerous meanings within the context of art, theatre, film, literature, philosophy and sociology. Some usages are descriptive and others prescriptive. Little in the way of a core meaning relates these usages though they do revolve around an understanding that a break has taken place with the period, the practices and culture conventionally labelled as the modern.

Offering alternative answers to the questions of when modernity began and ended and its essential features and character, our various postmodernisms have provided a narrative of dissatisfactions and disenchantment with modernity, of tensions within it that have led to rejection, breakdown, crisis, rupture and eventually a transition to a postmodern age and society. Postmodernism indicates the belief that a new age has begun which transcends the modern and which both explains contemporary behaviour and attitudes and offers a radically new set of experiences, practices and life worlds for its inhabitants. The move from the modern to the postmodern worlds, like that from the classical to the medieval to the modern, were at first imperceptible. But unlike these transitions, and more in line with the development of the Renaissance and Enlightenment movements, postmodernists are conscious of the change. They use it in either a laudatory or pejorative fashion, wringing hands like Nietzsche, Bell, Jameson and MacIntyre or welcoming its newness and its open possibilities like Lyotard, Derrida, Vattimo and Jencks, (Descombes, 1987; Lawson, 1985; Vattimo, 1988). This self-consciousness does much to save post-modernism from the accusation that it is the by-product of a faulty periodization and from the response that the postmodern is no different from the modern or late modern experiences.

The ramifications of a break with modernity and the claimed emergence of a new postmodern world have been weighed by numerous scholars outside political science for over a decade (Baudrillard, 1984; Baynes et al., 1987; Berman, 1983; Featherstone, 1985, 1988; Fekete, 1988; Hassan, 1985; Huyssen, 1984; Jencks, 1977; Kolb, 1986; Kroker and Cook, 1988; Lyotard, 1984; MacIntyre, 1984, 1988). The problematic is how, if at all, order, meaning, legitimacy and morality can exist once absolutism, objectivity, certainty, foundations, commensurability, unity and the prioritized self, are deconstructed? Put more positively, how are society, politics and morality possible when we accept partiality, relativity, uncertainty, the absence of foundations, incommensurability, pluralism, fragmentation and polyculturalism? Efforts within political science to grapple with postmodernism have come largely from theoreticians (Connolly, 1988; Bell, 1976; Jameson, 1984; Ryan, 1988a, 1988b). Yet because post-modernists see the new tendencies not only best exemplified in culture but regard culture as a determining agent we should expect to find the most valuable application of this approach to be in the study of political culture.

This suspicion is fulfilled when we compare a typification and caricature of the postmodern world with the political and cultural changes already observed in contemporary society. Postmodernism is seen to signify a society exhibiting discontinuity between economy, society and polity; the transfer to a postindustrial, information and consumer economy; a reorganization of middle-class employment, income, expenditure and attitudes, especially to work and leisure; heightened conflict between the private and public realms; an eclectic and amorphous culture exhibiting plurality, mixed lifestyles and new attitudes based on immediate gratifications, fantasy, novelty, play, hedonism, consumption and affluence. A postmodernist politics and political culture would highlight a dissatisfaction with modern politics, its sameness, customary allegiances, its predictability, bureaucracy, discipline, authority and mechanical operation, and would stress the emergence of a politics featuring difference, dealignment and realignment, unpredictability, freedom, delegitimization and distrust, power and spontaneity.

So, when applied to politics, postmodernism offers an explanatory paradigm to fit new political phenomena and beliefs variously identified and treated in the recent work on party and class realignment, growing distrust in government, the emergence of new classes, new political movements, and changing political attitudes, the re-emergence of ideology, rhetoric and charisma, and growing power of the media in creating and maintaining new political practices. Fearful of such trends the conservative and traditionalist political response is to seek to maintain order amongst collections of narcissistic, hedonistic, alienated strangers by creating legitimacy and consensus out of private lives fashioned by distrust of politicians and government and the appeal of the private. In practice the successful reactionary politician in the postmodern age concentrates upon political nostalgia, perhaps romanticism, nationalism or theism; upon the invention of tradition (Hobsbawm and Ranger, 1983), on the manufacture and transmission of information and knowledge to present a recognizable and believable world and on recreating ideologies and alliances between ever-changing individuals, movements and groupings. Radical post-modernists, alternatively, see in the new age the approach of a new pluralistic and democratic politics in which tolerance and freedom flourish in communitarian and democratic political activity, which utilizes the new open and public space vacated by the old politics and the consumer society (Bernstein, 1976, 1986); in a fashion reminiscent of the ideas of Hannah Arendt (Arendt 1959, 1961, 1970; Connolly, 1988; Dallmayr, 1984; Bianchini, 1987a, 1987b; Forbes, this volume).

Contemporary political culture: a review of contributions

Five essays in this volume address the theme of postmodern political culture. Bryan Turner argues that: 'Bell largely anticipated, and to some extent worked out, many of the leading issues in the current debates about modernism, postmodernism, and postindustrial society and the rise of narcissistic consumerism.' In so doing Daniel Bell is seen to have sketched the main elements of a political culture defined as postmodern (Bell, 1973, 1976). Turner's picture of new forms of political behaviour and his history of the attendant economic and social changes reveal a remarkable consensus with the description of recent history provided by Inglehart. Where the postmaterialist and postmodernist theses part company is in their characterization of the new culture. While to Inglehart the major change and cleavage is between materialist and postmaterialist attitudes, to Turner the dichotomy is between modernist and postmodernist culture. While postmaterialism is a unified field of attitudes, postmodernism refers more generally to the absence of unity and identity in contemporary culture. In short, a postmodern culture is one with no linear pattern of change nor an identifiable form but is rather a picture of fragmentation, multidirectional change and a psychedelic collage of contemporary attitudes, values and beliefs. Empirical testing of this hypothesis would be difficult in the absence of a unified field of attitudes, but already evidence gained from existing sources is proving fruitful.

Taking as his data set research designed to test the postmaterialist thesis against Swedish young people, Bo Reimer has argued that: 'the value orientations of young people, being directed towards *immediacy*, cannot be contained inside a materialist/postmaterialist value construction.' Arguing that the present value systems of young people are increasingly led by consumer and lifestyle needs that encourage diversity of value orientations, Reimer concludes:

> In this postmodern consumer culture, it seems we have to take into account *a different type of socialization* than that proposed by the Inglehartian model; a socialization that is continuous, forever faced with new, changing situations, leading to diverse value orientations.

Reimer finds that Inglehartian 'collective goals' are less popular than the 'individual values' tested by Milton Rokeach amongst Swedish young people, who seem to prefer 'pleasure', 'an exciting life', 'mature love' and 'looking good'. In the postmodern 'zeitgeist' of the young 'a multitude of possibilities, undreamed of by older generations', opens up. Whole lifestyles may be tried, discarded and replaced, all in the search for 'the ultimate' (Chambers, 1986). All of this – designer clothes, the latest music, style in cars, domestic things, food, holidays – is financially expensive. Postmaterialists have discovered that a high income is required to maintain the quality of life they desire, an element of materialism is a precondition for postmodernism in a postmodern world (Marsh, 1975: 21–39). Ronald Inglehart's interaction with Reimer makes a fitting postscript to this collection. Careful and considerate in style and keeping an open mind on the possibility of change in value priorities, Inglehart argues that 'postmaterialism fits particularly well with postmodernism'. Indeed:

> Though the materialistic/postmaterialistic dimension does *not* encompass any culture as a whole, it seems to be an important factor contributing to the evolution of postmodernist culture that has been discussed by various contributors to this volume.

Introduced originally as an aesthetic concept, the concept found fertile ground in the areas of art, literature, sociology and philosophy. But like the concept of the Renaissance, the Postmodern Age or

Condition has struck a chord across many disciplines and cultures (Featherstone, 1988). As with the Renaissance it now makes sense to ask whether the aesthetic movement is tied to any economic, social, political or wider cultural changes (Hassan, 1985; Huyssen, 1984). As Reimer argues, the suggestion that there may be a postmodern culture sounds absurd, as it seems to belong to a different universe of discourse. But not only is this response dispelled on examination but the concept invites us to read our recent history in a completely new light. Modern history can be presented as the imposition of a universalizing civilizing culture by elite groups who use knowledge and culture as power (Elias, 1978, 1982, 1983; Bourdieu, 1984; Huyssen, 1984). To some like Foucault, self-contained and self-disciplined individuals are created, whose minds, bodies and behaviour are subject to regimes of surveillance, discipline and control. Medicine, psychology, architecture, social work can be seen as parts of the modernizing process that subjected individuals to technical rationality (Foucault, 1967, 1977, 1981, 1984). Yet to others the unforeseen consequence of the civilizing process, of education, of exposure to the market-place of the new, consumerism, technological rationality and efficiency, has been the production of plurality, disunity, polyculturalism, and all on a global scale. Within this world groups jockey for power and status by searching for symbolic distinction. By having the latest style or lifestyle, the 'difference' or 'distinction', groups may increase their 'cultural capital'. The body and the home become the scene, the 'habitus', where political, economic and social conflict are fought out at the cultural level (Honneth, 1986). Postmodernism does not recognize a gradual change in value priorities in the contemporary world but a turmoil of values and preferences, the by-product and waste of centuries of the modernizing process. In the postmodern world the individual is exposed to an unending mass of images, experiences, lifestyles, options, distinctions, voices and choices that make a nonsense of a moral or social order. As MacIntyre points out (1984), in such a culture the language of honour and duty, good manners, and virtues such as benevolence, courage and justice, is unintelligible, only the language of preferences, attitudes and feelings is effective. In response, the recreation or renewal of value discourse and the virtues is now the self-conscious aim of postmodernist politicians as well as intellectuals (Fekete, 1988: i–xix) on both the right and the left (MacIntyre, 1988). In his essay, Turner traces postmodernism back to Nietzsche and the late nineteenth century, and draws a parallel with the Culture of the Baroque.

Ian Forbes's essay 'Nietzsche, Modernity and Politics' elaborates the connection between Nietzsche and Postmodernity. While working with a narrower notion of culture than Reimer, Forbes connects

Nietzsche's prophetic vision of the crisis of modernist culture with two postmodern movements, surrealism and feminism. Surrealism represented 'a more open-ended view of the possibilities and functions of art' and in politics it was a celebration of 'nothing'. In both areas surrealism refused to enclose culture or meaning, it praised the absurd, the grotesque, the different, the antithesis to reason, order and form. Feminism, like surrealism, aims to repudiate conventional politics and by pastiche, parody and deconstruction makes the traditional political culture unfamiliar: 'It sees a political culture which cannot be improved or adjusted; it must be vacated.' In the place of political culture feminism offers no collectivist alternative only a plurality of perspectives, a celebration of the new, personal choice and options (Jagger, 1983; Fraser and Nicholas, 1988: 390–1).

According to Kyösti Pekonen the continuous encounter with the 'new' in the modern situation does not always produce radical and progressivist solutions but can be reactionary, romantic, shallow and conservative. In his essay Pekonen finds the crisis in contemporary Finnish political culture lying in the absence of the political, or rather the truly political. Stressing the importance of symbols and the discourse of signs in postmodernism he argues that his examples:

> reveal politics becoming more abstract, the personalization of politics, and the role of image, which all emphasize the growing importance of political imagery. A growing reliance upon political imagery suggests that the ability of electoral politics to continue giving meaning depends on political identities and identifications where people make these symbolically, or imagine their future through symbols.

In a world of cultural fragmentation and plurality, whose tradition is only nostalgia and revival, most individuals are left experimenting with attitudes, lifestyles and culture in an effort to locate a fulfilling 'habitus'. The body and the home are the main theatres of pleasure, to which political attitudes are appended (Bourdieu, 1984: 432–40). Political attitudes become a part of lifestyle, a consumption in the search for the new.

Comparative political science has always provided the most fertile ground for political cultural research and does so again here in the essay by N.J. Rengger on 'Incommensurability, International Theory and the Fragmentation of Western Political Culture'. Contemporary international theory he considers to be premised on modernist assumptions of rationalism, positivism and pragmatism. Culturally, this theory has been ethnocentric and Western in origin. What is explored is the hypothesis that the current crisis of Western political culture, as defined by Alasdair MacIntyre and revealed in the antifoundational philosophy of Richard Rorty, mirrors a crisis not only in international theory but also in the practice of international relations (Rorty, 1979, 1987). Rengger concludes that 'Western political culture is not only internally fragmented, its paradigmatic status in the international system that grew out of it is increasingly under strain, if it has not already collapsed'. The process of postmodernization may be as global as that of modernization (Robertson and Lechner, 1985).

Collectively these efforts to introduce and apply postmodernism to political science remain highly speculative and are presented as an effort to open a more detailed and rigorous debate. The opening essays in the collection deal with more conventional topics and approaches, offering criticisms and revisions in equal doses. Brian Girvin opens the debate by offering a defence of the general functionalist hypothesis that:

> The disruption caused by political systems since the 1960s will be interpreted as a normal feature of political evolution, when new values and ideas are absorbed, modified, or discarded by the society, rather than the portent of a fundamental realignment in political or social terms.

Applied to Ireland, Britain and the USA, this traditional hypothesis gains qualified approval.

A more radical departure from the dominant paradigm of the 1960s appears in Richard Topf's essay on 'Political Change and Political Culture in Britain, 1959–1987'. Here the conventional paradigm of the 'civic culture' is critically reviewed and left with little of substance intact, with the central arenas of devastation lying in the areas of methodology, the database, and data analysis. Of even greater interest Topf produces some original contemporary evidence from his joint work at Nuffield College with Adrian Heath (Heath and Topf, 1986, 1987; see also Topf and Jowell, 1988). From this new data we learn that high levels of cynicism about politics have persisted from the 1959 *Civic Culture* survey to the present in Britain, and that despite realistic assessments of the low level of influence participation would have, British citizens still felt that they ought to subscribe to political activism at various levels. Of central significance is the finding that education was a great predictor of cultural allegiances, and, increasingly, a trend towards 'moral libertarianism' and 'economic inegalitarianism'.

The debate on postmaterialism and the pivotal role of culture in explaining relationships between the new economy and new political movements is opened with 'Neoconservatism and Value Change in the USA: Tendencies in the Mass Public of a Postindustrial Society' by Michael Minkenberg and Ronald Inglehart using previously unpublished data acquired by the latter. Taking the emergence of new right movements as a new phenomenon and not 'a revival of conservatism', the essay argues that neoconservatism 'is a reaction against a fundamental change in culture and values and that it does not reflect the old cleavages expressed in class and partisan lines but a new cleavage based on value change.' Economic change and the experience of welfare democracy and participation in the new consumer society lessened the attraction of socialism to the old working classes. Neoconservatism is in fact 'a coalition of forces which see their common enemy in the postmaterialist oriented strata of the new left, and their new political agenda'. Neoconservatism includes parts of the 'old left' who felt challenged by the 'new left', and traditional conservative groups. Socialist parties meanwhile seem to attract the new postmaterialists in both the working and middle classes, especially those who are highly educated, working in the service and public sectors. Eroded political allegiances and classes have been replaced by new right alignments reflecting a heightened concern with 'nationalism, law and order, family, religion and bourgeois morality' plus confidence in the values of industrial capitalism and progress. Drawing support from materialists across all classes and generations these new alliances seem threatened in the long run only by the declining size of the old working class and the generational replacement of materialists by postmaterialists.

Two effects that further relate changes in political culture to new movements and new politics are provided by Detlef Jahn and Rüdiger Schmitt. In 'From "Old Politics" to "New Politics": Three Decades of Peace Protest in West Germany', Schmitt challenges the idea of 'continuity' in the peace protest movements of the last four decades, preferring to explain the various waves of protest in terms of 'changes which have been taking place in the West German political culture over the past twenty years'. What characterizes the new wave of protesters is a 'distrust against political authorities' and a positive orientation to political participation, to activism rather than the passive value orientation traditionally associated with German political culture.

In his essay on German and Swedish trade unions, Detlef Jahn has concluded that: 'changes in the political culture and in structural conditions, lead to a redefinition of the normative resources of trade unions and their role in society.' Stranded by the rate of change in a modernized society; orientated by 'instrumental-rational' and 'materialist' logic, most trade unions have found themselves unable to provide an attractive field of values and allegiances in non-economic areas. With some blue collar and most white collar workers developing new attitudes and lifestyles, the new trade unions can either decide to 'broaden their policy concerns to encompass non-work place and non-work issues such as consumer questions, living conditions etc. or suffer internal division and decline'.

Brief mention can be given to several workshop papers that could not, unfortunately, be included in this collection. Of greatest significance were two papers that illustrated the point that political cultures are not 'given' but are products of human activity. Phillip Daniels in 'The Cultural Foundations of a Free Market Economy: Mrs Thatcher's Experiment' (1987) explored the recent effort by the Conservative party in Britain to inculcate a new set of behaviour patterns, value systems and political attitudes. While behaviour has been changed through alterations in the tax system, extending house and share ownership, easing access to private education and health care, this has been aided by the creation and reinforcement of an 'enterprise culture' that sets high store by profit-making, material possession, effort and reward maximization, or possessive individualism. Alternatively, for the area of social policy, we could also usefully explore the recent recreation of a culture of independence or 'self-dependence', as coined by J.S. Mill. In this high value is placed upon self-help, personal responsibility, private consumption, individual rights and freedom of choice, and cultural approbation is attached to welfare dependence, social responsibility, public provision, social rights and the lack of options. Either way, government policy has not been neutral in regard to political culture, but both educative and instrumental. Using both carrots and sticks, education and propaganda, the economic and social policies of the Thatcher government are aimed at transforming political attitudes, values and behaviour (Hall, 1988b; Kavanagh, 1987).

According to Franco Bianchini the attempt to create political cultures appropriate to a postmodern age is not the preserve of the right, and he illustrated this with case studies of the cultural policies of the left in Rome in the 1970s and the Greater London Council before its demise (Bianchini, 1987a, 1987b). In both cases socialists tried to create a hegemonic culture by embracing diversity, by 'establishing a dialogue between the party and the new movements', 'to try to overcome their exclusivism, to respond to political apathy . . .', to fight capitalism also on the terrain of 'personal politics'; and 'consumerism' and 'to unite the fragments, constructing a new consensus around the socialist project'. This attempt to reconstruct a socialist strategy upon postmodernist assumptions will be high on the agenda of debate both within political science and socialist parties in the near future.

Changing values and value conflicts in the political culture of Portugal was introduced as a paper by Jorge Vala-Salvador and Jose M. Leite-Viegas, with a supporting methodological essay by Professor Franz-Wilhelm Heimer sketching out a new interdisciplinary scheme for political cultural research (Heimer, 1987; Vala-Salvador and Leite-Viegas, 1987). The more traditional culture of Ireland was discovered by P.R.O. O'Carroll from Cork, with a special reference to populism, and, by contrast, the rapidly created and changing culture of the newly industrialized colony of Singapore was analysed by John Money from the University of Glasgow (O'Carroll, 1987; Money, 1987). In 'The Paramount Importance of Cultural Sources' Knudsen traced the traditions of foreign policy studies that rely upon cultural sources. In addition he constructed a model that hypothesizes a strong causal relationship between cultural/societal forces and foreign policy orientation and between situational/contextual factors and foreign policy behaviour respectively, giving illuminating evidence from American political cultural and foreign policy decisions (Knudsen, 1987). Finally, Olaf Johansson from Umea, Sweden produced an interesting paper on 'Political Culture, the Mass Media and Change in Sweden: Reactions to the Assassination of the Swedish Prime Minister'.

Conclusions

From a reading of the essays presented in this volume and the current literature several tentative conclusions and suggestions for future research can be made. First, political culture, individual values and value priorities are going through a series of profound changes in the contemporary world. Secondly, that if there is a pattern of change it is in the fragmentation of old cultures and the proliferation of new values, attitudes and attendant behaviour, lifestyles and political movements in their place. Thirdly, that the emerging character of contemporary political culture is pluralistic, anarchic, disorganized, rhetorical, stylized, ironic and abstruse (Kroker and Cook, 1988; Featherstone, 1988; Held, 1987: 241–2). Fourthly, political scientists need to follow some recent political theorists and address the concepts and issues surrounding such notions as modernity, late-modernity and postmodernity (Connolly, 1984, 1987, 1988; Blumenberg, 1983; Habermas, 1981, 1984, 1987; Kolb, 1986; Baynes et al., 1987; Rundell, 1987). In the area of political science study it is as evident as ever that work needs to continue on the concept and paradigms of, and methodology for, the study of political culture, for here plurality and incommensurability are all too obvious. Our survey confirms that old political allegiances, cleavages and alliances are weakening and new ones emerging to the extent that it is now sensible to speak of 'old' and 'new' politics, an 'old' and 'new' right, and an 'old' and 'new' left, for instance. Within both right and left parties the new alliances cut across boundaries so that the new right appeals to the old right groups, and to both old materialists and the recently 'embourgeoisified' amongst the working classes.

In this complex position allegiances will continue to be hard to maintain and will be in constant need of reorganization in the face of generational, lifecycle and period effects. Increasingly, it is likely that the new class of young professionals, the highly educated public servant, private sector managers, technocrats and politicians, with both postmaterialist and materialist value priorities will set the agenda for the new politics, and energy, ethnicity, ecology, gender, rearmament and lifestyle issues will dominate this new agenda. But it is possible to overstress the degree/scope of change, to confuse changes in value priorities for changes in values, and to underestimate the levels of authority in both old politics and traditional values. What we are witnessing is the cumulative effect of gradual changes in value priorities and behaviour causing major stress on parties and old pressure groups. But the concomitant of the increasing priority given to private life, to the immediacy of lifestyle and consumption, the attractive and qualitatively rewarding, could be growing distrust and the delegitimization of politics, parties, government and the state (Connolly, 1984; Blumenberg, 1983). So far evidence suggests that the state can adapt and continue as guardian of the moral order of the political society perhaps with increased power and options.

Finally, we should be increasingly aware that in a postmodern world of plurality and confusion, of information and the media, the opportunities for culture creation are growing. Indeed, as Michael Ryan has observed, 'what postmodernism as a movement has discovered is that what were thought to be effects in the classic theory of representation can be causes; representations can create the substance they supposedly reflect' (1988b: 560). In a world suffering from cultural dissonance and confusion new opportunities arise for the political impressario to create value agendas, cultures and charismatic personalities. One scenario for the future is a world full of 'designer cultures' created for the needs of groups, presented by media persons, film and pop stars, advertisers, sportsmen, evangelists and millionaires, to fill the cultural void left by the collapse of cultural traditions. Political culture in a postmodern world may become more like a script and less an inherited narrative for life.[2] Irrespective of ideological and party allegiances, the politics of postmaterialism and postmodernism have and will intrude into and shape political behaviour and institutions in the contemporary world.

Notes

1. Amongst the most interesting research centres on political culture there are the Unit for Mass Communications at Gothenburg; the Arnold-Bergstraesser Institute in Lisbon; the Institute for Social Research at Michigan; Nuffield College, Oxford; the Glasgow Media Group; the Birmingham Centre for Contemporary Cultural Research.

2. At the time of going to press the British Broadcasting Corporation were carrying a television series on this theme entitled '3 Minute Culture'. The author and introducer, Michael Ignatieff, wrote of the contemporary media and politics, 'In a culture of amnesia, messages are imprinted, not by narrative's enchantment, but by repetition', not by 'catharsis but cleverness'. He writes, 'Right across the media, we have replaced narrative with flow, connection with disconnection, sequence with randomness. The cost is to our memory' (Ignatieff, 1989).

References

Almond, Gabriel A. (1954) *The Appeals of Communism*. Princeton: Princeton University Press.

Almond, Gabriel A. (1983) 'Communism and Political Culture Theory', *Comparative Politics*, 15 (2): 127-8.

Almond, G. A. and Verba, S. (1963) *The Civic Culture: Political Attitudes and Democracy in Five Nations*. Princeton: Princeton University Press.

Almond, G. A. and Verba, S. (eds) (1980) *The Civic Culture Revisited*. Boston: Little, Brown.

Almond, G. A. and Powell Jnr, G. B. (1984) *Comparative Politics Today: a World View*. Boston: Little, Brown.

Arendt, Hannah (1959) *The Human Condition*. New York: Doubleday Anchor.

Arendt, Hannah (1961) *Between Past and Future*. London: Faber & Faber.

Arendt, Hannah (1970) *On Violence*. London: Allen Lane.

Baker, Kendall L., Russell, J.D. and Hildebrandt, K. (1981) *Germany Transformed: Political Culture and the New Politics*. Cambridge: Harvard University Press.

Barnes, Samuel H. and Kaase, M. (eds) (1979) *Political Action: Mass Participation in Five Western Democracies*. London: Sage.

Baudrillard, Jean (1984) *In the Shadow of the Silent Majorities*. New York: Semiotext.

Baynes, Kenneth, Bohman, James and McCarthy, Thomas (1987) *After Philosophy: End or Transformation*. Cambridge, Mass: MIT Press.

Beer, Samuel (1982) *Britain Against Itself: the Political Contradictions of Collectivism*. New York: Norton.

Bell, Daniel (ed.) (1964) *The Radical Right*. New York: Doubleday.

Bell, Daniel (1973) *The Coming of Post-Industrial Society*. New York: Basic Books.

Bell, Daniel (1976) *The Cultural Contradictions of Capitalism*. London: Heinemann.

Berman, Marshall (1983) *All that is Solid Melts into Air: the Experience of Modernity*. London: Verso.

Bernstein, Richard (1976) *The Restructuring of Social and Political Theory*. New York: Harcourt Brace Jovanovich.

Bernstein, Richard (1986) *Philosophical Profiles*. Cambridge: Polity Press.

Bianchini, Franco (1987a) 'G.L.C./R.I.P. Cultural Policies in London, 1981-1986', *New Formations*, 1: 103-17.

Bianchini, Franco (1987b) 'Cultural Policy and Changes in Urban Political Culture: the "Postmodern Response" of the Left in Rome (1976-1985) and London (1981-1986)', paper presented to the workshop on Politics and Culture, ECPR Joint Sessions, Amsterdam.

Blumenberg, Hans (1983) *The Legitimacy of the Modern Age*. Cambridge, Mass: MIT Press.

Bourdieu, Pierre (1984) *Distinction*. London: Routledge & Kegan Paul.

Braungart, M. and Braungart, R.G. (1986) 'Life Course and Generational Politics', *Annual Review of Sociology*, 12: 205–31.

Brittan, Samuel (1975) 'The Economic Contradictions of Democracy', *British Journal of Political Science*, 5: 129–59.

Brittan, Samuel (1977) *The Economic Consequences of Democracy*. London: Temple Smith.

Brittan, Samuel (1988) *A Restatement of Economic Liberalism*. London: Macmillan.

Brown, Archie (ed.) (1984) *Political Culture and Communist Studies*. London: Macmillan.

Brown, Archie and Gray, J. (1979) *Political Culture and Political Change in Communist States*. London: Macmillan.

Butler, David and Stokes, Donald (1971) *Political Change in Britain: Forces Shaping Electoral Change*. Harmondsworth: Penguin.

Chambers, Iain (1986) *Popular Culture: the Metropolitan Experience*. London: Methuen.

Christoph, J. (1965) 'Consensus and Cleavage in British Political Ideology', *American Political Science Review*, 59: 629–42.

Connolly, W.E. (ed.) (1984) *Legitimacy and the State*. Oxford: Basil Blackwell.

Connolly, W.E. (1987) *Politics and Ambiguity*. Madison: University of Wisconsin Press.

Connolly, W.E. (1988) *Political Theory and Modernity*. Oxford: Basil Blackwell.

Crewe, Ivor, Sarvick, B. and Robertson, D. (1977) 'Partisan Dealignment in Britain 1964–74', *British Journal of Political Science*, 7 (2): 129–90.

Dallmayr, Fred. R, (1984) *Polis and Praxis: Exercises in Contemporary Political Theory*. Cambridge, Mass.: MIT Press.

Daniels, Phillip (1987) 'The Cultural Foundations of a Free Market Economy, Mrs Thatcher's Experiment', paper presented to the workshop on Politics and Culture, ECPR Joint Sessions, Amsterdam.

Descombes, Vincent (1987) *Modern French Philosophy*. Cambridge: Cambridge University Press.

Durkheim, Emile (1933) *The Division of Labour in Society*. Toronto: Macmillan.

Easton, David (1965) *A Systems Analysis of Political Life*. New York: Wiley.

Elias, Norbert (1978) *The Civilizing Process*. Vol. 1: *The History of Manners*. Oxford: Basil Blackwell.

Elias, Norbert (1982) *The Civilizing Process*. Vol. 2: *State Formation and Civilization*. Oxford: Basil Blackwell.

Elias, Norbert (1983) *The Court Society*. Oxford: Basil Blackwell.

Fagan, R. (1969) *The Transformation of Political Cultures in Cuba*. Stanford: Stanford University Press.

Featherstone, Mike (1983) 'Consumer Culture', *Theory, Culture and Society*, 1 (3): 1–189.

Featherstone, Mike (1985) 'The Fate of Modernity: an Introduction', *Theory, Culture and Society*, 2 (3): 1–5.

Featherstone, Mike (1987) 'Lifestyle and Consumer Culture', *Theory, Culture and Society*, 4 (1): 55–70.

Featherstone, Mike (1988) 'In Pursuit of the Postmodern: an Introduction', *Theory, Culture and Society*, 5 (2/3): 195–216.

Fekete, John (ed.) (1988) *Life after Postmodernism*. London: Macmillan.

Flanagan, Scott C. (1980) 'Value Cleavages, Economic Cleavages and the Japanese Voter', *American Journal of Political Science*, 24 (2): 178–206.

Foucault, Michel (1967) *Madness and Civilization: a History of Insanity in the Age of Reason*. London: Tavistock.

Foucault, Michel (1977) *Discipline and Punish: the Birth of the Prison*. London: Allen & Unwin.

Foucault, Michel (1981) *The History of Sexuality*, Vol. 1. London: Pelican.

Foucault, Michel (1984) *The History of Sexuality*, Vols 2 & 3. Paris: Gallimard.

Fraser, Nancy and Nicholson, Linda (1988) 'Social Criticisms without Philosophy: an Encounter between Feminism and Postmodernism', *Theory, Culture and Society*, 5 (2/3).

Geertz, C. (1983) *The Interpretation of Cultures*. New York: Basic Books.

Goldthorpe, John H., Lockwood, David, Beckhofen, Frank, and Platt, Jennifer (1968) *The Affluent Worker: Industrial Attitudes and Behaviour*. Cambridge: Cambridge University Press.

Gramsci, Antonio (1971) *Prison Notebooks: Selections*. Tr. Q. Hoare and G.N. Smith. New York: International Publishers.

Habermas, Jürgen (1976) *Legitimation Crisis*. London: Heinemann.

Habermas, Jürgen (1981) 'Modernity versus Postmodernity', *New German Critique*, 8 (1).

Habermas, Jürgen (1983) 'Neoconservative Culture Criticism in the United States and Western Germany', *Telos*, 56: 78–89.

Habermas, Jürgen (1984) *Reason and the Rationalisation of Society*. London: Heinemann.

Habermas, Jürgen (1987) *The Philosophical Discourse of Modernity*. Cambridge: Polity Press.

Hall, Stuart (ed.) (1976) *Resistance through Rituals: Youth Subcultures in Post-war Britain*. London: Hutchinson.

Hall, Stuart (1980) *Culture, Media and Language*. London: Hutchinson.

Hall, Stuart (1988a) 'The Toad in the Garden: Thatcherism among the Theorists', in C. Nelson and L. Grossberg (eds), *Marxism and the Interpretation of Culture*. London: Macmillan.

Hall, Stuart (1988b) *The Hard Road to Renewal: Thatcherism and the Crisis of the Left*. London: Verso.

Harrop, M. and Miller, W.L. (1987) *Elections and Voters: a Comparative Introduction*. London: Macmillan.

Hassan, Ihab (1985) 'The Culture of Postmodernism', *Theory, Culture and Society*, 2 (3): 119–32.

Heath, A.F. and Topf, R.G. (1986) 'Educational Expansion and Political Change in Britain: 1964–1983', *European Journal of Political Research*, 65: 991–1017.

Heath, A.F. and Topf, R.G. (1987) 'Political Culture', in R. Jowell, S. Witherspoon and L. Brook (eds), *British Social Attitudes: the 1987 Report*. Aldershot: Gower.

Hebdige, D. (1979) *Subculture: the Meaning of Style*. London: Methuen.

Heimer, Franz-Wilhelm and Leite Viegas, Jose Manuel (1987) 'Nailing the Pudding to the Wall: Towards an Interdisciplinary Approach to Political Culture', paper presented to the workshop on Politics and Culture, ECPR, Joint Sessions, Amsterdam.

Held, David (1984) 'Power and Legitimacy in Contemporary Britain', in G. McLennan, D. Held and S. Hall (eds), *State and Society in Contemporary Britain*. Cambridge: Polity Press.

Held, David (1987) *Models of Democracy*. Cambridge: Polity Press.

Hobsbawm, Eric and Ranger, T. (1983) *The Invention of Tradition*. London: Cambridge University Press.

Honneth, Axel (1986) 'The Fragmented World of Symbolic Forms: Reflections on Pierre Bourdieu's Sociology of Culture', *Theory, Culture and Society*, 3 (3): 55–66.

Huyssen, Andreas (1984) 'Mapping the Postmodern', *New German Critique*, 33; 5–52.

Ignatieff, Michael (1989) 'Cleverness is All', *The Independent*, Weekend Magazine, 7 January: 25.

Inglehart, Ronald (1977a) 'Values, Objective Needs and Subjective Satisfaction amongst Western Publics', *Comparative Politics*, 9 (4): 429–58.

Inglehart, Ronald (1977b) *The Silent Revolution*. Princeton: Princeton University Press.

Inglehart, Ronald (1981) 'Post-Materialism in an Environment of Insecurity', *American Political Science Review*, 75 (4): 880–900.

Inglehart, Ronald (1982) 'Changing Values in Japan and the West', *Comparative Political Studies*, 14 (4): 445–79.

Inglehart, Ronald (1985) 'New Perspectives on Value Change: Response to Lafferty and Knutsen, Savage and Böltken and Jagodzinski', *Comparative Political Studies*, 17 (4): 485–532.

Inglehart, Ronald and Flanagan, Scott C. (1987) 'Value Change in Industrial Societies', *American Political Science Review*, 81 (4): 1289–1319.

Jagger, A. (1983) *Feminist Politics and Human Nature*. Brighton: Harvester.

Jameson, Frederick (1984) 'Postmodernism, or the Cultural Logic of Late Capitalism', *New Left Review*, 146: 53–92.

Jancar, B. (1984) 'Political Culture and Political Change', *Studies in Comparative Communism*, 17 (1): 69–82.

Jencks, Charles (1977) *The Language of Postmodern Architecture*. New York: Rizzoli.

Kaase, Max (1982) 'The Concept of Political Culture: its Meaning for Comparative Research', *EUI Working Paper*, 30.

Kavanagh, Dennis (1971) 'The Deferential English: a Comparative Critique', *Government and Opposition*, 6 (3): 333–60.

Kavanagh, Dennis (1972) *Political Culture*. London: Macmillan.

Kavanagh, Dennis (1974) 'An American Science of British Politics', *Political Studies*, 22 (3): 251–70.

Kavanagh, Dennis (1980) 'Political Culture in Great Britain: the Decline of the Civic Culture', in Almond and Verba (1980).

Kavanagh, Dennis (1983) *Political Science and Political Behaviour*. London: Allen & Unwin.

Kavanagh, Dennis (1985) *British Politics: Continuities and Change*. Oxford: Oxford University Press.

Kavanagh, Dennis (1987) *Thatcherism and British Politics: The End of Consensus?* Oxford: Oxford University Press.

King, Anthony (ed.) (1976) *Why is Britain becoming Harder to Govern?* London: British Broadcasting Corporation.

Knudsen, Baard (1987) 'The Paramount Importance of Cultural Sources: American Foreign Policy and Comparative Foreign Policy Research Reconsidered', *Cooperation and Conflict*, 22: 81–113.

Kolb, David (1986) *The Critique of Pure Modernity*. Chicago: Chicago University Press.

Krisch, H. (1986) 'Changing Political Culture and Political Adaptability in the German Democratic Republic', *Studies in Comparative Communism*, 19 (1): 41–53.

Kroker, Arthur and Cook, David (1988) *The Post-Modern Scene*. New York: St Martin's Press.

Lash, Scott and Urry, John (1987) *The End of Organized Capitalism*. Cambridge: Polity Press.

Lawson, Hilary (1985) *Reflexivity: the Postmodern Predicament*. London: Hutchinson.

Leiss, William (1983) 'The Icons of the Market Place', *Theory, Culture and Society*, 1 (3): 10–21.

Leite-Viegas, Jose Manuel (1987) 'Telenovelas: do modelo de recepção à diversidade de reconhecimento', *Sociologia*, 2: 13–46.

Lipset, Seymour M. (1960) *Political Man*. London: Heinemann.

Lipset, Seymour M. and Rokkan, Stein (1967) *Party Systems and Voter Alignment*. New York: Free Press.

Lyotard, Jean François (1984) *The Postmodern Condition: a Report on Knowledge*. Minneapolis: University of Minnesota Press.

MacIntyre, Alasdair (1984) *After Virtue: a Study in Moral Theory*. 2nd edn. London: Duckworth. (First edition 1981.)

MacIntyre, Alasdair (1988) *Whose Justice? Which Rationality?* London: Duckworth.

Mackenzie, W.J.M. (1967) *Politics and Social Science*. Harmondsworth: Pelican.

Mackenzie, W.J.M. (1978) *Political Identity*. Manchester: Manchester University Press.

Mann, Michael (1970) 'The Social Cohesion of Liberal Democracy', *American Sociological Review*, 35 (3): 423–39.

Mann, Michael (1973) *Consciousness and Action among the Western Working Class*, London: Macmillan.

Marsh, Alan (1975) 'The Silent Revolution, Value Priorities and the Quality of Life in Britain', *American Political Science Review*, 69: 1–30.

Marsh, Alan (1977) *Protest and Political Consciousness*. Beverly Hills: Sage.

McKendrick, Neil, Brewer, John and Plumb, J.H. (1982) *The Birth of Consumer Culture*. London: Europa.

Meyer, A.G. (1983) 'Cultural Revolutions: the Uses of the Concept of Culture in Comparative Communist Studies', in Symposium on Political Culture, *Studies in Comparative Communism*, 16 (1/2): 1–8.

Money, John (1987) 'Political Culture, Economic Growth, and Regime Stability: the Remarkable Case of Singapore, 1945–1985', paper presented to the workshop on Politics and Culture, ECPR Joint Sessions, Amsterdam.

Miliband, Ralph (1973) *The State in Capitalist Democracy*. London: Quartet Books.

Miliband, Ralph (1983) *Capitalist Democracy in Britain*. Oxford: Oxford University Press.

Müller-Rommel, Ferdinand (ed.) (1989) *New Politics in Western Europe*. Boulder, Colorado: Westview Press.

Norton, Philip (1985) *The British Polity*. London: Longman.

O'Carroll, J.P. (1987) ' "Moving Statues" and Political Change in the Republic of Ireland', paper presented to the workshop on Politics and Culture, ECPR, Joint Sessions, Amsterdam.

Offe, Claus (1985) *Disorganized Capitalism*. Cambridge: Polity Press.

Parkin, Frank (1972) *Class Inequality and Political Order*. London: Paladin.

Parsons, Talcott (1966) *Societies: an Evolutionary Approach*. New Jersey: Prentice Hall.

Parsons, Talcott and Shils, Edward (eds) (1951) *Towards a General Theory of Action*. Cambridge, Mass.: Harvard University Press.

Pateman, Carol (1973) 'Political Culture, Political Structure, and Political Change', *British Journal of Political Studies*, 1 (3): 291–305.

Pateman, Carol (1980) 'The Civic Culture: A Philosophic Critique', in Almond and Verba (1980).

Patrick, Glenda M. (1984) 'Political Culture', in Giovanni Santori (ed.), *Social Science Concepts: a Systematic Analysis*. London: Sage.

Robertson, Roland and Lechner, Frank (1985) 'Modernization, Globalization and the

Problem of Culture in World-Systems Theory', *Theory, Culture and Society*, 2 (3): 103–18.

Rokeach, Milton (1973) *The Nature of Human Values*. New York: Free Press.

Rokeach, Milton (1979) 'Change and Stability in American Values 1968–1971', in M. Rokeach (ed.), *Understanding Human Values: Individual and Societal*. New York: Free Press.

Rorty, Richard (1979) *Philosophy and the Mirror of Nature*. Princeton: Princeton University Press.

Rorty, Richard (1987) 'Posties', *London Review of Books*, 3 September: 11–12.

Rose, Gillian (1988) 'Architecture to Philosophy – the Postmodern Complicity', *Theory, Culture and Society*, 5 (2/3): 357–71.

Rose, R. (1965) *Politics in England*. London: Faber & Faber.

Rundell, John (1987) *Origins of Modernity: the Origins of Modern Social Theory from Kant to Hegel and Marx*. Cambridge: Polity Press.

Ryan, Michael (1988a) *Culture and Politics*. London: Macmillan.

Ryan, Michael (1988b) 'Postmodern Politics', *Theory, Culture and Society*, 5 (2/3): 559–76.

Suhonen, Pertti (1985) 'Approaches to Value Research and Value Measurement', *Acta Sociologica*, 28 (4): 349–58.

Symposium on Political Culture (1983) *Studies in Comparative Communism*, 16 (1/2).

Topf, Richard and Jowell, R. (1988) 'The New Public Morality', in R. Jowell, S. Witherspoon and L. Brook (eds), *British Social Attitudes: the 1988 Report*. Aldershot: Gower.

Tucker, R. (1973) 'Culture, Political Culture and Communist Society', *Political Science Quarterly*, 88 (2): 173–90.

Turner, Bryan S., Abercrombie, Nicholas and Hill, Stephen (1980) *The Dominant Ideology Thesis*. London: Allen & Unwin.

Vala-Salvador, Jorge and Leite-Viegas, J.M. (1987) 'Political Culture in Urban Portugal: Research Findings on Value Patterns', paper presented to the workshop on Politics and Culture, ECPR, Joint Sessions, Amsterdam.

Vattimo, Gianni (1988) *End of Modernity: Nihilism and Hermeneutics in Post-Modern Culture*. Cambridge: Polity Press.

Weber, Max (1968) *Economy and Society*. New York: Bedminster Press.

Welch, Stephen (1987) 'Issues in the Study of Political Culture', *British Journal of Political Science*, 17 (4): 479–500.

White, S. (1979) *Political Culture and Soviet Politics*. London: St Martin's Press.

Wildavsky, Aaron (1985) 'Changes in Political Culture', *Politics*, 20 (2): 95–102.

Wildavsky, Aaron (1987) 'Choosing Preferences by Constructing Institutions: a Cultural Theory of Preference Formation', *American Political Science Review*, 81 (1): 3–21.

Winch, Peter (1958) *The Idea of a Social Science and its Relation to Philosophy*. London: Routledge & Kegan Paul.

2

Change and Continuity in Liberal Democratic Political Culture

Brian Girvin

Since 1945 many liberal democratic states have experienced numerous changes in their societies. These changes have affected the balance of power between states, the relationship between classes within individual states, and the dynamics of the political system itself. Many of these trends have accelerated since the early 1960s, leading to the view that this decade constitutes a fundamental point of departure in the political experience of the postwar liberal democratic political systems (Caute, 1988; Inglehart, 1977). In turn, it has been urged that new values, new types of economic organization and new forms of cultural expression have emerged from this process. Postindustrial society, postmaterialist values and postmodernist culture have in common the belief that there is a radical disjuncture between the bourgeois, industrial and materialist dominance of high capitalism and new identifiable trends (Bell, 1973, 1976; Inglehart, 1977; Hassan, 1985).

It would be difficult to dispute that many new trends are in evidence; what might be questioned is the radical nature of the changes and their implications for political action and behaviour. There is always a tension between the pressure of change and the resistance induced by the traditional elements of continuity. The disruption caused to many political systems since the 1960s, illustrated below by the breakdown of the Keynesian welfare consensus in the United Kingdom and America, can be interpreted as a normal feature of political evolution, when new values and ideas are absorbed, modified, or discarded by the society, rather than the portent of a fundamental realignment in political or social terms. As Stearns (1984) has argued the importance of the changes detected has frequently been exaggerated and the prevalence of continuity has been understressed. These changes, though important, are neither unique nor major and can, it will be argued here, be assimilated historically within the framework established during the early nineteenth century. This can be illustrated by the continuing influence of liberal individualist values, the dominance of capitalist economic organization, and in somewhat different circumstances by the ability of traditional social forces, such as the Roman Catholic

Church in the Republic of Ireland, to resist changes affecting its moral teaching.

In addition, too much stress has been placed upon the impact of economic change. As Bell (1980) has suggested, the rhythm of change within the economic, political and cultural domain has to be disaggregated. Each sphere operates within a distinct set of categories, assumptions, and structures which do not necessarily affect the rhythm of the other sphere. Consequently the process of change is more complex and less uniform comparatively than is sometimes allowed, and too much emphasis on change understates the importance of countervailing features within each system, as the cases of the United States, the United Kingdom and the Republic of Ireland illustrate. Thus, the roles of tradition, class, religion and nationalism have also to be understood in the context of change and not as passive recipients of that change; the dialectic of change involves the interaction between both stable and unstable elements.

The civic culture as the political culture

There is usually a strong association in modern liberal democratic states between the continuity of traditional norms and values and the stability of the society. Almond and Verba (1963) developed the concept of the civic culture, which sought to define the conditions necessary for the achievement of stability. The civic culture, which can be taken as one expression of political culture, pays close attention to values and attitudes current in the society. There is a strong tendency to stress those factors within a society which reinforce continuity, stability and socialization.

The use of culture frequently causes confusion, but here it refers to

> the system of beliefs about patterns of political interaction and political institutions. It refers not to what is happening in the world of politics, but what people believe about those happenings. And these beliefs can be of several kinds: they can be empirical beliefs about what the actual state of political life is; they can be beliefs as to the goals or values that ought to be pursued in political life; and these beliefs may have an important expressive or emotional dimension. (Verba, 1965: 516)

Political culture consequently can be applied more generally than the civic culture which tends to be limited to the developed liberal democratic states. Thus, Almond and Verba in the classic statement emphasize those factors in the culture which reinforce system maintenance (1963: 12); there is consequently '. . . an ordered subjective realm of politics which gives meaning to the polity, discipline to institutions and social relevance to individual acts'. The stress on the integrity of the civic culture is weakened by Almond and

Verba's insistence that the stability of the civic culture is dependent on a dual relationship within the political system between an activist elite and a passive mass. Without this duality, the viability of the political system can, it is claimed, be brought into question (Almond, 1980: 16).

The civic culture remains a powerful analytical tool, recognized even by critics (Almond and Verba, 1980). But it has limited application because it is bound by the political environment of the late 1950s and early 1960s. Its elegance remains both its strength and weakness because it helps explain the stable nature of some states during the early 1960s, while finding subsequent changes far more recalcitrant to its analysis. Political culture, as distinct from but embracing the civic culture, is perhaps less elegant in its formulation, but it does draw attention to the values prized by societies and the political behaviour to which these give rise. It does not, unlike the civic culture, offer a normative criterion for evaluating the democratic status of an individual state. Political culture in this sense attempts to identify those factors in a political system which have a formative political influence on the individual, the group and the society; it further seeks to evaluate the importance of certain values and norms over the long and short term.

While there are numerous meanings for the concept of political culture, it has been used continuously to examine and explain quite diverse political contexts; including those of the Soviet Union and the British working class (White, 1979; Jessop, 1974). Moreover, political culture has been invaluable in explaining the rationale for political conflict based on religion, race or nationality, areas somewhat outside the scope of the traditional civic culture approach. In this sense, all values are of equal analytical importance in that political culture is an attempt to understand why this group acts in a specific way, while another, perhaps quite similar, behaves quite differently (Rosenbaum, 1975).

By appropriating the concept of political culture and subsuming it under the civic culture, Almond and Verba reduced its effectiveness as an explanatory concept for both change and continuity. The civic culture examined stable political cultures, particularly those of Britain and the United States, but neither explained the possibility of instability nor the role that change would play in such a stable environment. The onset of change in the 1960s seriously questioned the validity of the civic culture. Many of the responses to these changes, whether positive or negative, implicitly accepted the civic culture model and predicted that democracy was endangered, that many states were becoming ungovernable, and that there were limits to growth (Hirsch, 1976; Brittan, 1977). If the civic culture approach is accepted in its original form there would have been cause for concern not least because some of the prerequisites identified for political stability were being undermined. Yet unprecedented change, if this it was, need not endanger the long-term stability of a political system if a mechanism is available for internalizing change without endangering the maintenance of core values, even if in attenuated form. This long-term stability will be assured if a society can adapt to the changes while simultaneously experiencing continuity in an overall context (Dowding and Kimber, 1983).

Macro-, meso- and micropolitical culture

This mechanism can be detected if individual political cultures are understood in terms of a broadly macro- and a microlevel of organization. A political culture is a shared pattern of beliefs within which there may be many subcultures but a common source of values which inform those beliefs. The presence of subcultures means that a political culture is not homogeneous in the sense that diversity does not exist, but it does mean that there is an irreducible core to which most, if not all, make reference. Since early in the nineteenth century this 'irreducible core' has been associated with a strong sense of national identity which large numbers of individuals have been able to share. In contrast, this common sense of identity has established the basis for differentiation and enmity between groups that do not share such an identity. The centrality of national identity as a focus for loyalty underpins the continuity of a political culture and provides an important building block for the cohesion of system maintenance. Rustow has suggested that among the emerging liberal democracies, political stability requires this sense of identity: '. . . it simply means that the vast majority of citizens in a democracy – to-be – must have no doubt or mental reservation as to which political community they belong' (1970: 350). This sense of belonging is the key to the macropolitical culture, allowing conflict, often serious conflict, to be mediated without the break up of the political culture or the common sense of identity. Thus serious political upheaval, such as experienced in the United States during the 1960s, does not entail the break up of the system; whereas in other states without a shared identity, such as Northern Ireland, political order may collapse.

The macropolitical culture is rarely questioned by members of the nation. This is what Collingwood (1940: 40–8) has described as 'absolute presuppositions'; those values or meanings which remain uncontested within any group, but in this case within the polity. All individual nationalisms create their absolute presuppositions in the process of growth, usually asserting the ancient origins of its identity (Martin, 1978; Armstrong, 1982). National identity provides the grounding for the modern macropolitical culture, because its emergence can be associated with a series of developments which have their origin in the early nineteenth century. Industrialism, nationalism and mass-democracy blend within the modern state structure to create what Giddens (1985: 132–5) has described as '. . . bordered power containers'. This phenomenon marks the beginning of the modern world, at first in Western Europe but subsequently transmitted to most of the world. A national state has become the objective of most nationalities, and many conflicts within states are a consequence of the absence of or disputes within this common identity.

The macropolitical culture reflects the long-term certainties of the collectivity which in the modern world is usually expressed through nationalism. Within this macro area there will be other norms such as religious belief, political symbols and the forms of interpersonal behaviour which also have a long-term impact. The macropolitical culture also provides an essential condition for political activity, establishing the rules of the game which prove acceptable to most participants. It is at this level that the macropolitical culture and that of the micro begin to interact. The rules of the game are long-term processes but, unlike the core values, these rules can and are contested by different groups within a political system. The rules of the game are established at an intermediary level between the macro and the micro; what might be characterized as a mesolevel. While the macrolevel is fairly static, that of the meso is open to influence from the on-going political debate and struggle at the microlevel. The changes which occurred in American and British politics since the mid-1970s had their most immediate impact on the microlevel of the political culture, what might be characterized as the day-to-day political struggle. However, the success of new style conservatism in both these states also affected the mesolevel in that the rules of the game were changed. This created a climate, where new ideas of what is possible and necessary emerge, which is consistent with traditional values yet appears better equipped to respond to everyday politial requirements.

It is at the microlevel that 'normal' political activity takes place; and where change is most immediately detected. At this level, elections are fought, policies elaborated and governments elected or rejected. All of this can occur without affecting the rules of the game or the macrolevel (for example, the continuing importance of a set of constitutional norms). The rules of the game are both organic in that they are structured by the macrolevel certainties but are also hegemonic in that they are adjusted by the influence of the dominant political forces at the microlevel. Thus, the nature of power at the microlevel will have an important effect on how the rules evolve. If changes at the microlevel are not absorbed by adjusting the rules, there is a danger of social instability and perhaps a threat to the political culture itself. A revolutionary situation is the most potent example of this disjunction between the levels, suggesting that the macropolitical culture may not be able to sustain its legitimizing functions. In these circumstances the authority of the macropolitical culture breaks down and the basis for a radical redefinition of that culture emerges.

Such eventualities are rare among the liberal democratic states. In most of these states, as illustrated below by Britain, the United States and the Republic of Ireland, the absorbing effect of the political culture has been considerable. The three levels of political culture have proven capable of responding to change in such a way as to permit the continued transmission of core values while quite radical changes have taken place at the microlevel which have in turn adjusted the rules of the game (for example, universal franchise). While there is tension between change and continuity at the different levels, once these core values are not directly threatened by changes at the microlevel, the assimilative power of the political culture remains quite strong. Once the core values are threatened, as has been the case in the Republic of Ireland, over divorce and birth control, the changes will be resisted by traditional social forces. Moreover, it is conceivable that under some circumstances changes can take place at the macrolevel which, if they have been accepted and assimilated at the lower levels, will transform the political culture without impairing its continuity or stability (Dowding and Kimber, 1983). The acceptance of the welfare state in postwar Britain provides one example of how the mesolevel might assimilate change at the microlevel. This is a long-term process and is unlikely to occur within a single generation. In the context of changes since the 1960s, it is important also to appreciate the strength of continuity while recognizing the processes of change.

Tradition and resistance to change in the Irish Republic

The strength of continuity in a political system is highlighted in the case of the Irish Republic. Perhaps uniquely among Western Euopean democracies, Ireland's political culture is characterized by long-term stability and a high degree of internal cohesion. Until very recently deviant subcultures have been rare, apparently unnecessary in a homogeneous society. For over a century that political culture, at each of its levels, has given expression to a number of central values which have been successfully internalized by the society. These include religion, nationalism, an authoritarian political style and an antiliberal ideology (Chubb, 1969; Garvin, 1981). In particular, religion and nationalism conjoined to create an identity which differentiated Ireland from the United Kingdom. Thus, while Ireland had adopted many aspects of British government, its judicial system, and aspects of its culture, it has maintained a distinct political culture which allowed the society to evolve separately from its neighbour. Moreover, the strength of this political culture facilitated the integration of the community during the years immediately after independence (Prager, 1986; Girvin, 1986a).

The consensual nature of the political culture reinforced continuity, a continuity that at times bordered on stagnancy. There was always the danger that radical change would seriously disrupt such a society, and destabilize its political system. The changes which occurred in Ireland during the 1960s were far more profound that those experienced by other liberal democratic states. There was a rapid transition, concentrated into two decades, from a traditional agrarian society to a modernizing industrial society (Murphy, 1984). As a consequence of these changes there was a widespread challenge to the traditional values closely associated with the growth of a new middle class stratum within the society. This stratum gave expression to individualism, secularism, and liberalism as well as providing a constituency for changes in some of the political parties.

This liberal grouping challenged the dominance of the traditional sectors of the society from the late 1960s. Throughout the 1970s divisions based on a cleavage between traditional and liberal groups began to become salient. Surveys revealed that the electorate was divided between those who continued to subscribe to traditional and authoritarian values and those who identified with liberal and modern values. These divisions correlated strongly with age, education and occupation as well as political support. Those over 45, with basic formal education, living in rural areas and working in low-skilled occupations tended to retain traditional values, while the better educated, the young, those living in urban centres and skilled or professionals were decidedly more liberal (Fogarty et al., 1984).

This growing liberalism confronted the powerful Roman Catholic Church with an awkward choice. As one of the main beneficiaries of the traditional culture, its dominance was being eroded by the new trends. Moreover, moral issues, with which the Church was particularly concerned, were moving on to the political agenda and creating divisions within the political system. The Church could accept these changes and adapt to them or it could confront and attempt to neutralize them. Prior to this it was possible for Whyte (1974) to conclude that '. . . the religious factor hardly comes into a discussion of politics in Ireland today'. The Church had exercised hegemonic influence over the society since before independence, to the extent that much of Ireland's social legislation reflected Catholic teaching. Until the late 1960s this influence had reflected the Church's importance in the society; thereafter, with the emergence of new social forces, the Church's role proved more problematic.

For most of the 1970s the traditional groups were on the defensive and the Church was unable to prevent the introduction, and later the extension, of the right to obtain and purchase contraceptives. In addition, public opinion appeared to be moving in a more liberal direction and, on a number of moral issues, an increasing proportion of the electorate was favourable to change. It was also possible that the hierarchy would not actively oppose legislation which ran counter to Catholic teaching. This apparent accommodation with pluralism and liberalism was short lived. During the late 1970s the Church rethought the implications of its strategy and developed a more assertive stance. The primary concern was loss of influence; there was an increasing danger that the hierarchy would become simply another interest group rather than the arbiter of policy. Furthermore, the Vatican, under the direction of John Paul II, was pursuing conservative policies, particularly on moral issues. Pressure also emerged from traditional Catholics who feared the erosion of the denominational nature of much of Irish society. By the early 1980s a large number of lay activist groups had emerged promoting the Catholic viewpoint on a wide range of issues.

The organization of an antiliberal majority was extremely successful. Between 1979 and 1986 the political influence of Irish liberalism waned and in two decisive referenda traditional values were reinforced. The first of these took place in 1983 and involved the placing of a constitutional prohibition on abortion; the second, in 1986, was over an attempt to remove the constitutional ban on divorce. On both issues the traditional view triumphed; the divorce referendum was probably the more important as it was generally assumed that the liberal view would be carried without serious opposition. In fact, only a third of those who voted supported the proposal to introduce divorce. The vote for and against the liberal positions in each referendum was almost exactly the same, roughly two-thirds supporting the traditional view and a third the liberal. The failure of the divorce referendum demonstrates the continuing attractiveness of traditional values in Irish society. It also emphasizes the influence which the Roman Catholic Church exercises. But it also shows how weak liberalism is despite the changes which have occurred. Those advocating change lost the political argument during the campaign. When the referendum was announced in April 1986 the opinion polls detected growing support for the proposal to change the constitution. Between April and June when the referendum took place, support for change declined by an average of twenty points in virtually every subcategory in the surveys. In an eight-week period the liberal position was challenged by traditional values, contained and then overwhelmed. The anti-divorce message was readily accepted by rural residents. However, a major reason for failure was the inability of those promoting change to convince women and sections of the working class that change would not have long-term negative consequences for the society (Girvin, 1987a).

The outcome of the divorce referendum indicates that a large section of the society continues to support the Church against an increasingly liberal state. The state and most of the Dublin-based social and economic elites supported change, but most other sectors of the society were mobilized against them. Irish society remains informed by religious motifs and values to an extent uncommon within the European context. This reflects one of the central features of the society; the sense of identity between priest and people is a popular one and ensures the continued influence of theocratic norms. Liberalism, although stronger than it was two decades ago, has a clearly restricted appeal.

Despite the emergence of this cleavage, Ireland's political culture has remained intact. Indeed, one reason for the rejection of liberalism has been the widespread belief that the changes promoted would impair the integrity of the macropolitical culture itself. The form that Irish liberalism takes is believed by a majority to weaken an essential sense of Irishness still associated with nationalism and religion. To change these would have made Ireland too similar to Britain, and this would have undermined Ireland's distinctiveness. It cannot be doubted that Irish political culture changed over the past twenty-five years at the microlevel, but those changes have been refracted through the political culture assimilating those which do not impair it while rejecting others considered threatening. This meshing of modern and traditional norms is not contradictory, but reflects the complex nature of change in this political culture. There does remain a tension between the defence of the traditional values of the majority and the demands for change by the liberals. Currently, this tension is contained at the microlevel of the political culture. The failure of the liberals in recent years to force change probably means that the tension will be maintained here without impairing the integrity of the political culture itself. This continues to be achieved because, despite serious diffences, both liberals and traditionalists continue to identify with the central values of the political culture and hence continuity is assured.

The fragmentation of political cultures in Northern Ireland

Discontinuity rather than continuity remains the most characteristic feature of Northern Ireland. Whereas in many liberal democratic states it is possible to identify a range of subcultures or political cultures which are segmented, these features are not incompatible with the unified nature of the macropolitical culture (Rosenbaum, 1975: 36–63). This diversity can exist within the political culture even though the segmentation is intense and divisive. In other states or systems this diversity in unity is absent, and in the absence of an integrating set of values a number of distinct political cultures may emerge. Northern Ireland, though part of the United Kingdom, possesses neither a unified political culture nor does it share fully in the political cultures of either Great Britain or the Irish Republic. In contrast to the Irish Republic, where religion and nationalism have provided the integrating elements of the political culture, these values provide the main focus for conflict and cleavage in Northern Ireland. Two political cultures have emerged based on a set of values which make accommodation extremely difficult if not impossible. In each case the political culture integrates its designated population and mobilizes its political resources, the consequence of which is the alienation of the other political culture. The symbols of one political culture are not only alien to the other, but are so structured as to reinforce the differences.

The United Kingdom and the Republic of Ireland are generally regarded as being among the most stable political systems in Western Europe, yet within the former there is a relatively small subunit where conflict has been endemic for over a century. The main source of the conflict rests on the differing political values embraced by the majority Protestant and Unionist population, and the minority Catholic nationalist population. The religious and political elements have meshed on both sides to create political cultures, the aim of which is to deny the value of the other's fundamental beliefs. What is absent as a result are the building blocks necessary to underwrite the legitimacy of the state and reinforce the stability of the political system. In most other parts of Europe the existence of a unified political culture enhances both legitimacy and stability, allowing the political system the opportunity to overcome crises and establish continuity (Grew, 1978). In Northern Ireland, Rustow's (1970: 350) condition for political stability, that the majority have no reservations as to the political community they belong to, is simply not fulfilled.

Two sets of identities were generated in Northern Ireland during the nineteenth century: Nationalist and Unionist. Two hostile political cultures align themselves along a fault line based on the confrontation between 'bordered' faiths (Martin, 1978: 107). This relationship, which is central to the conflict, is a 'conflict of irreconcilables'; and

is composed of rival forces which have had a taste of total victory and desire to taste it yet again. For the aim is not tolerance and compromise but victory. This unifies both sides and disciplines them amongst themselves as the prospect of a lost battle embroils the likelihood of total and permanent defeat. Such an anticipation increases violence and bitterness and creates a tendency to spirals of escalating bitterness. (Martin, 1978: 109)

This is given a specific focus in the constitutional aims of the contending groups: Nationalists believe that a unified Ireland is an essential prerequisite for realizing its identity, while for Unionists the continued link with Great Britain serves the same purpose.

In most other societies in Europe socialization is concerned with transmitting values which enhance stability and continuity. In Northern Ireland each of the political cultures does transmit values which achieve these ends within its respective political culture, but simultaneously destabilizes the political system and the society. There is an effective 'socialization into conflict' within each community, a process which is reinforced by the recourse to violence. Between 1914 and the early 1980s, the formative political experience in every decade has been associated with violence between the communities. This cycle of violence has engendered and hardened traditional responses based on secure values and familiar patterns of behaviour; the prevalence of violence has prevented the growth of trust which lays the basis for a civic culture in other liberal democracies (Rose, 1971: 327–55). Other factors have contributed to this outcome; segregated education, the reluctance to mix socially, and low levels of community integration. Rose (1971) found that the two communities had very little contact and even less in common. Such is the influence of this segregating process that most Catholics and Protestants believe it would make a considerable difference if an individual changed their political affiliation or their religion.

The return to violence after 1968 simply reinforced these trends and increased their saliency. Identity became the most important focus for loyalty and mobilization. Nationalists have always maintained a fairly clear conception of their identity as Irish, but this has not always been as clear with Unionists. However, under the pressure of events, Unionists now overwhelmingly perceive themselves as British. This sense of Britishness does not involve accepting the British state as the legitimate source of political authority. As with their Nationalist counterparts, the Unionists in Northern Ireland maintain the right to determine their own expression of political order. In 1978, some 85 per cent of the Unionists agreed with the statement that a 'loyalist is loyal to Ulster before the British government' (Moxon-Browne, 1983). This disjunction has been reinforced since the signing of the Anglo-Irish Agreement in 1985. Thus, for Unionists loyalty to its political culture takes priority, when necessary, over loyalty to the state. This is also reflected in the political culture of the Nationalists, although with a quite different emphasis. There may be differences within each of these political cultures, but these are over tactics and do not provide linkages between the two political cultures. As a consequence each political culture operates as a powerful defence of values which are taken to be threatened by the opposing one. Both also deny the legitimacy of the other's aims and objectives, believing that victory for the other means defeat for itself. There is little room for consensus politics in such a fragmented society.

The intractability of the conflict has to be sought in the nature of these divisions. Serious conflict has been a feature of many European states in the past; although some of these have been resolved through violence this has not usually endangered the continuity of the political culture or the state. More recently forms of conflict resolution through accommodation have become widespread. Indeed, one of the features of Northern Ireland which attracts most attention has been the elusiveness of similar resolutions. In Austria the Proporz system became an effective mechanism after 1945 to accommodate the class differences which existed between left and right and which had led to a Civil War in 1934. A consociational model has been adopted in Belgium and the Netherlands in recognition of the existence of separate subcultures, often making incompatible demands on the state. Consociationalism, federalism and pillarization have all been offered as models for resolving the modern Irish conflict, yet none of them have attracted significant support. Divisions based on class, language, or religion can have serious consequences for a political system, yet they are not intractable problems, as the examples of Switzerland or the Netherlands suggest. In these cases there is little doubt concerning national identity *despite* the differences based on class, religion or language. A consensual approach to conflict resolution was possible precisely because of the common sense of identity. The differences in these cases are reflected through sub-cultures or cultural segmentation within a political culture which retains, at least at the macrolevel, a common set of political values.

It is the absence of these common values in Northern Ireland which makes it difficult to resolve the conflict. Consensual models of conflict resolution have tended to fail where this source of identity is weak or missing. The absence of trust between communities reinforces the basic hostility evident through conflict. Northern Ireland may not be typical of politics in Western Europe, but it is possible to identify strong linkages between it and many other regions of the world. The conflict between the Turkish state and its Kurdish minority is but one analogy which could be drawn. As ethnic differentiation continues to be central to the political culture and socialization in most postcolonial states, the process of state building will probably open up divisions based on similar criteria to those operational in Northern Ireland (Tilley, 1985).

Finally, Northern Ireland also draws attention to the inappropriateness of the postmaterialist model in the face of national divisions. Once the most modern region in Ireland, Northern Ireland has been progressively deindustrialized. It has a large service sector and it could be suggested that intergenerational change, based on the introduction of a welfare state, expanded educational opportunities and sectoral change, might have contributed to the political conflict that has ensued since 1968. There is certainly a coincidence between this and the 'events' of the late 1960s; however, the symbols, objectives, and lines of cleavage are traditional and concentrate on national conflict rather than on the aims of the new politics. For Northern Ireland, as for the Irish Republic, continuity and traditionalism continue to carry more weight than the alternatives.

Political change in stable political cultures:
Britain and the United States

The tension between continuity and change is well represented in the postwar experience of two of the most liberal democratic states. For Almond and Verba, Britain and the United States are the basic models for the civic culutre: '. . . there exists in Britain and the United States a pattern of political attitudes and an underlying set of social attitudes that is supportive of a stable democratic process' (1963: vii). Yet, by the end of the 1970s considerable doubt was being cast on the ability of either state to maintain this stability. In the short term it appeared that the political cultures in Britain and the United States had experienced a degree of change which contrasted sharply with the experience of the period 1945 to 1960 (Abramowitz, 1980; Kavanagh, 1980). However, if a longer term perspective is taken the changes which occurred do not appear as unprecedented. Between 1932 and 1945 the political culture in both countries was changed by the twin pressures of economic depression and war. The New Deal in the United States and the welfare state in Britain fundamentally changed the lower order context for political behaviour. Conservative elites, institutions and policies were replaced by a new consensus which valued affluence, growth and redistribution. These changes did not disrupt the macropolitical culture but they did change the rules of the game as a consequence of the changed nature of political power at the microlevel. This was appreciated by the conservative parties when they returned to government during the 1950s; they were unable, but were also unwilling, to change the direction of policy. This reflected the extent to which the culture had internalized these political changes. These were of such fundamental significance that they changed the behaviour of both elites and the masses. This may explain why, during this period, the masses appeared quiescent; in general the social environment in Britain and the United States had been restructured to favour the non-property owning sections of the society and they consequently felt little urgency to become involved in the political process. This was not a sign of passivity but reflected the belief that what had been achieved was of benefit to them (Girvin, 1987b).

Once that environment began to change and the older certainties were challenged, the electorate became less passive. Britain and the United States faced different challenges during the 1960s, yet the assertion of Democratic and Labour party dominance appeared to confirm the leftward trend in politics. However, this decade marks the end of the unquestioned acceptance of the postwar consensus; by 1970 in both countries the consensus on welfare, employment and government had been seriously shaken. Although the problems were different the traditional policy responses appeared inadequate. In addition, the failure of the Democrats and the Labour party to resolve long-standing problems provided the opportunity for a conservative revival. From the mid-1960s to the late 1970s the major political forces in both societies were faced with a series of crises which undermined political stability. The American experience was the most dramatic: the Vietnam war, civil rights and political assassination questioned the veracity of governmental structures. In the United Kingdom, economic decline, industrial confrontation and the war in Northern Ireland pointed to a loss of direction which threatened the integrity of the state.

In both countries old forms of political loyalties broke down. In the United States the race issue and to a lesser extent the Vietnam war weakened the Democratic party in the south; what was once a one-party electoral arena became a potential two-party region. This dealignment of traditional political forces paralleled the emergence of new political groups associated with the anti-war and civil rights movement. Mainly middle class, the so-called new politics were essentially moral movements which stressed the issues of the counter-culture (feminism, ecology and pacifism). This movement was particularly influential within the Democratic party and moved the political agenda towards its objectives during the 1970s, in the process of which the party alienated its traditional supporters further. These changes gave the right an opportunity to organize a new governing coalition which could frame its own policy agenda (Peele, 1984).

In Britain the postwar consensus came under pressure at much the same time. The commitment to full employment, rising incomes and the welfare state was seriously questioned. At one level the difficulty was associated with rising expectations from the state, while the economy could not supply the means to meet these expectations. One feature of the process is what Beer (1982) has called 'pluralistic stagnation': this rests on the failure of the more traditional group politics to respond to the changing nature of the political system. The postwar collectivism proved unable to absorb the new social forces which emerged. This was accompanied by class decomposition and the collapse of deference, which contributed to greater volatility in electoral behaviour and consequently to greater political uncertainty. The growth of a new populism among the middle classes, particularly the university educated, had a similar impact to that of the new politics in the United States. The Labour party attracted this new force and by the early 1970s had assimilated many of its political objectives; in doing so a basic contradiction arose between the new and old adherents of the party (Crewe, 1982).

The years between 1968 and 1974 were crucial in both countries for the right. In each case a conservative party was elected on a programme which appeared to challenge the 'left' consensus. However, in each case the administration retained a greater commitment to the consensus than appeared from the rhetoric. In both cases the radical promise remained unfulfilled. The collapse of the Heath and the Nixon administrations undermined the attempt to formulate new electoral alignments, and questioned the ability of the right to govern. By the mid-1970s conservative politics had suffered disarray and public opprobrium. It is questionable if these events amounted to a total rejection of conservatism. It might be suggested that these were short-term set-backs rather than a long-term trend towards the left. Both governments had compromised conservative values; worse, both failed in their efforts. Following electoral defeat the right had to reassess its strategy (Girvin, 1987b).

What occurs in both Britain and the United States by the end of the 1970s is what may be described as the normal process of political change. Change takes place within a basically stable framework (over the long term), but with considerable short-term instability. As a result of the oil crisis, the recession and the world-wide inflation some basic governmental assumptions were challenged. For the first time in over forty years it became possible to overturn the prevailing policy consensus and replace it with a new (and conservative) one. Conservatism based its political success on addressing the concerns of a significant proportion of the electorate. On moral, economic and foreign policy issues there was an increasing congruence between conservative policy and mass opinion. However, the key to Reagan's and Thatcher's success centred on their promise to curb inflation; this allowed conservatives to appeal to a wider constituency than had hitherto been the case (Ladd and Lipset, 1980; Girvin, 1988).

To attribute recent conservative success in both countries simply to economic issues would be to ignore the changes which have occurred within public opinion. During the 1970s in particular, there was a clash between two contending sets of values to dominate the political agenda. At first the left or liberal view appered to become dominant, but the emergence of the new right challenged this and quickly replaced it with a clear agenda of its own. This was followed by the election of conservative governments in both countries and their subsequent re-election. There has been a partial implementation of the conservative programme since then; but more importantly the policy agenda has shifted somewhat to the right, particularly on economic issues and foreign policy. Both the Democrats and the Labour party are now echoing, albeit in their own terms, much of what was once a preserve of the conservatives (Krieger, 1986).

While change has taken place within the United Kingdom and the United States, it remains difficult to evaluate its impact on the long-term evolution of the political culture. If conservative values come to dominate the routine levels of political behaviour it is possible that this would seriously affect the structure of the political culture. However, what is striking about both states is the sense of continuity within the political culture, the extent to which a movement to the left or right is constrained by a deeper set of values within that community (Norton, 1985: 25–34, 350–64; Taylor-Gooby, 1985, 1987a, 1987b). American political culture has successfully assimilated the drive to the left beginning with the New Deal continuing through the civil rights movement and the great society, but culminating in the failure of Carter's neocorporatist extension of liberalism at the end of the 1970s. Similarly, British political culture assimilated much of the drive to the left from the mid-1960s, but a political reaction during the latter half of the 1970s effectively blocked further changes in that direction. The success of conservative governments can, in part, be attributed to the rejection of some liberal policies by significant sections of the electorate.

That there has been a swing to the right is unmistakable. In both countries there has been a reassertion of nationalism. This has been complemented by an insistence on the value of the market in economic life, and an emphasis on individualism absent since the 1930s. In foreign policy the movement to the right has been reflected in the advocacy of a strong defence posture towards the Soviet Union and an assertion of the moral superiority of liberal values. Finally, conservatives have stressed a set of moral norms which concentrate on such traditional areas as the family, law and order and religion. It would be mistaken, however, to see this movement to the right as a total rejection of the postwar consensus. The political culture internalizes development discreetly and, as with the left earlier, provides a bulwark against rapid change.

The progress of the right has not been as rapid as either the Conservative or Republican parties would like. In Britain, the Conservative party continues to receive public approval on a number of economic issues, such as inflation and public spending. However, attempts to change the structure and nature of the welfare state have been strongly resisted. The proposed 'poll tax', changes in education and health policy and the consequences of an increasingly centralized state suggest that Thatcherism, even with a significant majority, is encountering more resistance than at any time since 1979. In the United States, the 'Reagan Resolution' has had a significant impact on economic and foreign policy, but its overall success has been limited to a restricted agenda. Moreover, the 'Irangate' controversy has partly undermined the continuing effectiveness of the right's agenda. Despite recent foreign policy successes, Reagan's personal popularity remains relatively low. Recent polls have also indicated growing scepticism towards the right's economic policies. Furthermore, the administration has found it difficult to mobilize opinion on moral issues where individual choice is believed to be primary (abortion in particular). These trends have been short term and their main impact in both Britain and the United States has been on the micropolitical culture and on the routine life of politics. To an extent the rules of the game have been altered by the advance of the right, but not radically. In an overall context the microculture and the rules of the game have absorbed elements from both sides of the political spectrum over the past twenty-five years, without these changes transforming the macro-political culture. As a consequence of both the stability and flexibility of these two systems new developments have been assimilated, without the legitimacy of the core values being impaired (*Guardian*, 1986; *Public Opinion*, 1986; *Wall Street Journal*, 1988).

Conclusion: the continuity of political culture

This chapter has deliberately emphasized the strength of continuity in a number of liberal democratic states. To do so is not to ignore the importance of change; indeed, a central aspect of this process is that precisely because of the strength of continuity in the political culture changes are assimilated without core values being transformed in the short term. Change with continuity reinforces the stability of the political culture. Consequently the challenges faced by many liberal democratic states during the 1970s and 1980s, while real, did not disrupt the political culture at the macrolevel. The most sustained changes have occurred at the microlevel, and it is here that new forms of political organization, new lifestyles and new ideas have had the greatest efffect. Some of these changes have been transmitted to the mesolevel of the political culture where the rules of the game have been altered. This has occurred because the political culture in most societies proved resilient enough to assimilate the changes without disturbing essential core values. Even with short-term instability, as occurred during the late 1960s and early 1970s, long-term stability has been maintained. However, without the existence of the central precondition of common identity and values available such stability cannot be assured, as the case of Northern Ireland attests. The Republic of Ireland draws attention to the difficulties which new values have in penetrating an almost static political culture; despite the microlevel conflict on moral issues the society remains remarkably stable. In Britain and the United States long-term stability has been reinforced, especially in the latter, due to the assimilative effect of the political culture.

Successful assimilation is based on a number of conditions. The extent to which the political culture reflects adequately the sense of national identity within the community is central; if the political culture cannot attract loyalty then change poses real difficulties. This is closely related to the nature of change itself; if change is imposed externally or promoted too rapidly it will be resisted. If change is perceived as threatening core values it will almost certainly be rejected. Despite this, change is normal within most political cultures. Given the nature of the modern world this is to be expected. To effect assimilation there must be a meshing of the new with the existing structures in such a way as to allow changes to penetrate the system while retaining the core values of the society.

The main avenue for such assimilation is through the mesolevel of a political culture. The microlevel provides the terrain for the immediate conflicts over distribution, values or political order. Conflict can be confined at this lower level without penetrating above it; and most conflicts are resolved or contained here. The mesolevel provides an intermediary level where decisive shifts at the microlevel can be recognized by the political culture. The effect of such a shift will be to reorder the rules of the game and present the political culture with the possibility of changing quite significant elements of its structure. In effect, the mesolevel transmits to the macrolevel the outcomes of crucial conflicts at the microlevel. This process is very gradual. It can be assumed that a fundamental change at the microlevel will be reflected quite quickly at the mesolevel, while the macrolevel will take much longer to be affected by these changes. In this context lower order changes can be accomplished in the lifetime of single political generations, while significant changes at the macrolevel are unlikely to occur outside a long historical period.

It is only when changes cannot be accommodated at the mesolevel that they will be rejected or (in rare circumstances) the attempt to do so will bring about a political reaction which if it leads to revolution will destroy the existing political culture and create the conditions for a new one with values and assumptions based on the revolutionary experience. The destruction of political cultures is a rare phenomenon once it becomes embodied in a nationalist framework, though the possibility should not be excluded (Hitler's Germany is a probable case in point). More often the pace of change and assimilation will be regulated by specific elements of the political culture. Thus the relative flexibility of the American constitutional structure can be compared to the inflexibility of that in the Irish Republic. Both constitutions reflect quite different priorities placed on the political culture by the society. Change has usually been assimilated easily in the British case, possibly the classic reformist state, precisely because accommodation has been a primary element in the political culture since the eighteenth century. The very circumstances which created stability in Great Britain contributed to the long-term instability in Northern Ireland.

Each of the case studies presented here illustrates a different facet of continuity, whether that focuses on stability or instability. The studies also draw attention to the long-term forces which mould the political culture of an individual state or nation. In particular the macropolitical culture establishes an historical context which each generation has to confront. This context can be changed over time, but only if the changes can be assimilated within the contours that are already well established.

References

Abramowitz, Alan I. (1980) 'The United States: Political Culture under Stress', pp. 177–211 in Almond and Verba (1980).

Almond, Gabriel A. (1980) 'The Intellectual History of the Civic Culture Concept', pp. 1–36 in Almond and Verba (1980).

Almond, Gabriel A. and Verba, Sidney (1963) *The Civic Culture*. Princeton: Princeton University Press.

Almond, Gabriel A. and Verba, Sidney (eds) (1980) *The Civic Culture Revisited*. Boston: Little, Brown.

Armstrong, J.A. (1982) *Nations before Nationalism*. Chapel Hill: University of North Carolina Press.

Beer, Samuel H. (1982) *Britain Against Itself*. London: Faber & Faber.

Bell, Daniel (1973) *The Coming of Post-Industrial Society*. New York: Basic Books.

Bell, Daniel (1976) *The Cultural Contradictions of Capitalism*. New York: Basic Books.

Bell, Daniel (1980) *Sociological Journeys*. London: Heinemann.

Biever, B.F. (1976) *Religion, Culture and Values*. New York: Arno Press.

Brittan, Samuel (1977) *The Economic Contradictions of Democracy*. London: Temple Smith.

Caute, David (1988) *Sixty-Eight*. London: Hamish Hamilton.

Chubb, Basil (1969) *The Government and Politics of Ireland*. Stanford: Stanford University Press.

Collingwood, R.G. (1940) *An Essay on Metaphysics*. Oxford: Oxford University Press.

Crewe, Ivor (1982) 'The Labour Party and the Electorate', pp. 9–49 in D. Kavanagh (ed.), *The Politics of the Labour Party*. London: Allen & Unwin.

Dowding, Keith and Kimber, Richard (1983) 'The Meaning and Use of Political Stability', *European Journal of Political Research*, 11 (3): 229–43.

Fogarty, Michael, Ryan, Liam and Lee, Joseph (1984) *Irish Values and Attitudes*. Dublin: Dominican Publications.

Garvin, Tom (1981) *The Evolution of Irish Nationalism*. Dublin: Gill & Macmillan.

Giddens, Anthony (1985) *Violence and the Nation State*. Cambridge: Polity Press.

Girvin, Brian (1986a), 'Nationalism, Democracy, and Irish Political Culture', pp. 3–28 in B. Girvin and R. Sturm (eds), *Politics and Society in Contemporary Ireland*. Aldershot: Gower.

Girvin, Brian (1986b) 'Social Change and Moral Politics: the Irish Constitutional Referendum 1983', *Political Studies*, 34 (1): 57–79.

Girvin, Brian (1986c) 'National Identity and Conflict in Northern Ireland', pp. 105–34 in B. Girvin and R. Sturm (eds), *Politics and Society in Contemporary Ireland*. Aldershot: Gower.

Girvin, Brian (1987a) 'The Divorce Referendum in the Republic, June 1986', *Irish Political Studies*, 2: 91–6.

Girvin, Brian (1987b), 'Conservatism and Political Change in Britain and the United States', *Parliamentary Affairs*, 40 (2): 154–71.

Girvin, Brian (1988) 'Conservative Politics in a Liberal Society: the Case of the United States', pp. 164–92 in B. Girvin (ed.), *The Transformation of Contemporary Conservatism*. London: Sage.

Grew, Raymond (ed.) (1978) *Crises of Political Development in Europe and the United States*. Princeton: Princeton University Press.

Guardian (1986) 'Marplan Survey of Political Attitudes', October 7.

Hassan, Ihab (1985) 'The Culture of Postmodernism', *Theory, Culture and Society*, 2 (3): 119–31.

Hirsch, Fred (1976) *The Social Limits to Growth*. Cambridge, Mass: Harvard University Press.

Inglehart, Ronald (1977) *The Silent Revolution: Changing Values and Political Styles among Western Publics*. Princeton: Princeton University Press.

Jessop, Bob (1974) *Traditionalism, Conservatism and British Political Culture*. London: Allen & Unwin.

Kavanagh, Dennis (1980) 'Political Culture in Great Britain: the Decline of the Civic Culture', pp. 124–76 in Almond and Verba (1980).

Krieger, Joel (1986) *Reagan, Thatcher and the Politics of Decline*. Cambridge: Polity Press.

Ladd, E. C. and Lipset, S.M. (1980) 'Anatomy of a Decade', *Public Opinion*, 3 (6): 2–9.

Martin, David (1978) *A General Theory of Secularization*. Oxford: Basil Blackwell.

Moxon-Browne, Edward (1983) *Nation, Class and Creed in Northern Ireland*. Aldershot: Gower.

Murphy, Detlef (1984) 'Vor der Agrarkolonie zur Industriegesellschaft', pp. 194–219 in Peter Reichel (ed.), *Politische Kultur in Westeuropa*. Frankfurt: Campus Verlag.

Norton, Philip (1985) *The British Polity*. London: Longman.

Peele, Gillian (1984) *Revival and Reaction*. Oxford: Oxford University Press.

Prager, Jeffrey (1986) *Building Democracy in Ireland*. Cambridge: Cambridge University Press.

Public Opinion (1986) 'Opinion Roundup', 9 (3): 27–39.

Rose, Richard (1971) *Governing without Consensus*. London: Faber & Faber.

Rosenbaum, Walter A. (1975) *Political Culture*. London: Nelson.

Rustow, D.A. (1970) 'Transitions to Democracy', *Comparative Politics*, 2 (3): 337–63.

Stearns, Peter N. (1984) 'The Idea of Postindustrial Society: Some Problems', *Journal of Social History*, 17 (4): 685–93.

Taylor-Gooby, Peter (1985) *Public Opinion, Ideology and Social Welfare*. London: Routledge and Kegan Paul.

Taylor-Gooby, Peter (1987a) 'Welfare Attitudes: Cleavage, Consensus and Citizenship', *Quarterly Journal of Social Affairs*, 3 (3).

Taylor-Gooby, Peter (1987b) 'Citizenship and Welfare', in R. Jowell, S. Witherspoon and L. Brook (eds), *British Social Attitudes: the 1987 Report*. Aldershot: Gower.

Tilley, Charles (1985) 'War Making and State Making as Organised Crime', pp. 169–91 in P.B. Evans, D. Ruescheymeyer and T. Skocpol (eds), *Bringing the State Back In*. Cambridge: Cambridge University Press.

Verba, Sidney (1965) 'Comparative Political Culture', pp. 512–60 in L.W. Pye and Sidney Verba (eds), *Political Culture and Political Development*. Princeton: Princeton University Press.

Wall Street Journal (1988) 'Wall Street Journal/NBS Poll', January 26.

White, Stephen (1979) *Political Culture and Soviet Politics*. New York: St Martin's Press.

Whyte, John H. (1974) 'Ireland: Politics without Social Bases', pp. 619–51 in R. Rose (ed.), *Electoral Behaviour: a Comparative Handbook*. New York: Free Press.

3

Political Change and Political Culture in Britain, 1959–87

Richard Topf

It is no longer fashionable to write of paradigms in the social sciences. Inevitably, however, at a given time within any field of research there are accepted wisdoms put forward in the textbooks, and unquestioned conventional truths which form the basis for further research. Inevitably also, such accepted wisdom incorporates theoretical models of the social world, expressed in particular terms of discourse. It is perhaps precisely the mark of their acceptance that in time the theories, and the concepts and notions which characterize them, become the lingua franca of the textbooks.

The notion of political culture has experienced precisely this fate in the political science literature. Although theorists at the forefront of research may question the usefulness of the concept (Kaase, 1982), British and American textbooks reveal no such doubts about political culture. In all four editions of *Politics in England*, Rose heads a chapter 'Political Culture', and most recently writes:

> A political culture is a more or less harmonious mixture of the values, beliefs and emotions dominant in a society . . . that influence support for authority and compliance with its basic political laws. Collectively, the values, beliefs and emotional symbols that constitute the political culture of England are 'a system of tacit understandings'. (1985: 127–8)

Kavanagh's recent book on British politics also heads a chapter 'Political Culture', and offers a very similar notion:

> Every political system is embedded in a political culture. At one time, historians, anthropologists, and political scientists spoke of a 'national character'. Now we are more likely to refer to the political culture – the values, beliefs, and emotions that give meaning to political behaviour. These are the values which create dispositions for people to behave in a particular way or which provide justifications for behaviour. (1985: 46)

In their standard American textbook, Almond and Powell write:

> A political culture is a particular distribution of political attitudes, values, feelings, information and skills. As people's attitudes affect what they will do, a nation's political culture affects the conduct of its citizens and leaders throughout the political system. (1984: 37)

It is this conventional notion of political culture which provides the starting point for this chapter. Its central characteristics are clear enough. The political culture of a society is composed of the political attitudes, values, feelings, information, skills, which form the Weltanschauung of political actors, and give meaning and justification to their actions. It is, therefore, a concept embedded in a type of theory which relates 'orientations' to action. Almond has claimed that the notion of political culture is 'not a theory but a set of variables which may be used to construct theories' (1980: 26). It will be argued later that this is far from being the case. Indeed, a major problem of conventional usage arises out of the failure of many analysts to render explicit the conceptual framework which they necessarily adopt.

Crucial to this notion of political culture is that it is amenable to analysis and measurement by social survey methodologies. It is held to be axiomatic that we may approach political culture by asking individuals about their attitudes, values, and so on, and aggregate their responses. This is not to say, with Scheuch (1969), that we must necessarily commit the individualistic fallacy of generating causal arguments from aggregated data to collective characteristics. It is quite proper to argue, as Verba has done (1980: 401), that the distribution of attitudes, etc., is a legitimate 'macrocharacteristic'. I shall pursue these points later. For the moment the claim is that there remains in currency a conventional notion of political culture which is used in attempts to explain contemporary political processes and structures.

The origins of the convention: civic culture and stable democracy

It was to be expected that in the years following the Second World War, social scientists sought to analyse the conditions for political stability. For liberal democrats, as Verba notes (1980: 407): 'this concern for the question of why some democracies survive while others collapse', flowed naturally enough from puzzles about recent events in Germany and Italy, as well as from doubts about contemporary French stability.

Undoubtedly the most ambitious of these projects was Almond and Verba's *The Civic Culture* (1963). Reflecting on this project some twenty years after the research was conducted, Almond remarked (1980: 15) that it was the invention of a new research technology – survey research methodology – which served as stimulus and catalyst for the work. As the original subtitle stated, *The Civic Culture* was a study of 'political attitudes and democracy', a study in 'micropolitics', as the authors described it. They put the theoretical relationship between societal attitudes and stable democracy thus:

By moving constantly from characteristics of the political system to frequencies of particular attitudes within the system to the pattern of attitudes within individual members of the system, one can hope to develop plausible, testable (and, perhaps, in a preliminary way, tested) hypotheses about the relationship between what we call political culture and the workings of political systems. (1963: 43–4)

Thus, for Almond and Verba it was the concept of political culture which provided the crucial link between micro- and macro- politics:

We would like to suggest that this relationship between the attitudes and motivations of discrete individuals who make up political systems and the character and performance of political systems may be discovered systematically through the concepts of political culture we have sketched out. (1963: 33)

The authors were aware that the notion of political culture may not be devoid of ambiguities. But, they wrote:

Here we can only stress that we deploy the concept of culture in only one of its many meanings: that of psychological orientation toward social objects. When we speak of the political culture of a society, we refer to the political system as internalised in the cognitions, feelings, and evaluations of its population. People are inducted into it just as they are socialised into nonpolitical roles and social systems . . . the political culture of a nation is the particular distribution of patterns of orientation toward political objects among the members of the nation. (1963: 14–15)

At this juncture, only one element of the analytical framework must be highlighted. The thesis posits that by the study of individual orientations towards political objects, an hypothesis may be developed about the relationship between the political culture, from which those orientations are derived, and the political system. The political system is defined as 'a system of action . . . the unit of the political system is the role' (Almond, 1970: 32–5). Thus, underpinning this entire analytical framework is a theory of political culture defined in terms of role behaviour.

It needs no rehearsal here that Almond and Verba found one particular form of political culture to be exemplary of stable liberal democracy – the civic culture. Civic culture – note, significantly for later analysis that the authors (1963: 6) accredit the concept of civility to Shils – is a mixed 'modernizing-traditional' one, found, above all, in Britain. It shares the 'rationality-activist' model of political partici-pation and involvement, fused with passivity, traditionality and commitment to parochial values (1963: 31–2). In civic cultures, the individual *homo civicus* (Dahl, 1961: 223–5) sustains a belief in the 'myth of civic competence' (Almond and Verba, 1963: 479–81) which ensured his loyalty to the political system. Above all, there was an essential 'balance':

That required that all citizens be involved and active in politics, and that their participation be informed, analytic, and rational. [But] only when combined in some sense with their opposites of passivity, trust, and deference to authority and competence, was a viable, stable democracy 'possible'. (Almond and Verba, 1980: 16)

Thus: 'The democratic citizen is called upon to pursue contradictory goals: he must be active, yet passive; involved, yet not too involved; influential, yet deferential' (Almond and Verba, 1963: 479).

The empirical base

The civic culture thesis rests upon two primary empirical variables, the stability of political systems and the characteristics of the political cultures. However, as critics have noted, stability was asserted rather than demonstrated from empirical data,[1] and it is the survey-based analysis of political orientations which forms the core of the empirical study.

Central to the civic culture thesis is the focus on the relationship between political trust, civic competence, political efficacy and political participation. Put briefly, it was argued that the 'balance' between political acquiescence and activism was maintained because individuals in their roles as citizens felt a mythical competence to influence political decisions should they wish to do so. But they did not so wish very often, and they trusted the political system to be fair and responsive to their demands. This balance was found in the exemplary stable democracies of the United States and, particularly, Britain.

Political change: decline and crisis

The first major repetition of Almond and Verba's survey of British political culture was not carried out until 1974. Alan Marsh, a social psychologist, conducted a study whose focus was on 'unorthodox' political behaviour and political protest (Marsh, 1977).[2] He found that a majority of the respondents expressed low levels of interest in political affairs, distrust of established political institutions and low levels of political efficacy (see Table 1).

Marsh reported that in 1974:

Twenty-three percent [of respondents] will not even read the political section of newspapers and a cumulative 69 percent will do no more than talk about it; the remaining third do get involved to some degree, but only 8 percent have ever had anything to do with an election campaign. (1977: 58)

In answer to the question: 'How much do you trust the government in Westminster to do what is right?', some 61 percent of respondents

Table 1   *Levels of political cynicism 1959–86*

Percentage of population who agree that:	1959 (%)	1974 (%)	1986 (%)
People like me have no say in what government does	–	61	71
Politics and government so complicated that cannot understand what is going on	58	74	69
MPs lose touch with the people quickly	–	67	66
Parties only interested in votes, not opinions	–	67	70
British government of any party cannot be trusted to place needs of country above interests of own political party	–	60	57
$N =$	(953)	(1,802)	(1,548)

Sources: *Civic Culture* study, ICPR edition, 1974; *Political Action* study 1979, ICPSR edition (also Barnes and Kaase, 1979); *British Social Attitudes* survey, 1986

replied 'only some of the time', or 'almost never'. Sixty percent said that 'almost never' or 'only some of the time' did they believe that people in politics speak the truth, and the same percentage said they believed that British governments of either party placed party interests above the needs of the country and its people.

Turning to what Marsh interpreted as indicators of political efficacy, 63 percent replied that they 'agree strongly' or 'agreed' that 'people like me have no say in what government does', 75 percent that 'sometimes politics and government seem so complicated that a person like me cannot really understand what is going on', and 74 percent agreed that 'generally speaking, those we elect as MPs to Westminster lose touch with the people pretty quickly'.

Marsh offered no direct comparisons with Almond and Verba's data, but concluded that:

> Political trust is at a much lower ebb than would seem healthy from Almond and Verba's view at least, for a democratic society; more particularly so since competence has remained high. But perhaps the British political community has proved to be, in a sense, more mature than given credit for. No riots have broken out, only the growth of the potent political attitude: politically competent cynicism. (1977: 232)

Marsh's focus on 'protest potential' represented part of a general movement among social scientists in the 1970s who were reporting very major changes in the political cultures and processes of Western democracies. A new orthodoxy came to prevail (Kavanagh, 1983: 320; Duncan, 1983: 4; Nordlinger, 1981: 69), the central feature of which was the view that Britain and the United States, once the exemplars of stable democracy, instead were seen as the leading examples of the decline and crisis of liberal democracy.

Unsurprisingly, Marsh's findings soon came to play a central role in such analyses of British decline and crisis, often with less optimistic interpretations than his own. Rose (1985: 135) and Beer (1982: 116) both reproduced Marsh's tabulation on political trust in their own works. Beer, eminent among writers in the conventional, political culture genre, reaffirmed that he considered 'political culture to be one of the main variables of a political system', and went on to argue that:

> Analytically, the fundamental change is the change in the political culture. The rise of the new populism and the coincident decline of the civic culture constitute the main background conditions that precipitated the other dysfunctions . . . (1982: 4–5)

These other dysfunctions were pluralist stagnation, crises of authority and related crises of the political system.

Other analysts have reversed this causal argument. Huntington (1975) held that in the United States the rate of growth in public expenditure correlated with a decline in the level of 'public consent', thence to a decrease in governmental authority, and hence crisis of democracy. Somewhat similarly, O'Connor, a neo-Marxist (1973), and Brittan (1975), a neo-Liberal, held that internal contradictions in the liberal democratic system itself generated a loss of public trust in the governmental system, and thus crisis.

Each of these analysts advanced theses correlating changes in the political culture with other changes in political systems. However, although several supported their arguments with empirical evidence, such as Marsh's work, none of the more prominent analysts advancing this thesis themselves engaged in survey research, yet alone attempted to replicate the civic culture survey. Thus in Kavanagh's important review of the literature in 1980, whilst underestimating the broader impact of the civic culture project for British political scientists, he rightly noted that:

> In spite of the popularity of the cultural approach, many of the writings are backed by scanty evidence. Indeed, it is chastening to realise how little good data there are at all. . . . If students of British politics have fed off Almond and Verba's descriptive data for too long, this is largely because later writings have been based on so little empirical research. (1980: 162–6; cf. Kaase, 1982)[3]

Political change in the 1980s

Equally serious for many such students has been the failure of the purported crises of British and American political systems to manifest themselves. Certainly it is widely recognized that during the last decade Britain has been undergoing a period of significant political change. Compared to the stability of the 1950s and 1960s, opinion polls on support for political parties have fluctuated widely from month to month, and there have been large swings in by-elections and general elections. Voters are more likely than they were to switch their vote between parties from one election to another, whilst the proportion of the electorate who say that they are strongly attached to any one of the political parties has fallen quite dramatically.

At the same time, there has been a steady decline in the numbers who support either of the traditional, two major parties. In the 1987 general election, almost half of the registered voters (45 percent) did not vote for either the Conservative or Labour party. The geographical distribution of votes has also changed markedly, such that there is much talk of a Britain of two nations, the South and the rest. In 1987, in the South the Conservatives polled 51 percent of the votes and Labour 22 percent, whilst in Scotland the Conservatives polled 24 percent and Labour 42 percent.

These changes in voting patterns are paralleled by equally significant changes in the party system itself, and in the ideological stances of the parties. At least until after the 1987 general election, most analysts were convinced that Britain had moved to a three-party system. The politics of consensus which was seen as the style of the 1950s and 1960s, when voters were wont to complain that they could not distinguish between the two major parties, has been replaced by accusations of ideological extremism of the right and left, and the advancement of 'commitment' as a virtue.

Listing the evidence of political change of this kind is easy enough, and a considerable psephological literature has emerged offering explanations, often in heated debate over both rival theories and interpretations of the data.[4] Thus, structuralists point to sociodemographic changes, such as the decline in the size of the British working class, whilst rational choice theorists prefer evidence of declining party identity and the rise of issue voting. Neither of these approaches is satisfactory, and attempts to combine both approaches raise major analytical problems which are all too often glossed over.

Singularly absent from such explanations of change over the last decade is any systematic attempt to apply the notion of political culture, despite its continued exposition in the textbooks. Commenting upon contemporary changes and their possible direction, Rose writes:

> The most important of all political changes – alterations in the values and beliefs of the political culture – are the most difficult to anticipate. Yet once the meaning of politics alters, then much else alters in consequence. (1985: 397)

However, in his earlier chapter on political culture, the tenor of Rose's analysis emphasizes continuity rather than change. Even in 1985 he continued to draw upon survey data of research conducted by Almond and Verba in 1959, and Marsh in 1974, to present his account of contemporary Britain. Of course, it may well be appropriate to do this if the stable nature of British political culture is demonstrated by comparison with more recent data, and I shall show below that, in some respects, this is indeed the case. But Rose did not follow this course, nor did he resolve the question of how political culture may be related to changing political behaviour over the last decade, if the characteristics of that culture themselves remain largely unchanging.

British political culture today

Fortunately, it is now possible to begin to fill in some of the lacunae in reliable time-series data. Marsh, writing of a time just before the announcement of the February 1974 general election, reported disturbingly low interest in politics affairs among his respondents. In the 1980s some 30 percent of the population report that they have 'a good deal', or 'quite a bit' of interest in politics generally, and three-quarters reported following the 1983 general election and caring about the result.[5] Whilst these are very general indicators, at least it would not appear that in the mid-1980s respondents express any lower levels of political interest than Marsh identified.

In 1982, Beer drew upon Marsh's 1974 data to conclude that:

> In the light of the survey evidence it is no exaggeration to speak of the decline of the civic culture as a 'collapse'. The change in attitudes towards politics and government since the 1950s has been deep and wide. (1982: 119)

In 1986, *British Social Attitudes* replicated a number of such questions about attitudes towards the political system and the way the country is run. As Table 1 shows, taken together the answers tend to confirm the picture of widespread public cynicism. When asked, 'How much do you trust a British government of any party to place the needs of this country above the interests of their own political party?' 57 percent replied 'only some of the time' or 'almost never'. Two related questions yielded even more cynical answers. Respondents were asked whether they agreed or disagreed with the statements that 'generally speaking, those we elect as MPs lose touch with people pretty quickly' and that 'parties are only interested in people's votes, not in their opinions'. On both of these statements the great majority of respondents gave what are clearly cynical or disillusioned responses: 70 percent agreed with the first and 66 percent with the second statement.

These answers indicate that the widespread political cynicism and lack of deference, reported by Marsh, continue at much the same level today. Importantly, however, there is little evidence that trust in politics and politicians has ever been much higher. Analysis of Almond and Verba's own 1959 survey of Britain reveals that 58 percent of respondents agreed then that 'people like me don't have any say about what the government does' and 83 percent agreed that 'all candidates sound good in their speeches but you can never tell what they will do after they are elected' (*Civic Culture* study, ICPR edition, 1974).

It has to be concluded that Almond and Verba were incorrect in their original characterization of the British civic culture as one with high levels of deference and respect for the political authorities. The cynicism identified in the 1970s was also present, but unstressed, in the 1959 survey (Heath and Topf, 1987). Moreover, whilst political cynicism is inevitably associated with measures of party identity and sympathy, nonetheless, there is scant evidence that people want major changes to our present political system. Only 31 percent of respondents expressed a preference for a change to some electoral system allowing more proportional representation of parties, and 52 percent single-party government to coalitions.

Political obligation and political action

I have emphasized that the civic culture thesis rests upon the purported relationship between political orientations and actions. In the *Civic Culture* study, one key battery of questions asked people what they thought they would do about the passing of an unjust or unfair law. Table 2 shows that in 1959, 34 percent said they would do nothing, falling to 29 percent in 1974, and down to 10 percent by 1986.

In both surveys, respondents were also asked if they had ever carried out any of the activities which they said they would, faced with

Table 2   *Levels of political action 1959–86*

Percentage of population who would or have acted by:	would			have			would never		
	1959 (%)	1974 (%)	1986 (%)	1959 (%)	1974 (%)	1986 (%)	1959 (%)	1974 (%)	1986 (%)
Signing a petition	19	22	65	–	23	34	–	23	–
Contacting their MP	–	–	52	–	–	11	–	–	–
Going on a protest or demonstration	–	25	11	–	6	6	–	43	–
Doing nothing	34	–	10	94	–	56		n.a.	

In 1959, $N = 953$; in 1974, $N = 1,802$; in 1986, $N = 1,548$

Sources: as Table 1

injustice or unfairness. In 1959, 94 percent said that they had not, compared with 1986, when the percentage saying they had not had fallen to 56 percent. One in three of all respondents claimed to have signed a petition, and one in ten to have written to their Member of Parliament. But an average of well below 5 percent said that they had ever performed any of the other activities listed.

Such responses would hardly seem to confirm a collapsing civic culture with citizens distrustful of conventional political participation. But they do pose a dilemma for the conventional notion of political culture. Most citizens express the view that they have very little say over what the government of the day does, yet at the same time, they say that they would act upon perceived injustices. Moreover, the form of political action in which they see themselves as engaging is in no way unconventional, as Marsh's thesis of protest potential suggested. Overwhelmingly, people opt for conventional activities such as signing petitions and writing to Members of Parliament, despite their seeming rejection of participation through the major political parties.[6]

At first this may seem like Almond and Verba's myth of civic competence (1963: 481) by which citizens believe they have some influence over the political process which, in reality, they do not. On the contrary, however, these data suggest that citizens suffer from no such delusions, and believe that they would engage in political activities in full recognition of the likely limitations on their influence.

Strength is added to this interpretation when we turn to a further batch of recent questions which specifically asked people to rank the effectiveness of types of political activity intended to influence government. The ranking people chose corresponded neither to the ranking of activities they said they would engage upon were they faced with injustices, nor with their reports of what, if anything, they had done in practice. Signing petitions was by far the most popular on the first two counts, but ranked third in effectiveness below contacting the media, and contacting one's Member of Parliament. Fifty-eight percent thought that contacting the media would be very, or quite, effective, but only 15 percent said that that is what they would do, and only 3 percent said they had ever done so.

This picture raises more questions than it answers. First, within the terms of the conventional interpretation of the data, there is the myth of civic competence, the increasing disparity between 'action potential' and reported activity itself. Ninety percent of respondents now say that they would do something about the passage of unjust or unfair legislation, yet only 56 percent say that they have ever done so, and well below 10 percent have done anything more 'active' than petitioning or contacting their Member of Parliament.

Then there are further anomalies, between preferred types of political action and beliefs about their effectiveness, and between 'action potential' and beliefs about efficacy. Thus petitioning, by far the most popular type of activity, is seen as being effective by less than half the respondents, and is regarded as ineffective even by some 45 percent of those who say they have petitioned. Similarly, some 90 percent of respondents say that they would attempt to influence government over an unjust or unfair law, whilst 75 percent say that they believe they have no say in government decisions.

The political culture of activism

If conventional political culture theories are to explain recent changes in British politics, and if the tensions cited above are to be resolved, then much progress would be made if it were possible to discover cultural characteristics which differentiated the active few from the relatively inactive majority.

One characteristic that has long been considered central is education. Lipset, for example, notes with favour Dewey's philosophical treatise on this precise theme, and argues that:

> Education broadens man's outlook, enables him to understand the need for norms of tolerance, restrains him from adhering to extremist doctrines, and increases his capacity to make *rational* electoral choices. . . . The higher one's education, the more likely one is to believe in democratic values and support democratic practices. (1960: 56; emphasis added)

Almond and Verba used education as a principal variable, and concluded: 'The educated classes possess the keys to political participation and involvement, whilst those with less education are less well equipped' (1963: 381).

These analysts saw education as rendering citizens available for political participation, rather than determining the affective content of their participation. This conclusion was shared by Marsh (Marsh, 1977; Barnes and Kaase, 1979), who found that increasing levels of education were equally associated with both increasing conventional participation and with increasing 'protest potential' – the widening political repertory hypothesis of educational effects.

It has often been suggested that Britain is an exception to this kind of generalization. Kavanagah (1980: 134) reanalysed the original *Civic Culture* data to show that in some respects the British with least education expressed the highest political competence. Heath and Topf concluded from examining the 1979 and 1983 British Election Study data that there was:

> No evidence of substantial differences in the political norms and language of the educationally qualified and unqualified, and little of significant

differences in levels of either conventional or unconventional participation. Similarly, there is scant evidence that education leads to a weakening of party identification as predicted by cognitive theories of participation. (1986: 565)

The 1986 survey offers new data. As Table 3 shows, graduates are three times as likely as the educationally unqualified to say that they had a high level of interest in politics, and under 15 percent of graduates report having no interest compared with over half of the unqualified. Using a compressed measure of political cynicism,[7] less than 5 percent of graduates were very cynical compared with 28 percent of the educationally unqualified.

Table 3   *Levels of political interest by educational qualification, 1986*

| | | Level of education | |
Political interest	Degree (%)	Intermediate (%)	None (%)
High	61.5	32.6	19.9
Some	24.3	36.6	26.6
Little/none	14.1	30.9	53.5
$N =$	(115)	(744)	(686)

Chi-square = 157.6, 8 df

Source: British Social Attitudes survey, 1986

When we turn to the question of what respondents would do about unfair or unjust legislation, the educational gradient remains, but it is far less steep. Ninety-four percent of graduates say that they would engage in at least one form of political activity to resist injustice, compared with 86 percent of the unqualified, and this gradient remains even when controlling for age (although there is also an age effect). There are sharper differences in the types of political activity in which people say they would engage (Table 4). Eighty percent of graduates say that they would write to their Member of Parliament, compared with just over 40 percent of the unqualified, and, as Marsh also found, 24 percent of graduates say that they would join in a demonstration, compared with only 5 percent of the unqualified.

We find much the same gradients for political activity itself. Only 5 percent of graduates reported that they did not vote in the last election, as against 20 percent of the unqualified. Graduates were over three times as likely to belong to a political party, and over four times as likely to have canvassed in the election campaign. Whilst much the same proportions of each educational category said they had once acted to resist legislative injustices, some 38 percent of graduates said

Table 4   *Levels of political action by educational qualification, 1986*

| | Level of education | | | |
	Degree (%)	Intermediate (%)	None (%)	Chi-square
Percentage saying how they *would* act against an unjust or unfair law:				
Contact MP	79.6	56.3	42.1	68.1
Sign petition	71.2	68.9	58.7	18.5
Contact media	24.2	15.3	13.1	9.3
Join demonstration	24.2	13.2	5.3	48.9
Do at least one act	94.4	93.1	85.5	
Do nothing	4.3	6.8	14.5	37.8
Percentage saying how they *have acted* against unjust or unfair law:				
Contacted MP	29.4	10.8	7.7	48.6
Signed petition	52.8	36.5	28.6	29.3
Contacted media	8.6	3.3	1.3	20.6
Joined demonstration	16.6	7.3	2.2	45.2
Done at least one act	71.3	45.7	36.7	
Done nothing	28.7	54.3	63.3	49.7
Percentage *assessing* each act as *effective* in influencing government:				
Contacting MP	61.1	53.0	51.0	7.4
Signing petition	36.3	44.9	50.8	15.2
Contacting media	59.8	63.4	59.7	8.5
Joining demonstration	22.5	24.7	18.3	24.9
N =	(117)	(744)	(685)	

Source: *British Social Attitudes* survey, 1986

that they had done so more than once, compared with 7 percent of the unqualified.

The inconsistencies between these responses and beliefs about effectiveness remain for all educational levels (Table 4). Thirty-nine percent of graduates did not believe it would be effective to contact their Members of Parliament, 49 percent of the unqualified. Sixty-four percent of graduates thought it was not effective to sign petitions, although 71 per cent would do so, whilst 49 percent of the unqualified thought it ineffective but 59 percent said they would petition.

On the basis of these findings, it may seem that for Britain educational qualification is a significant indicator of the exemplary bearer of the civic culture. The better educated are more interested in politics and government, less cynical about them, are more likely to say they would engage in political activities within conventional norms, and are more likely to say they have in practice done so on more than one occasion.

However, all these differentiations are ones of degree, and must be set against the gradient of the educationally qualified in the population as a whole, which still comprises well under 10 percent graduates and almost half unqualified.[8] When we turn to consider the politically active as a group, we find that in relation to the distribution of educational qualifications as a whole, graduates are significantly overrepresented, comprising 54 percent of activists. But by the same measure, almost half of activists are non-graduates, and over a quarter have no educational qualifications. Similarly, activists are significantly less cynical about the political process, but nonetheless, over half are very or fairly cynical.

The problem of political action

Almond and Verba proposed that:

> The subjectively competent citizen has not necessarily attempted to influence the government, but he is more likely to have made such attempts than is the citizen who does not consider himself competent. [He has] a reserve of influence. He is not the active citizen: he is the potentially active citizen. (1963: 481)

A key finding presented in *The Civic Culture* was the claim of 24 percent of respondents that they believed an attempt of theirs to influence Parliament would be successful (1963: 480). It is questionable as to whether or not Almond and Verba were ever justified in making this claim,[9] but certainly all subsequent evidence suggests that they were mistaken about the nature of the myth of civic competence.

The central feature of that myth is not that citizens accredit themselves with unwarranted, potential influence over governmental affairs. Rather it is that they say they would act, and say so in ever-increasing numbers, and that to a much more limited extent they say that they have acted, even though they do not believe they have influence. They act in ways which they do not consider especially effective, nor even, potentially, the most effective of the courses of action available to them.

Clearly something is awry with the analytical framework, and the most obvious problem relates to the interpretation of 'action' itself. Conventional usages of the concept of political culture hinge upon the relationship between orientation and action – between culture, and the system defined in terms of the role. The notion of the role developed in the political culture literature derived primarily from Parsons's version of systems functionalism. In his seminal article, Almond wrote:

> The unit of the political system is the role. The role, according to Parsons and Shils, '. . . is that organised sector of an actor's orientation which

constitutes and defines his participation in an interactive process' [1951: 23].
It involves a set of complementary expectations concerning his own actions
and those of others with whom he interacts. Thus a political system may be
defined as a set of interacting roles, or as a structure of roles, if we
understand by structure a patterning of interactions. (1970: 32)

It is this concept of political action which informs that of 'orientations
towards political action', that in turn is central to the conventional
theses on democratic stability. Whilst a detailed critique of the *General
Theory of Action* per se is not possible here, the key themes can be
quickly established. 'Social systems' and 'personality systems' are
systems of action, in contradistinction to 'cultural systems', which are
systems of symbolic patterns. And 'action' here means 'motivated
action', where motivations are conceived psychoanalytically, as the
expenditure of energy on:

> Orientations involving cognition of and cathectic attachment to certain
> means and goal objects and certain more or less implicit and unconscious
> 'plans' of action aimed at the acquisition of cathected relationships to goal
> objects. (Parsons and Shils, 1951: 111)

Put at its simplest: 'The theory of action . . . conceives of . . . behaviour
as oriented to the attainment of ends in situations, by means of the
normatively regulated expenditure of energy' (1951: 53). Now, insofar
as this Freudian grounding in notions of energy flows and gratifications
serves to strengthen the heuristic usefulness of Parsons's earlier
theories of rational action, they are perhaps harmless enough. But the
dichotomization of motivations into 'drives' and 'need-dispositions',
and then the identification of 'values' with need-dispositions, all add
up to an analytical model which places the political system – defined in
terms of the allocation of values – firmly in the sphere of 'need-
dispositioned' motivations to action.

Thus, political action becomes axiomatically analysed in *zweckrational* terms. That is to say, the social scientists' interpretations of the
reasons for political actions by actors are reconstructed in the
instrumentally rational terms of goals, satisfactions, and so on. Such
explanatory theories, therefore, wedded neatly with contemporary
notions of empirical democracy theory, which held that 'politics' is an
activity directed at the articulation and realization of interest demands.
Political action became by its very nature instrumentalist:

> We are interested in participation that involves attempts (successful or
> otherwise) to influence government . . . Participation is important to us as
> the key *instrumental* political act by citizens in a democracy. (Verba et al.,
> 1978: 301; emphasis added)

It is in the context of this notion of political action, held to be
constitutive of the political system itself, that the conventional

interpretation of orientations towards such action must be assessed. Hence, we find the unresolved dilemma of apparent dissonance between survey responses reporting how people would act, how they have acted, and what they consider effective. Those tensions arise because action is interpreted in instrumentally rational terms. Indeed, for the coherency of the theory, this must be so.

However, this is not the only possible interpretation of the data. Instead of attempting to fit responses to questions about political participation into a rationalistic framework held to be constitutive of the political system, they may be interpreted as expressions of 'values', or better, of positions in the moral order, constitutive of the political culture. Rather than orientations towards *zweckrational* action, they may be measures of what people believe they ought to do, that is, what they feel a moral obligation to do, even though as individuals, they may not always fulfil their obligations.

I am not simply proposing that people are reporting what they believe the ideal citizen ought to do, always provided that they believe it is also rational and effective so to do. Rather, what I am proposing is that the rationalistic framework is itself inappropriate. The moral order which informs beliefs about action relates to what the conventional theory would term 'role definitions', and I would prefer to call political identities.

Such an interpretation removes one dilemma by shifting the 'would do' batteries of responses to the realm of political culture rather than treating them as indicators of action constituting the political system. It explains why people say they would do things which they have not done in practice, namely, because it is what they believe citizens ought to do. It also sets out a framework for explaining why some people act politically in ways which from a rationalistic perspective appear to be 'irrational', that is, when people do not believe in the effectiveness of their own activities. The basis of this latter interpretation would be that the activities are morally grounded, expressions of political identity. Thus, for example, the data makes it reasonable to conclude that petitioning is an expressive act which is meaningful to citizens who identify with that aspect of the political culture, irrespective of its effectiveness.

Such an analytical approach to resolving some of the tensions in development of the civic culture thesis is not anathema to that thesis in its original form. As I noted above, Almond and Verba drew heavily on Parsonian theory, which in turn emphasized the 'normative' elements of culture systems. Thus Parsons wrote that:

> A society must constitute a social community that has an adequate level of integration or solidarity. . . . This community must be the 'bearer' of a cultural system sufficiently generalized and integrated to legitimize

normative order. Such legitimation requires a system of constitutive symbolism which grounds the identity and solidarity of the community, as well as beliefs, rituals, and other cultural components which embody such symbolism. (1969: 19)[10]

Writing of the significance of the Kennedy assassination for the American political system, Verba himself wrote of the event revealing:

> A level of commitment to politics both more intense than that revealed by the usual public-opinion-surveying techniques, and of a somewhat different order. . . . The kind of primordial emotional attachment that is necessary for the long-term maintenance of the political system . . . is not the rather fragile support that is based solely on a calculation of interests; it is support based on a . . . less rational sort of attachment. (1965: 358–60)

Verba's neo-Durkheimian analysis of the Kennedy assassination was much influenced by Shils's earlier work on the British coronation (1953), both focusing on political ceremonies and rituals as acts of communion within civil religion (Bellah, 1968), through which citizens reaffirm their national identities. The theoretical problems raised by such approaches cannot be pursued here (cf. Lukes, 1977), and neofunctionalism is not being offered as an alternative theory to solve the problems of the civic culture thesis.

However, it serves as a reminder that the continual emphasis upon instrumentalist action, which the mass survey techniques have tended to engender, if for no other reason than selecting the concrete nation-state as the unit of analysis tempts analysts to lose sight of the core problem of cultural renewal and change. Political culture theorists hold the political culture as the repository of norms and values – the moral order. But the theory requires these to be realized through process, or action. The adoption of role-theory resolves the problem of this realization, by making role-holders the bearers of the moral order, and then making citizenship into a type of role.[11]

Political culture: the form of the moral order

It is clear that the conventional notion of political culture has served its term – useful or not – for the study of political stability. The questions which demand attention now, at least with regard to Western democracies, are no longer about stability but about changes in value systems and ideologies, and related changes in political participation and political party support.

The concept of political culture will continue to serve as a valuable analytical tool for the study of these changes, once it is divested of its rationalistic baggage. We may then attend to the central project, implicit even in the theoretical framework underpinning the civic culture thesis. This involves the study of the form of the moral order constitutive of the dominant political culture, by which the state is legitimated, and the identification of political processes by and through which these cultures are renewed and changed. Equally important, such studies must attend to the location of subcultural variations, and their relationship to legitimation and change. In other words, through the analysis of political culture and shared political identities, the project may approach questions about communities, groups and perhaps even individuals, who, through their actions, are citizens in the widest sense of the term (Pranger, 1968).

One approach has already become clear. Measures of education have been shown to serve as significant indicators of the likelihood of political participation in this wider sense. But the association of educational qualifications with political activism, which is in any case only partial, does not of itself further our understanding of recent changes in political culture. To pursue this further, we must escape the unduly limited notion of which values are relevant, inherited from the civic culture paradigm (Natchez, 1985: 138–45).

This idea is far from novel. Lipset (1963: 207ff.) has made valiant attempts to deploy Parsons's pattern variables in the comparative study of democratic political systems. It must suffice here to say that Lipset's analysis paralleled that of Almond and Verba not only in drawing upon the same theoretical framework,[12] and thus presenting the same difficulties I have already outlined, but also in attending primarily to problems of political stability.[13]

Inglehart's seminal thesis about the emergence of postmaterialism also linked changing values and their expression through political participation (1977: 4).[14] In *Political Action*, Inglehart and colleagues (Barnes and Kaase, 1979) further developed his initial thesis in a search for relationships between basic values and political participation. However, they were forced to conclude that: 'There was no association between value orientations and conventional participation' (1979: 287ff.), and only a most modest one with so-called protest potential.[15]

Recent work on value clusters in Britain offers new insights into the form of the moral order.[16] So far, this has focused upon what have come to be regarded as two of the basic value clusters associated with liberal democracy, namely 'moral traditionalism', and 'economic egalitarianism'. The first of these relates to such things as respect for authority, for traditional values, and for the rule of law. The second relates to beliefs about the distribution of wealth and income in society, about the equality of social justice, and about the basis of social conflict.

Ranking moral traditionalism on a scale ranging from libertarians through conformists to authoritarians, the predominant British disposition in the 1980s must be regarded as authoritarian.[17] On the other hand, similarly ranking economic egalitarianism, a majority of the population express egalitarian convictions.[18] For present purposes, of course, the significance of such findings is their relevance for political culture and identities.

Table 5   *The moral order: traditionalism and egalitarianism by cynicism and activism*

	Moral traditionalism			Economic egalitarianism		
	Liber-tarian	Conform-ist	Authori-tarian	Left	Centre	Right
Political cynicism						
Very (%)	20.3	55.0	24.7	39.8	52.6	7.6
Fairly (%)	22.8	58.2	19.0	23.9	57.9	18.1
Not (%)	25.5	55.4	19.0	7.0	49.2	43.9
	Chi-square = 5.9, 4 df; *p* = 0.2078			Chi-square = 179.5, 4 df; *p*<0.0001		
Political activism						
Very (%)	36.7	49.7	13.5	21.4	55.2	23.4
Fairly (%)	22.7	57.4	19.9	22.0	53.3	24.7
Not (%)	29.7	58.1	22.1	23.9	55.0	21.0
	Chi-square = 25.3, 4 df; *p* < 0.0001			Chi-square = 2.5, 4 df; *p* = 0.6525		

Source: *British Social Attitudes* survey, 1986

It is common for conventional accounts of political culture to associate moral traditionalism with dispositions towards the democratic political process. Both Lipset's position on the benefits of education, and to some extent Inglehart's on postmaterialism, suggest that moral libertarianism is a democratic virtue, whilst moral authoritarianism threatens liberal democracy. Implicit, at least, in such interpretations is the view that moral authoritarianism may be a psychological trait offering a foothold to authoritarian ideologies. It may well be expected, therefore, that moral libertarians, who hold the more radical positions on authority, would be particularly concerned about the responsiveness of politicians and governments to the democratic process. If so, they would rank somewhat higher on the index of political cynicism than moral authoritarians.

We find, however, that the composite measure of political cynicism shows a very weak statistical relationship with moral traditionalism (see Table 5). On the other hand, when we turn to political activism, we do find a marked correlation with moral traditionalism, although there was none between political cynicism and political activism. Libertarians are more than twice as likely as authoritarians to be politically active; proportionally few activists are moral authoritarians. This would suggest, counterintuitively, that the values measured by the index of moral traditionalism are not salient for political cynicism.

An equally surprising relationship emerges with economic egalitarianism. As Table 5 also shows, unlike moral traditionalism, this value index correlates very strongly with political cynicism. Only 8 percent of the very cynical were on the right of the egalitarian index, compared with 44 percent of respondents who were not cynical. Moreover, again unlike moral traditionalism, there was no association whatsoever between the index of economic egalitarianism and that for political activism. Those on the left and on the right of the scale were equally likely, and unlikely, to be active.[19]

There can be no doubt that these are significant findings for the form of contemporary, British, political culture, although no firm conclusions may be drawn based upon such single point data.[20] A beginning may be made by considering the demographic distribution of the two value indices, and as the new databases develop, much work remains to be done.

Figure 1 illustrates the sociodemographic distribution of the two

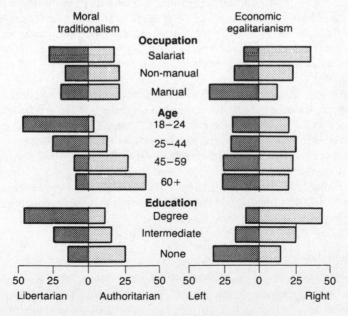

Figure 1 *The demographic distribution of the moral order*

Source: *British Social Attitudes* survey, 1986

value indices.[21] It shows that like political cynicism, occupational class is not significantly associated with moral traditionalism, but it is strongly associated with economic egalitarianism. Just 10 percent of the salariat are on the left of the egalitarian scale, compared with 35 percent of manual workers. Similarly, 36 percent of the salariat are on the right, compared with 13 percent of manual workers.[22] If may well be, therefore, that egalitarianism remains a feature of 'class politics' (cf. Minkenberg and Inglehart, this volume).

In contrast to occupational class, age parallels political activism and not cynicism. As may be seen, almost none of the youngest cohort in the 1986 survey were moral authoritarians, whilst under 10 percent of those over sixty years old were moral libertarians. There was no association with the index of economic egalitarianism. Of course, at this stage in the project we have no way of addressing the crucial questions which have become such a part of the postmaterialism debate, as to whether these effects are intergenerational, life cycle, both, or neither. All that does seem noteworthy is that they are sustained even for the youngest cohort, which has reached maturity knowing only one Prime Minister and her government in power.

Significantly, educational qualification, which was identified earlier as closely related both to political activism and to positions on the moral order, distinguishes respondents along both value indices. As may well be expected, only some one in ten graduates were found to be moral authoritarians, and only 15 percent of those with no educational qualifications were moral libertarians. Such results are much in line with what the theories of both Lipset and Inglehart may have predicted.

However, in the case of economic egalitarianism, the relationship is reversed. Contrary to conventional expectations, very few graduates proved to be in favour of economic egalitarianism, compared with a third of respondents with no educational qualifications. Moreover, the educational effect remained, albeit less significantly, when controlled for occupational class. Thus, at least in Britian, it would seem that increasing levels of education are being paralleled by a commitment to inegalitarian values rather than the redistributive and consensualist values predicted by civic culture theorists.

Conclusions

This suggests some tentative conclusions about the relationship between contemporary British political culture and political change over the last thirty years. Contrary to much conventional writing, it is clear that political cynicism has been a long-standing feature of British political culture, rather than a behavioural disposition towards political action (or apathy). Expressions of cynicism and distrust are indicative neither of increasing political distrust, nor of a destabilizing protest potential which emerged only during the 1970s. Few people wish for radical change in the present political system. There is little evidence indeed of a collapsing moral order of the civic culture.

On the contrary, British political culture is changing in the direction of a more widespread sense of political obligation than a generation ago, accompanied by increasing expressive participation, engaged in despite cynicism about its instrumental effectiveness.

Importantly, such participation is not through the once-conventional mode of support for and through a two-party political system. Over the last generation, the Conservative and Labour parties combined have lost some 18 percent of their electoral support. Yet, as we have seen, in 1986 nine out of ten respondents said that they would act in some way to attempt to influence a perceived legislative injustice, and almost half report that they have attempted to influence government policy. Whilst there are good reasons to be cautious about such measures as indicators of true levels of political action and potential for action, such reasons do not apply to their reliability as indicators of the moral components of contemporary political culture.

At the same time, socioeconomic and demographic changes have meant an increasing proportion of the polity with better education, and a decreasing proportion in unskilled occupations. Both of these structural characteristics are associated with positions in the moral order. Education correlates with both economic egalitarianism and moral traditionalism, as well as with political activism. Occupation correlates with the egalitarianism but not with moral traditionalism. Moral traditionalism, but not egalitarianism, is significantly associated with political activism.

From this emerges a picture of contemporary political space in which mass and elite political cultures diverge. Contemporary political activists are underrepresentative of the extent of moral authoritarianism in the mass culture, whilst they overrepresent the moral libertarianism shared, principally by the young, better educated salariat. Conversely, when we turn to economic egalitarianism, contemporary political activists are at present representative of left–right distribution within mass culture, but not of the pronounced inegalitarianism of the better educated, occupational elite.

Assuming present demographic trends in education and occupation continue, and that political activists continue to arise principally from the better educated, then the expectation would be that political elites will come increasingly to espouse an unfamiliar matrix of moral libertarianism and economic inegalitarianism which is remote from contemporary mass culture along both indices.

However, there are inherent moral tensions in sustaining moral libertarianism together with economic inegalitarianism, some of which in 1989 are already beginning to emerge on the British political agenda. They surface in particular in relation to social policy and the legitimacy of the welfare state, in part because practical moral libertarianism entails a degree of social and political equality, whilst economic inegalitarianism does not axiomatically endorse anticollectivism.[23]

Further tensions arise from the advancement by a 'new right', Conservative government (Kavanagh, 1987; cf. Minkenberg and Inglehart, this volume), of anti-collectivist policies which threaten the very stage of the theatre in which morally libertarian, political actors, are seeking to express their identities. Economic inegalitarians may not be convinced by T.H. Marshall's definition of citizenship in terms of social rights and equality (Marshall, 1950; Lipset, 1963). But once having perceived themselves as being citizens with moral obligations, a continuingly reducing role for the state also cuts back their scope for political participation, except for that canalized through political parties.

Quite apart from such tensions, assumptions premised solely upon demographic trends serve to perpetuate the analytical naïvete of conventional interpretations of the political process. The analysis of political culture as the form of the moral order, through which collective political identities are reproduced, in no way entails the notion that culture is solely a societal product, with a political system concerned with the authoritative allocation of societal values (Easton, 1965).

I have argued elsewhere that the role of the state is central to an understanding of the processes of cultural reproduction (Topf, 1986). Gellner has suggested that:

> At the base of the modern social order stands not the executioner but professor. Not the guillotine, but the (aptly named) doctorat d'état is the main tool and symbol of state power. The monopoly of legitimate education is now more important, more central than is the monopoly of legitimate violence. . . The state is, above all, the protector, not of a faith, but of a culture. (1983: 34, 110)

Gellner relates the inevitability of such an educational monopoly to the needs of the labour market in late industrial society. In Britain in 1989 the government of the day includes in its rhetoric a commitment to promulgate a new 'enterprise culture', and it has advanced much the same arguments to justify radical change in all levels of the British educational system. For the first time, British schools will have a 'national core curriculum', determined by the state, whilst further and higher education is to be more closely controlled.

The empirical evidence reviewed here shows education to be central both to changes in the moral order of the political culture, and to the reproduction of that culture through political participation. It suggests, also, that for a growing proportion of citizens, such participation is itself a moral good. The British state may well be equipping itself with powerful tools to attempt to extend its influence and accelerate the rate of cultural change. Such attempts are likely to have but superficial success if they fail to recognize that the moral order of the political culture now embraces the economic order also.

Notes

1. Almond and Verba proposed that: 'A brief glance at history will tell which [countries] are the more stable' (1963: 479), and concluded that 'Great Britain and the United States are the two relatively stable and successful democracies'. Pateman suggests that for Almond and Verba, stability means no more than 'the infrequency of unconstitutional changes of regime' (Almond and Verba, 1980: 99, n. 7). It is this stipulative view that subsequent writers within the stable democracy tradition have also adopted. For further discussion see Barry (1970).
  2. Marsh's survey was later included in the eight-nation study, *Political Action*, of Barnes and Kaase (1979). The statistical materials cited here are taken from the ICPSR (Inter-university Consortium for Political Science Research) data set, with the adjustments to the sample made by those authors (1979: 23).
  3. Fortunately, the situation is now improving rapidly. The *British Social Attitudes* survey series has included increasing amounts of political culture material since its inception in 1983. An Anglo-German study of political culture is currently in progress, supported by the Anglo-German Foundation, and first results should be available by 1989.
  4. See, for example, Kavanagh (1985), Rose (1985), Heath et al. (1985), Rose and McAllister (1986), Kavanagh (1986), Crewe (1986), Heath et al. (1987).
  5. In the British Election Study 1983, 70 percent of respondents said that they read about the campaign in the newspapers, and 75 percent said that they 'cared a good deal' about which party won the election (Butler and Kavanagh, 1984). In the *British Social Attitudes* survey 1986, 73 percent of respondents said that they read a daily newspaper at least three times a week, 29 percent said that they had 'a great deal' or 'quite a lot' of interest in politics, whilst only 13 percent said none at all.
  6. An essential element of the thesis diagnosing the decline and crisis of the British civic culture was the purported loss of British deference and the rise of 'populism' manifesting itself in 'protest potential'. The *British Social Attitudes* studies have not replicated Marsh's questions on unconventional political activities, but the *European Values* survey in 1981 did so exactly. Table 6 shows the same leap between 1974 and 1981 in the numbers of people who say that they would petition, and that they have done so, but otherwise the same low levels of reported unconventional activity. Thus even if what was interpreted as 'protest potential' in the late 1970s was indeed indicative of potential activity, and that will be challenged later, then there is no evidence that that potential has manifested itself in action.
  7. For details see Heath and Topf (1987: n. 6).
  8. Precise figures are difficult to estimate. Heath and Topf (1986: Table 3) calculated 5 percent graduates and 54 percent unqualified for 1981. The 1986 *British Social Attitudes* survey indicates 8 percent graduates and 44 percent unqualified.

Table 6 Levels of political protest 1974–81

	have done		might do		would never do	
Percentage of population who say that they have or would:	1974 (%)	1981 (%)	1974 (%)	1981 (%)	1974 (%)	1981 (%)
Sign petition	23	63	22	28	23	9
Attend lawful demonstration	6	9	25	33	43	58
Join boycott	6	6	25	31	51	63
Join unofficial strike	5	8	16	16	72	76
Occupy building	1	2	13	10	80	87
Break windows, etc.	1	2	2	1	96	97
Fight with the police	0	1	4	3	95	96

Sources: Marsh survey, 1974, European Values survey, 1981 (see notes 2 and 6 above)

9. On the basis of their own data, when asked how successful people believed their attempts would be, 49 percent said it was not at all likely, or impossible.

10. Translated into the terms of the civic culture thesis, 'community' becomes commensurate with 'nation'. The conflation of the analytical notion of community with that of nation, as concretized by nation-state boundaries, presents particular problems which I have discussed elsewhere (Topf, forthcoming).

11. This analytical framework has the merit of tidiness, but works only if the analyst predetermines the coterminosity of political culture qua nation and political system qua state.

12. It differed, however, amongst other things, in drawing entirely upon secondary materials and presenting a largely historical analysis, whilst eschewing the survey methodology. Lipset characterizes Britain as embodying: 'a strong emphasis on ascriptive, elitist, particularistic, and diffuse values' (1963: 216). He draws on sources ranging from Bagehot to Shils, for example, to emphasize, like Almond and Verba: 'The protection from populist criticism which an elitist system gives to all who possess the diffuse status of "leaders"' (1963: 221).

13. Thus Lipset concludes: 'The particular distribution of different value orientations in Britain would seem to be congruent with the stability of an industrialized democracy, since it legitimates open participation by all groups in the economy and polity, while the diffuse elitism rewards all with a claim to high postion' (1963: 224). I have already shown that this would seem to be a singularly mistaken view of British political culture, certainly by the 1960s.

14. The thesis itself, which became closely related to theories about the decline and collapse of the civic culture, and the continuing debate it has engendered, need no rehearsal here. For Britain, Heath and Topf (1986: 560–4) demonstrated that educational qualifications, and not Inglehart's key measures of formative affluence, were the best indicators of his composite measure of postmaterialism. Moreover, the education gradient was even steeper for measures of other values associated with moral libertarianism.

15. For Britain, the coefficient was as low as 0.18.

16. See Abrams et al. (1985), Heath and Topf (1986, 1987), Jowell and Topf (1988).

17. For example, some three-quarters of the population favour schools teaching children to obey authority, and stiffer prison sentences for lawbreakers; less than a tenth disagree. Similarly, two-thirds favour censorship to uphold moral standards, and believe

that the young lack respect for traditional British values, whilst less than a fifth disagree (Heath and Topf, 1987).

18. For example, 65 percent believe that ordinary working people do not get a fair share of the nation's wealth; just 14 percent disagree. Fifty-nine percent believe that there is one law for the rich and one for the poor; 22 percent disagree (Heath and Topf, 1987).

19. As would be expected, attitudes towards economic egalitarianism discriminate powerfully between party-political sympathies, but the effects remain even when controlling for party sympathy.

20. The *British Social Attitudes* series provides one basis for time-series data. The results of a comparative, Anglo-West German study should become available in 1989.

21. Figure 1 is based directly upon Table 7 below, the respective chart bars merely omitting the central position on each index.

22. For details of the occupational categories used, see Heath and Topf (1987).

23. Any analysis of the interrelationships between the moral order, political party ideology and rhetoric, and public perceptions of government policy, is well beyond the scope of this chapter. The tensions identified may be simply illustrated, however, by

Table 7   *The demography of the political culture*

	Moral traditionalism			Economic egalitarianism		
	Liber-tarian	Conform-ist	Authori-tarian	Left	Centre	Right
Occupational class						
Salariat (%)	29.6	52.5	17.9	10.3	53.3	36.4
Non-manual (%)	17.4	61.4	21.3	17.9	58.4	23.7
Manual (%)	20.8	57.7	21.5	34.7	52.1	13.2
	Chi-square = 16.6, 4 df; p = 0.0023			Chi-square = 97.5, 4 df; p>0.0001		
Age						
18–24 (%)	48.3	48.2	3.6	20.1	59.0	20.8
25–44 (%)	26.9	60.5	12.6	20.6	55.3	24.0
45–59 (%)	11.1	61.9	27.0	26.0	51.1	23.0
60 and over (%)	9.3	50.8	39.9	26.1	53.5	20.4
	Chi-square = 215.7, 6 df; p>0.0001			Chi-square = 7.3, 6 df; p = 0.2919		
Educational qualification						
Degree (%)	47.1	41.8	11.1	9.8	46.4	43.7
Intermediate (%)	26.0	57.8	16.2	16.6	57.6	25.7
None (%)	15.1	58.4	26.5	32.5	52.3	15.1
	Chi-square = 68.0, 4 df; p>0.0001			Chi-square = 81.2, 4 df; p>0.0001		

Source: *British Social Attitudes* survey, 1986

noting that in the 1986 *British Social Attitudes* survey, whilst 43 percent of respondents agreed with the moral proposition that government should redistribute income from the better-off to those who are less well off (and 25 percent had no view) (Q.B231.I), 79 percent agreed with the practical proposition that the government should spend more money to create jobs (and just 11 percent had no view) (Q.B231.B).

References

Abrams, M., Gerard, D. and Timms, M. (eds)(1985) *Values and Social Change in Britain.* Basingstoke: Macmillan.

Almond, G.A. (1970) *Political Development: Essays in Heuristic Theory.* Boston: Little, Brown.

Almond, G.A. (1980) 'The Intellectual History of the Civic Culture Concept', pp. 1–36 in Almond and Verba (1980).

Almond, G.A. and Powell Jnr, G.B. (1984) *Comparative Politics Today: a World View.* Boston, Little Brown.

Almond, G.A. and Verba, S. (1963) *The Civic Culture: Political Attitudes and Democracy in Five Nations.* Princeton: Princeton University Press.

Almond, G.A. and Verba, S. (eds) (1980) *The Civic Culture Revisited.* Boston: Little, Brown.

Barnes, S.H., and Kaase, M. (eds) (1979) *Political Action: Mass Participation in Five Western Democracies.* Beverly Hills: Sage.

Barry, Brian (1970) *Sociologists, Economists and Democracy.* London: Collier-Macmillan.

Beer, S.H. (1982) *Britain Against Itself: the Political Contradictions of Collectivism.* London: Faber & Faber.

Bellah, R.N. (1968) 'Civil Religion in America', pp. 331–93 in Cutler (1968).

Brittan S. (1975) 'The Economic Contradictions of Democracy', *British Journal of Political Science,* 5: 129–59.

Butler, D. and Kavanagh, D. (1984) *The British General Election of 1983.* London: Macmillan.

Crewe, I. (1986) 'On the Death and Resurrection of Class Voting: Some Comments on *How Britain Votes*', *Political Studies,* 34: 620–38.

Crozier, M.J., Huntington, S.P. and Watanuki, J. (1975) *The Crisis of Democracy: Report on the Governability of Democracies to the Trilateral Commission.* New York: New York University Press.

Cutler, D.R. (ed.) (1968) *The World Yearbook of Religion: the Religious Situation.* Vol. 1. London: Evans Brothers.

Dahl, R.A. (1961) *Who Governs? Democracy and Power in an American City.* New Haven: Yale University Press.

Duncan, G. (ed.) (1983) *Democratic Theory and Practice.* Cambridge: Cambridge University Press.

Easton, D. (1965) *A Framework for Political Analysis.* Chicago: University of Chicago Press.

Gellner, E. (1983) *Nations and Nationalism.* Oxford: Basil Blackwell.

Greenberg, B.S. and Parker, E.B. (1965) *The Kennedy Assassination and the American Public.* Stanford: Stanford University Press.

Heath, A.F., Jowell, R. and Curtice, J. (1985) *How Britain Votes.* Oxford: Pergamon Press.

Heath, A.F., Jowell, R. and Curtice, J. (1987) 'Trendless Fluctuation: a Reply to Crewe', *Political Studies,* 35: 256–77.

Heath, A.F. and Topf, R.G. (1986) 'Educational Expansion and Political Change in Britain: 1964-1983', *European Journal of Political Research*, 14: 543-67.

Heath, A.F. and Topf, R.G. (1987) 'Political Culture', pp. 51-69 in Jowell et al. (1987).

Huntington, S.P. (1975) 'The United States', in Crozier et al. (1975).

Inglehart, R. (1977) *The Silent Revolution*. Princeton: Princeton University Press.

Jowell, R. and Topf, R.G. (1988) 'Trust in the Establishment', pp.109-26 in Jowell et al. (1988).

Jowell, R., Witherspoon, S. and Brook, L. (eds) (1987) *British Social Attitudes: the 5th Report*. Aldershot: Gower.

Jowell, R., Witherspoon, S. and Brook, L. (eds) (1988) *British Social Attitudes: the 1988 Report*. Aldershot: Gower.

Kaase, M. (1982) 'The Concept of Political Culture: its Meaning for Comparative Research', *EUI Working Paper*, 30.

Kavanagh, D. (1980) 'Political Culture in Great Britain: the Decline of the Civic Culture', pp. 124-76 in Almond and Verba (1980).

Kavanagh, D. (1983) *Political Science and Political Behaviour*. London: Allen & Unwin.

Kavanagh, D. (1985) *British Politics: Continuities and Change*. Oxford: Oxford University Press.

Kavanagh, D. (1986) 'How We Vote Now', *Electoral Studies*, 5: 19-28.

Kavanagh, D. (1987) *Thatcherism and British Politics*. Oxford: Oxford University Press.

Lipset, S.M. (1960) *Political Man*. London: Heinemann.

Lipset, S.M. (1963) *The First New Nation*. London, Heinemann.

Lipset, S.M. (1964) 'Introduction', pp. i-xxii in Marshall (1964).

Lukes, S. (1977) *Essays in Social Theory*. London: Macmillan.

Marsh, A. (1977) *Protest and Political Consciousness*. Beverly Hills: Sage.

Marshall, T.H. (1950) *Citizenship and Social Class*. Cambridge: Cambridge University Press.

Marshall, T.H. (1964) *Class, Citizenship, and Social Development*. Chicago: Chicago University Press.

Natchez, P. (1985) *Images of Voting: Visions of Democracy*. New York: Basic Books.

Nie, N.H., Verba, S. and Petrocik, J.R. (1979) *The Changing American Voter*. Cambridge, Mass.: Harvard University Press.

Nordlinger, E.A. (1981) *On the Autonomy of the Democratic State*. Cambridge, Mass.: Harvard University Press.

O'Connor, J. (1973) *The Fiscal Crisis of the State*. New York: St. Martin's Press.

Parsons, T. (1969) *Politics and Social Structure*. New York: Free Press.

Parsons, T. and Shils, E. (eds) (1951) *Toward a General Theory of Action*. Cambridge, Mass.: Harvard University Press.

Pateman, C. (1980) 'The Civic Culture: a Philosophical Critique', pp. 57-102 in Almond and Verba (1980).

Pranger, R.J. (1968) *Action, Symbolism, and Order*. Nashville, Tennessee.

Rose, R. (1985) *Politics in England: Persistence and Change*. London: Faber & Faber.

Rose, R. & McAllister, I. (1986) *Voters Begin to Choose: from Closed-Class to Open Elections in Britain*. London: Sage.

Scheuch, E.K. (1969) 'Social Context and Individual Behaviour', in M. Dogan and S. Rokkan (eds), *Qualitative Ecological Analysis in the Social Sciences*. Cambridge, Mass.: MIT Press.

Shils, E. (1968) 'Ritual and Crisis', pp. 733-48 in Cutler (1968).

Shils, E. and Young, M. (1956) 'The Meaning of the Coronation', *Sociological Review*, ns. 1 (2): 63-81.

Topf, R.G. (1986) 'The Politics of Environmental Pollution: Professional Knowledge and the State', paper for the European Consortium for Political Research Workshops, Gothenburg.

Topf, R.G. (forthcoming) *British Political Culture*. Oxford: Philip Allan.

Verba, S. (1965) 'The Kennedy Assassination and the Nature of Political Commitment', pp. 349–60 in Greenburg and Parker (1965).

Verba, S. (1980) 'On Revisiting the Civic Culture: A Personal Postscript', pp. 394–410 in Almond and Verba (1980).

Verba, S., Nie, N.H. and Kim, J-O. (1978) *Participation and Political Equality: a Seven-Nation Comparison*. Cambridge: Cambridge University Press.

4

Neoconservatism and Value Change in the USA: Tendencies in the Mass Public of a Postindustrial Society

Michael Minkenberg and Ronald Inglehart

During the past several years, various Western countries have experienced a shift to the right. National elections in Britain, the USA, West Germany and (temporarily) France produced right-of-centre governments which share a commitment to return to traditional values, de-emphasizing the welfare state policies of their left-wing predecessors and re-emphasizing military strength, anticommunism and nationalism in foreign policy. Moreover, the electoral victories of Margaret Thatcher, Ronald Reagan, Helmut Kohl and Jacques Chirac were preceded and accompanied by neoconservative and populist 'new right' movements which introduced new issues and emphases in public debates over the past ten to fifteen years.

Whether these events reflect a long-term revival of conservatism in Western public opinion (Schumann, 1984; Habermas, 1985) or a temporary reaction to a long-term trend towards the left (Dalton et al., 1984) remains open for debate and shall be discussed below. However, there is little disagreement that conservatism has moved away from a defensive position in the face of liberal attacks and has increasingly dominated the agenda setting in public debate and policy (Steinfels, 1979; Habermas, 1982). The new qualities of contemporary conservatism which justify speaking of neoconservatism range from its message to its methods and mass support and must be seen in the light of fundamental social and cultural changes in Western societies. With the development of industrial capitalist societies toward a stage of 'post-industrialism', the exhaustion of the new welfare state, and intergenerational value change, a new cleavage of political conflict has emerged.

In this chapter, we will demonstrate the characteristics of neoconservatism at the mass public level. It is our thesis that neoconservatism (including the new right movements in various Western countries) is a reaction against a fundamental change in culture and values and that it does not reflect the old cleavages expressed in class and partisan lines but a new cleavage based on value change. Neoconservatism is not simply a revival of conservatism but a new coalition of forces which see their common enemy in the postmaterialist oriented strata of the 'new left', and their new political agenda. Neoconservatism includes part of the 'old left' who felt challenged by the new left, and traditional conservative groups. This reaction is expressed by a heightened concern with sociocultural values and issues (nationalism, law and order, family, religion and bourgeois morality), by support for the values of industrial capitalism, particularly the idea of progress, and by a general acceptance of the basic welfare state accomplishments (thereby distinguishing the 'new right' from the 'old right' which especially in the USA defined itself as the adversary of welfare statism).

Our analysis is based on a theoretical framework which allows for comparative research of neoconservatism as a mass public pheno-menon in all major advanced industrial democracies. However, in this contribution, we focus on the USA as a first case and starting point. As has been stated elsewhere, the process of change we are referring to is more advanced and visible in the USA than in other advanced industrial societies (Bell, 1973). Our database is the American cross-section survey of the Three-Nation study of *Generation and Politics* which has been conducted in the USA (1981), West Germany (1980) and the Netherlands (1981).

In order to measure neoconservatism we construct an additive index of neoconservatism with items representing a social force or concern which appears (negatively or positively) on the agenda of the new right. The same procedure is applied for the construction of an old conservatism index, based on items representing the old cleavage. The index construction will be validated by confirmatory factor analysis.

The next step involves the comparison of the frequency distribution of old conservatism and neoconservatism with regard to demographic and political variables. We expect the support pattern for neoconser-vatism to differ significantly from the one for old conservatism regarding crucial variables such as social status, occupational class, party identification, value orientation and religiosity. We hypothesize that 'new politics' factors, such as individual value orientations, are stronger predictors of neoconservatism than are 'old politics' factors, such as social class. Just the opposite holds true in the case of old conservatism. In order to test our hypotheses further and to determine the independent effects of the selected variables, we develop a recursive causal model based on OLS (ordinary least squares) multiple regression analysis. The results again are compared with the effects of our variables on the old politics version of conservatism in the USA. Finally, we draw some conclusions and discuss the meaning of our findings with regard to the future of conservatism in Western societies.

New classes, new politics and neoconservatism

The emergence of neoconservatism as the opposite pole to the postmaterialist new left on the new conflict axis is linked to structural changes – the change of the class structure and the exhaustion of the welfare state – and to individual changes – the rise of postmaterialist value orientations.

The transition of Western industrial societies into a phase of advanced industrial capitalism has been widely described (see discussion of literature in Lipset, 1981: 506f.). Sustained economic growth after the Second World War led to an unprecedented level of living standards and to an extension of the welfare state which in turn helped to alter the occupational structure and accelerated technological innovations. Further structural changes like urbanization, the expansion of educational opportunities and the increase of information resources added to the transformation process (Dalton et al., 1984: 5ff.). The concept of a 'postindustrial society' (Touraine, 1969; Bell, 1973) tries to capture the fundamental changes in the class structure of Western societies in which the decline of blue collar and agrarian occupations was countered by the rise of the service sector, especially professionals, technicians and scientists whose influence on social and economic change, intended and unintended, increases because of the increasing importance of theoretical knowledge. This emphasis on theoretical knowledge and those people who by their education, age and employment in personal services and the public sector play a significant part in 'postindustrial society', i.e. the 'new class' in the language of neoconservative writers (Schelsky, 1975; Bruce-Briggs, 1979), implies a shift away from traditional political conflicts in the area of economic production and distribution to areas of social planning, education and information processing.

Thus, class-based political conflict which emerged with the rise of industrial capitalism and democracy finally became institutionalized in that social cleavages and class struggle were successfully translated into political cleavages and struggles between parties and voting blocs (Lipset, 1981), changed its nature to the degree that social status and economic self-interest became a less reliable predictor for ideology and voting behaviour (Campbell et al., 1960: esp. ch. 13; Nie et al., 1976: 15–28). Still in 1960, Seymour M. Lipset could conclude: 'The most impressive single fact about political party support is that in virtually every economically developed country the lower-income groups vote mainly for the parties of the left, while the higher-income groups vote mainly for parties of the right' (Lipset, 1981: 234) and Robert Alford calculated a 'class voting index' which supported Lipset's statement with empirical evidence from four English-speaking democracies

(Alford, 1963). Since then, however, social class voting has declined almost continually in all major Western countries although short-term factors (current economic conditions, salient issues in campaigns, candidates) have caused some fluctuations, as Figure 1 indicates.

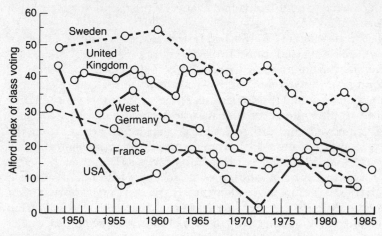

Figure 1   *The trend in social class voting in five Western democracies, 1947–86*

One particular aspect of these socioeconomic changes with important political implications is the exhaustion of the welfare state. With the success of the welfare state, the rise of the living standards of the working class and the social net which provides relative material security for the mass of the population, the welfare state has reached the point of diminishing marginal utility. Empirical evidence suggests that the higher the level of a country's economic development and success of the welfare state, the lower is the public support for classical workers' movement goals even among those who still profit most from the achievements of the welfare state (Inglehart and Flanagan, 1987). Economic motivations in national elections have not vanished but moved from individual self-interest (pocket-book voting) to concerns of the nation as a whole ('sociotropic voting') (Kinder and Kiewit, 1981; Lewis-Beck, 1986). Furthermore, at the level of high economic development the classic goals of the welfare state – egalitarian life structures – are in contradiction to its distinct methods – legal norms, public finance and bureaucracies. By accumulating power, the welfare state reaches beyond the economic realm into the private realm of the citizens and provokes opposition not only among its classical opponents (Offe, 1984; Habermas, 1985).

Under the conditions of postwar economic prosperity and internal and international security (relative to the insecurity of great economic crises and wars) among the Western countries, a value change has occurred which contributes to the decline of social class voting and tends to neutralize political polarization based on social class (Inglehart, 1977, 1983, 1984). As has been demonstrated, this phenomenon is largely attributable to intergenerational changes to the degree that considerable parts of younger age cohorts, having been raised in an environment of material saturation and security, developed value priorities which emphasize postmaterial issues such as a less impersonal, cleaner, more cultured society, a free personal life, and democratization of political, work and community life over materialist issues such as a stable economy, economic growth, fighting crime and maintaining the political order. Among the postwar generation (those born after 1945), the postmaterialists were as numerous as the materialists and they were mostly found among the students of Western populations. Recent studies show that postmaterialists by and large did not give up their value priorities when growing older, moving into professions and becoming part of higher socioeconomic strata although they can be characterized as 'underachievers' in the sense that their incomes and jobs do not correspond to the full potential of their affluent parental background and high education (Inglehart, 1981, 1986). As Figure 2 demonstrates, postmaterialism is due to inter-

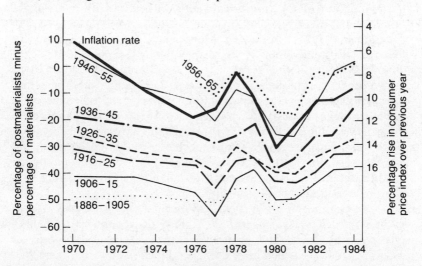

Both inflation rates and value indices are weighted according to population

Figure 2   *Value priorities and inflation rates in six West European countries, 1970–84*

Source: Inglehart, 1985: 510

generational effects on which period effects are superimposed rather than to lifecycle effects. Throughout the 1970s and early 1980s, younger age cohorts had a higher proportion of postmaterialists than older cohorts and their relative distance to each other was rather stable. The overall degree of postmaterialism, however, fluctuated across *all* generations in accordance with socioeconomic changes (Inglehart, 1985; see also Flanagan, 1982; Müller-Rommel, 1983; Bürklin, 1984).

The structural and individual changes outlined above have contributed to a redefinition of the political spectrum and ideologies and, accordingly, to realignment trends in Western party systems. The vast literature on political ideologies suggests that the left-right or liberal-conservative spectrum reflects fundamental orientations towards politics and society and that the underlying dividing line is to be found in attitudes towards change. The transition of the feudal order into a bourgeois–capitalist society, the Enlightenment and the French Revolution provide the historical context for the emergence of the left–right spectrum although its roots can be found in most premodern cultures of the world (Laponce, 1981).

Karl Mannheim has emphasized that conservative and progressive thought have been established as the two socially based and mutually related 'Weltanschauungen' in the modern world as a result of the differentiation of the traditional feudal order into diverse classes, interests and ideologies and through the coming of bourgeois society (Mannheim, 1927). Following Mannheim's approach and recent research (Epstein, 1966; Greiffenhagen, 1971; Grebing, 1971; Schumann, 1984) we define conservatism not simply as an antimodern movement but as the dialectical counterpart to political modernization (democratization, emancipation, self-government, etc.) which becomes mobilized in processes of differentiation and accelerated change. Here we can distinguish between two forms of conservatism: conservatism as the resistance to the idea of radical change of the social system and conservatism that takes necessary and even radical steps of systemic adaptation in order to maintain social and political power and privileges (Schumann, 1984: 376).

As conservatism emerged at the very moment of the rise of bourgeois society, it can be seen as the dialectical countermovement to the political, social and economic consequences of the ideas of bourgeois society which have been developed around the themes of liberty and equality. Conservatism in this mode becomes an 'intrinsic component of the liberal bourgeoisie when it [felt] its social position threatened either by internal differentiation or attack from without (the labor movement)' (Schumann, 1978: 812). In consequence, conservatism should not be reduced to so-called eternal conservative values but, as a type of 'situational ideology' (Huntington, 1957), it must be identified within historical conflict constellations. With the nationalist revolutions of the nineteenth century conservatism involved the defence of the church and privileged upper classes against the liberalism of the rising bourgeoisie; with the Industrial Revolution a new cleavage emerged which divided the conservative bourgeoisie (and remnants of the old order) against the workers' movement and its claim for participation and economic redistribution (Lipset and Rokkan, 1967). 'Left' became associated with the lower classes and allied elites which strove to change the society into a more self-governing egalitarian direction whereas 'Right' was associated with the upper and middle classes which were interested in maintaining and defending the status quo or a stable political order (Inglehart and Klingemann, 1976; Middendorp, 1978; Lipset, 1981).

With the educational revolution after the Second World War, the coming of postindustrial society and postmaterialism and the decline of social class voting, the class order and ideological expressions became inverted. While in the 1930s and 1940s high socioeconomic status cohorts in the USA were more conservative than the middle and lower status groups, the 'liberal' symbol became much more favourable at the top than at the bottom during the 1960s (Ladd and Hadley, 1978). A progressive, largely postmaterialist part of the 'new middle class' (students, non-manual employees in large enterprises, professionals in modern sectors including the growing public sector) supported the agenda of the new left, using government for objectives widely perceived as egalitarian, opposing the Vietnam war, struggling for civil rights, for women's and gay liberation, for environmentalism and democratization and promoting new lifestyles. As the new left, they moved into the Democratic party and contributed to the nomination of George McGovern as presidential candidate in 1972 which in turn brought down social class voting in the USA to an all-time low (see Figure 1). Similarly, in Western European countries the new left agenda, which is mainly based on postmaterialist issues, cuts across the traditional left–right spectrum and challenges the parties of the old left and their constituencies as the rise of the West German party of the Greens demonstrates; again, their support is drawn from upscale status groups (Bürklin, 1984; Inglehart, 1984).

Although especially in the USA and West Germany the new left tried to work through political parties, its roots are an anti-institutional protest and its organizational base still lies more with the new social movements than with the political parties (Brand, 1985; Offe, 1985). Despite their criticism of modern values like economic growth and technological progress the new left is not antimodern itself but rather a part of modernism in that its quest for democratization, autonomy and emancipation is a 'selective radicalization of "modern" values' and 'depends as much on the *accomplishments* of political and economic modernization as on criticism of its unfulfilled promises and *perverse effects*' (Offe, 1985: 853f., emphases in the original).

Neoconservatism, then, is bourgeois modernism becoming conservative itself in the face of this radical attack (Dubiel, 1985). As a response to the rise of postmaterialism and the related agenda of the new left, influential elites and a large proportion of Western publics have turned to the right and reacted with an increased emphasis on traditional, materialist values, and the 'old politics' agenda of economic growth, technological progress, a stable economic order, etc. The novelty of this mounting conservative response does not lie in the issues or the underlying philosophy itself but in the fact that it is an alliance of traditionally liberal groups, both at the elite level and the mass level, with traditionally conservative constituencies against the new challenge on the new, value-based conflict axis.

In the United States, the main carriers of this response are to be found among formerly liberal intellectuals and politicians, the working classes and the traditionally conservative old middle classes. Most prominent is a group of east coast intellectuals with a liberal or even radical biographical background who strongly reacted to the student protest movement of the 1960s and to whom the term neoconservatism was applied first (Harrington, 1976). They lay stress on traditional social and cultural values like authority, family, community, religion and American political tradition and, although they favour a certain degree of government intervention in the economy and a limited (conservative) welfare state, they are particularly concerned with the erosion of these values by the 'new class', with an expanded role of the government and too much social welfare (Moynihan, 1973; Bell, 1976). They advocate a capitalist market economy as the economic order appropriate to American democracy, and in foreign affairs issues promote a strong national defence and anti-Communist internationalism (Kristol, 1972; Podhoretz, 1980, 1981; for a discussion of the concepts see Steinfels, 1979). In general, these concepts are also supported by parts of the old left, working and lower middle classes, and there are strong ties between the neoconservative intellectuals, the old left in the Democratic party and the labour union leàdership (organized in the Committee for a Democratic Majority). While still adhering to an expanded role of government in economic affairs and social programmes, these elite groups and classes tend to be more conservative on social and cultural issues: they believe in traditional values related to family, law and order, patriotism and anti-Communism (Lipset, 1981; also Lipset and Schneider, 1983).

The concern for these issues is even more articulated among the new right, its supporters and constituencies (Crawford, 1980). The old middle classes, mainly consisting of self-employed craftsmen, small businessmen, real estate speculators and independent farmers were socially dominant for a long time and saw their values, derived from the Puritan–Protestant ethic, legitimized by American social and political institutions. However, with the coming of industrial mass society and the welfare state, began the decline of the old middle classes which became fully aware of this decline in the period of rapid social, economic and cultural change of the 1960s (Hughey, 1982). Supported by the old middle classes, a populist conservatism emerged which became politically relevant with the rise of the new right as well as the revival of conservative churches and fundamentalist movements such as the Moral Majority (Lipset and Raab, 1978; Hill and Owen, 1982; Liebman and Wuthnow, 1983). Populist conservatism struggles for the reinstitution of religious, particularly Puritan–Christian, social and moral values centred around themes like the family, home, safe neighbourhoods, public schools and moral education and demonstrates patriotism and strong anti-Communism. Although the neoconservative intellectuals and the leaders of the populist new right do not always share the same political concerns and have very different social and political backgrounds as well as different levels of conceptualization and partisan orientations, they see themselves as a 'working alliance' (Jeane Kirkpatrick, Irving Kristol, Howard Phillips and others in personal interviews) in the defence of American political traditions and institutions against post-New Deal liberalism in domestic and foreign policy (see also Schissler, 1983; Peele, 1985).

A similar redefinition of the political space at the elite and mass level is under way in Western European countries. In response to the democratization and reform politics of the student protest and the politics of the Brandt era, West German intellectuals have revived the distinctly German conservative idea of a strong state which keeps itself out of the party and social struggles and combined this position with the idea of economic growth and technological innovation (ideas traditionally alien to German conservatives) to what has been termed 'technocratic conservatism' (Greiffenhagen, 1971; Lederer, 1979). Like their American colleagues, they complain about the overload of government and the decay of bourgeois culture and values and try to counter the postmaterialist challenge especially in the educational realm by emphasizing the necessity of so-called 'Sekundärtugenden' like discipline, obedience, hard work, etc. (Fend, 1984). In the early 1980s, American and German neoconservatives have established contacts in joint meetings and conferences with a particular interest in foreign policy issues (Bossle, 1981; Rühle, 1982).

In France, 'neoliberals' are attracted by the socioeconomic platform of American conservatives and neoconservatives (Sorman 1983) and try to combine their proposals with the tradition of Gaullism. Moreover, the social Darwinist 'nouvelle droite' intellectual movement aggressively promotes the concepts of state authority and national prestige with reference to the German 'revolutionary conservatism' of the 1920s (Rémond, 1982; Christadler, 1983). At the mass level, the racist National Front which occasionally won more than 10 percent of the vote in various elections since its rise in 1985 has successfully established itself as the party of the extreme right at the right-wing endpoint of the new conflict axis.

The rearrangement of the political space in advanced industrial democracies is depicted in Figure 3, derived from a model of political cleavages and alliances by Claus Offe (1985: 858). On the old politics conflict axis which polarized left and right in economic and social class terms, the working class-based left with elements of the new middle classes opposes the conservatism of upper and old middle classes. With the new cross-cutting cleavage, the new left as composed of post-materialist new middle classes and groups not integrated in the job market (students, unemployed, etc.) splits from the old left and becomes a third force in the spectrum. In reaction to the post-materialists, the working class and the old middle classes move closer together and turn into the neoconservative alliance as the opponents to the new left in the new politics dimension. Here, new politics is understood in terms of the entire new conflict axis and not only in

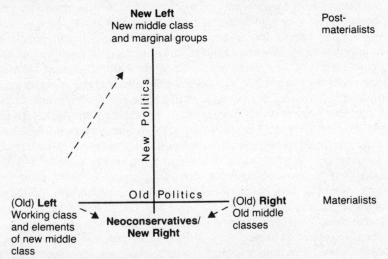

Figure 3   *A triangular model of the political spectrum: cleavages and forces*

Source: adapted from Offe, 1985: 858

terms of postmaterialist issues. The extreme version of the neo-conservative alliance is populist new right movements which capitalize on the radicalization of those parts of the old middle classes whose status is particularly threatened by the on-going social and cultural change. This model does not suggest that the old politics dimension disappears as a result of the new conflict axis but that its polarization and the ideological distance between old left and old right decreases in the face of the polarization on the new conflict axis. As to now, there is already empirical evidence that Western publics polarize more strongly on new politics issues than on old politics issues and that the left–right spectrum is in the process of redefinition (Inglehart, 1984).

Neoconservatism in the American mass public

Index construction
The limits for testing our hypotheses are obvious. We cannot expect to find all relevant items of the neoconservative intellectuals or the new right items in survey data. Even if we had a representative collection of issues, there remains the problem of identifying an 'ideology' at the level of the mass public. The empirical evidence for the modest degree of 'ideological conceptualization' and 'issue constraint' in the mass public vis-à-vis the elite cannot be ignored (Campbell et al., 1960; McClosky, 1960; Converse, 1964). However, in-depth interviewing has shown that even in the 'unideological' American public of the 1950s there existed a 'latent ideology of the common man' besides the articulated and explicit ideologies of political activists and elites (Lane, 1962); and survey analysis in the 1970s revealed a growing attitude consistency in the American public (Nie et al., 1976). For our purpose, it will suffice to demonstrate a relatively clear structure of the relevant items with the help of factor analysis.

As has been mentioned above, the database for our analysis is the American cross-section survey of the Three-Nation study of *Generation and Politics* of 1981 which is a follow up study of the 1975–6 *Political Action* study (Barnes and Kaase, 1979). From this follow restrictions in the items available for the index construction but a chance to use the same items which have been used elsewhere for conceptualizing the old politics and new politics dimension (Inglehart, 1977; Barnes and Kaase, 1979; Dalton et al., 1984). For distinguishing old politics from new politics items we use issue items and feeling thermometers for social and political groups. It could be argued that feeling thermo-meters are a less reliable predictor for one's overall political position than are issue positions since, as an expression of emotional ties, they are shaped more easily by circumstantial factors than are positions based on cognitions. However, panel studies show that affection and dislike for prominent political leaders are even more stable over time than are issue positions so that 'where political evaluations are concerned, a party "leader" issue flow may be dominant' (Converse and Markus, 1979: 48). In analogy we can assume that feeling thermometers for prominent social and political groups are at least as important in shaping one's ideological position as are issue positions.

The following issue positions are included in our analysis: equalization of income, government ownership of industries, government regulation of the economy, prohibition of inventions causing higher unemployment, equal opportunities for women, availability of abortion (for exact question wording see Appendix); and the groups included in the feeling thermometers are the Democratic party, the Republican party, big business, labour unions, blacks, the women's liberation movement, student protesters, the police, the military, the clergy and the Moral Majority. Each variable has been coded in a way that the higher the score of the respondent the more conservative he/she is. The results of the factor analysis (varimax rotation) as shown in Table 1 reveal a rather clear structure of the items with those variables loading high on the first factor (>0.30) representing the materialist, social class related old politics dimension and those loading high on the second factor representing new politics concerns and their counterforces, i.e. a sociocultural, establishment/anti-establishment variant of the left-right spectrum. Furthermore, we can assume that a redefinition of the political spectrum is indicated by our findings to the degree that the Republican party loads high on both factors and may have pulled big business over to the second dimension because of the perceived close ties between them, whereas the close link of the women's liberation movement, student protesters and blacks to the Democratic party has produced relatively high loadings for these groups on the first factor.

For the construction of the indexes we have given four values (1 to 4) to each variable the highest value being the most conservative response. For example, a value of 'four' was given to the range of 76 to 100 on the feeling thermometer for the Moral Majority and to the range of 0 to 25 on the feeling thermometer for the student protesters. Accordingly, the response 'strongly agree' on the income equality question was coded 'one' whereas the response 'strongly disagree' on the abortion question was coded 'four'. The neoconservatism index is an addition of all the recoded variables on the second factor with a loading >0.30 excluding big business, equality for women and government running industries and including blacks divided by the number of items after missing values have been deleted. Blacks have been included in the neoconservatism index because as a social group

Table 1   *Factor analysis of issue positions and feeling thermometers (pairwise varimax on two factors with normalized loadings)*

Variable	Old conflict axis	New conflict axis
Income equality	0.47	0.002
Industries run by government	0.42	0.02
Regulation of economy	0.55	−0.07
Prohibition of inventions	0.44	−0.06
Democratic party	0.48	−0.005
Labour unions	0.50	−0.09
Republican party	0.39	0.36
Big business	0.09	0.34
Equal opportunity for women	0.28	0.32
Availability of abortion	−0.006	0.41
Women's Lib. movement	0.40	0.34
Student protesters	0.26	0.36
Police	−0.10	0.51
Military	−0.14	0.52
Clergy	−0.15	0.48
Moral Majority	−0.18	0.36
Blacks	0.23	−0.04

Numerical entries are loadings on two dimensions only. Those loadings exceeding 0.30 have been boxed.

Source: Generations and Politics II, US data from the *Political Action* study.

they not only belong to the economically most deprived strata (which would justify including them with the labour unions in the old conservatism index) but have been attacked also on racist, i.e. sociocultural grounds particularly by the constituency of the new right and its predecessor, the George Wallace movement. On the other hand, big business has been excluded from the index since in the time of class conflict it was the opponent of the labour movement and thus clearly belongs to the old politics dimension. Also, the item equality of opportunity for women has been dropped from the neoconservatism index in order to avoid duplication, because it overlaps largely with the platform of the women's liberation movement. The old conservatism index has been constructed in the same way. It includes all highly loading variables of the first factor (>0.30) plus the big business variable minus the political party variables and the women's liberation movement variable. If the party variables had been included in the index, they would have distorted the relationship between the respondents' party identification and the index discussed in the OLS multiple regression model. The women's liberation movement is a target of the new right and its constituency and thus belongs to the neoconservatism index despite its high loadings on the first factor.

The index construction produced two scales with values between one (at the liberal pole) and four (at the conservative pole). For the following descriptive statistics we cut the whole range of either scale into three parts in order to separate liberals and conservatives in each dimension. On the old politics scale, respondents with values between one and two were defined as old liberals, those with values between three and four were defined as old conservatives. The same procedure was applied to the new politics scale thus creating a group of new liberals in the lower third and a group of neoconservatives in the upper third of the index. The middle third of each scale contains a centre group with no clear ideological leaning.

Table 2 displays the frequency distributions of liberals, the centre and conservatives in the old politics and new politics dimensions. Clearly the US public at the beginning of the 1980s is centre oriented in terms of the ideological orientations presented here. The centre group is the numerical majority, totalling two-thirds of the respondents in either conflict dimension. Moreover, there are more conservatives than liberals in either dimension. About one-fifth of the electorate could be classified as old conservatives, and almost one-third falls into the neoconservative category. These conservative groups, however, hardly overlap since only 53 respondents (7 percent of the sample after the exclusion of missing values) belong to both variants of conservatism.

Table 2   *Distribution of ideological orientations in old politics and new politics dimensions, USA 1981*

	Liberal	Centre	Conservative	Total
Old politics (%)	10.9	67.9	21.2	100.0
(N)	(104)	(648)	(202)	(954)
New politics (%)	5.6	63.3	31.1	100.0
(N)	(49)	(553)	(272)	(874)

Total $N = 1156$. Missing values have been omitted.

Source: as Table 1

Social and political attributes of old conservatism and neoconservatism in comparison

According to our theoretical framework, old politics issues reflect the socioeconomic cleavage of liberalism and conservatism in the USA. With the Great Depression and the New Deal, the ideological and partisan orientations became organized along class conflict lines. The Democratic party emerged as the party of liberalism, of the welfare state, income redistribution, organized labour and of the working and lower classes (including almost all blacks and many Catholics). The Republican party, on the other hand, opposed the New Deal liberalism and developed a conservative platform of limited government which was supported mainly by upper status Protestants and the old middle classes of small businessmen and self-employed craftsmen in the north-east and mid-west (Goldwin, 1967; Chambers and Burnham, 1967; Ladd and Hadley, 1978).[1] On the conflict axis based on value change and cutting across social class and partisan division, religiosity, generational differences and value orientations became the polarizing factor whereas social and partisan differences declined in importance and racial divides and union membership became almost insignificant (for an early analysis of the new politics dimension in the USA see Miller and Levitin, 1976). The socio-structural and sociocultural characteristics of the old politics and new politics orientations are depicted in Table 3. Old conservatism is mostly found among the old middle class, the upper status and upper educational strata whereas workers, lower status and lower educational groups are disproportionately liberal in the old politics, New Deal sense. This class-based polarization is neutralized, if not reversed, in the new politics dimension. Here workers and respondents with lower status and lower education display a rather high degree of conservatism.

But while there is a rather clear ideological polarization in the old politics between liberal workers and lower classes on the one hand and conservative middle and upper classes on the other, ideological differences in new politics orientations are sharpest in sociocultural and generational terms. Almost half of those who go to church every week, 40 percent of the oldest generation and nearly 40 percent of the respondents with a purely materialist value orientation are neo-conservatives. The same groups do not differ much from the nation as a whole when it comes to old politics orientations. On the other hand, those who rarely go to church, the youngest generation and the postmaterialists are more liberal in new politics terms than the nation as a whole. The fact that pure postmaterialists are the only group in which new liberals outnumber neoconservatives (by a margin of 2:1) underlines the high degree of ideological polarization between different value types and supports the notion of value-based conflict in the new politics dimension.

Finally, the relationship between party identification and ideological orientations, as shown in Table 4, demonstrates further differences between the two ideological dimensions. With regard to old politics, party identification and ideology are closely related. Democrats clearly exhibit liberal leanings while Republicans are

Table 3   *Social and political characteristics of old politics and new politics orientations, USA 1981*

	Old politics			New politics		
	Liberal (%)	Conservative (%)	(N)	Liberal (%)	Conservative (%)	(N)
Total	10.9	21.2	(954)	5.6	31.1	(874)
Occupational class						
Working class	15.5	7.3	(329)	2.0	36.5	(296)
Old middle class	6.6	38.8	(256)	5.4	29.5	(241)
New middle class	9.6	22.3	(301)	8.8	27.6	(283)
Social status						
Low	14.3	3.4	(202)	1.7	37.6	(173)
Middle	15.5	16.8	(310)	7.3	29.3	(287)
High	6.1	35.5	(360)	6.8	28.6	(339)
Education						
Grammar school	15.6	5.6	(231)	1.5	39.5	(194)
High school	13.9	13.2	(302)	0.7	31.5	(279)
College	6.0	35.6	(419)	11.0	26.5	(400)
Church attendance						
Never	14.4	24.8	(125)	8.9	22.3	(112)
A few times a year	15.4	17.8	(253)	7.0	22.3	(229)
Once/twice a month	14.7	21.1	(109)	3.0	31.0	(100)
Almost every week	5.1	22.9	(118)	0.0	31.1	(99)
Every week	7.3	20.8	(274)	0.8	47.9	(265)
Generations						
Pre new deal	7.7	17.4	(155)	0.8	40.5	(131)
New deal	10.1	24.6	(248)	4.4	37.4	(227)
Affluence	9.8	25.1	(275)	7.4	30.2	(258)
Protest	14.8	16.2	(271)	7.5	21.3	(253)
Value orientation						
Materialist	10.4	25.1	(395)	1.7	38.0	(353)
Materialist (mixed)	10.7	18.9	(317)	4.4	28.1	(295)
Postmaterialist (mixed)	12.3	17.4	(155)	6.7	28.2	(149)
Postmaterialist	12.2	16.2	(74)	29.4	14.7	(68)

The centre category has been omitted.

Source: as Table 1

predominantly conservative. Thus class-based polarizations between old conservatives and old liberals are reflected by party identification. This does not hold true concerning new politics orientations. Here ideological polarizations do not occur between Democrats and Republicans, but between partisans and independent partisans. Democrats and Republicans are rather conservative, independent Democrats and independent Republicans are rather liberal in new politics terms (compared to the nation as a whole). This finding underline the view that the new liberalism of younger, better educated and postmaterialist groups has added to a dealignment process in the 1970s (Miller and Levitin, 1976; Dalton et al., 1984). Our findings in Table 4 also suggest that the *de*alignment is partially neutralized by a

Table 4   *Party identification and ideological orientations, USA 1981*

	Old politics			New politics		
	Liberal (%)	Conservative (%)	(N)	Liberal (%)	Conservative (%)	(N)
Total	10.9	21.2	(954)	5.6	31.1	(874)
Strong Democrats	19.5	2.7	(113)	6.5	28.3	(92)
Democrats	11.9	11.9	(193)	5.4	31.4	(185)
Independent Dem.	15.9	10.3	(145)	13.8	26.1	(138)
Independents	9.2	20.2	(109)	5.1	31.3	(99)
Independent Rep.	8.3	29.7	(145)	5.3	22.7	(132)
Republicans	4.8	27.0	(126)	0.9	30.4	(115)
Strong Republicans	6.7	51.3	(119)	1.0	49.5	(105)

The centre category has been omitted.

Source: as Table 1

*re*alignment. The fact that strong Republicans are overwhelmingly conservative in either dimension indicates that the Republican party does not only provide the traditional political home for the upper social strata but is also attractive to neoconservatives who are rather lower class. Hence, the Republican party seems to adopt an ever-increasing and consistently conservative outlook in various policy dimensions whereas the Democrats remain ideologically heterogeneous.

The bivariate relationships between sociostructural, sociocultural and political attributes on the one hand, and the ideological scales on the other are summarized by the correlation coefficients depicted in Table 5. There is almost no correlation between neoconservatism and the old version which again suggests that we are dealing with very distinct versions of conservatism. The correlation between self-placement on a continuum from left to right is moderately positive with either version though 0.07 points higher with respect to neo-conservatism. This difference may indicate that the American public interprets the left–right spectrum more in terms of the new cleavage

Table 5   *Correlation matrix of old conservatism, neoconservatism and sociopolitical variables*

	Old conservatism	Neoconservatism
Neoconservatism	0.05	
Left–right self-placement	0.18	0.25
Party identification	0.38	0.14
Social status	0.35	–0.08
Education	0.34	–0.13
Family income	0.25	–0.01
Value orientation	–0.09	–0.28
Age of respondent	0.11	0.21
Religiosity	0.04	0.30
Race	0.19	0.07
Union membership	–0.18	–0.005
$N =$	(613)	(574)

Entries are Pearson product moment correlation coefficients.
For coding of variables and indexes, see Appendix.

Source: as Table 1

than in terms of the old one (Inglehart and Klingemann, 1976; Inglehart, 1987). However, since this difference is rather small and the left–right variable applies to either version, we will drop the left–right self-placement from further consideration.

Old politics variables such as party identification, social status, family income and union membership show the expected levels and direction of their relationship to old conservatism, whereas value orientation and religiosity are almost insignificant. Quite the contrary is true in the case of neoconservatism, which is most strongly related to value orientation and religiosity but not at all or very weakly related to social status, family income and union membership. Strikingly, although the feeling thermometer for blacks has been included in the neoconservatism index, the race variable is more relevant with regard to old conservatism: there is no clear ideological difference between blacks and whites in terms of the neoconservative issues. Furthermore, with regard to neoconservatism the education and age variables do not appear as significant as they do with regard to postmaterialism (Inglehart, 1977: 72–98). There is only a moderate negative relationship between level of education and neoconservatism and a moderate positive one between neoconservatism and age (which still is twice the strength of the relationship between age and old conservatism). Thus, neoconservatism is not simply the mirror image of postmaterialism but a response to it with its own distinctive social characteristics.

So far, we have provided evidence for the social and political characteristics of the two conservative variants on the basis of bivariate relationships. In order to test our hypothesis further that new politics variables are stronger predictors for neoconservatism than are old politics variables we want to estimate their independent effects on neoconservatism with the help of OLS multiple regression analysis. Therefore we develop a causal model which is derived from the theoretical framework presented above and variables and indexes discussed in the preceding pages (for the technique of regression analysis and causal modelling see Lewis-Beck, 1980; Achen, 1982; Asher, 1976; Berry, 1984; Davis, 1985).[2]

The model starts with the basic assumption that neoconservatism as a political ideology is directly determined by sociostructural factors and long-lasting orientations such as value orientations and, to a lesser degree, party identification which, in turn, are also determined by sociostructural forces. Thus, we specify that neoconservatism is mainly and directly affected by five factors: social status and party identification as factors representing the old politics dimension, age, religiosity and value orientation as factors representing the new politics dimension. Other factors which do not have a direct effect on neoconservatism, but are assumed to work indirectly through party identification, are race, party identification of the respondent's father and the respondent's union membership. Furthermore, social class and age are assumed to have direct effects not only on neoconservatism but also on party identification and value orientation and thus to work indirectly on neoconservatism as well. After having specified our model we obtain three equations, one for the dependent variable neoconservatism and two for the endogenous variables party identification and value orientation.

The path model in Figure 4 contains standardized OLS regression estimates which indicate the relative effects of the various variables.[3] Overall, about one-fifth of the variation in neoconservatism can be explained by direct effects of the five selected variables. Among these, religiosity and value orientation are the most powerful predictors for neoconservatism. The more religious or the more materialist the respondent's value orientation, other things being equal, the more conservative he or she is. That is, no matter how old the respondent or what social status he or she has obtained, religiosity or value orientation still explain more than twice the variation in neoconservatism as do either party identification or social status. And the fact that the direct effect of value orientation is twice the one of age differences means that, unlike in the case of value orientations, generational conflict plays a rather modest role in the struggle between protest movements and its neoconservative reaction. Hence, ideological differences in the new politics dimension are determined rather by religious and value orientations than by age differences. Finally, the

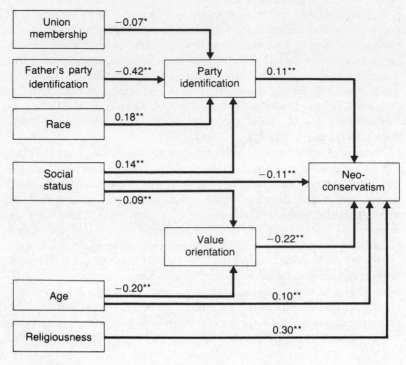

For equation 'Neoconservatism': $R^2 = 0.19$ $* p < 0.05$
                                  $N = 719$ $** p < 0.01$

Figure 4   *Path diagram neoconservatism (standardized OLS estimates)*

Source: as Table 1

signs and levels of the path coefficients demonstrate that neoconservatism is moderately related to a Republican party identification
and to a lower social status which, in turn, is related to a Democratic
party identification. The total effect of social status on neoconservatism
is –0.08 after adding its indirect effects (0.03) to its direct effect (–0.11).
Thus, status differences which determine directly neonconservatism
are partially neutralized by their relationships to party identification
and value orientation. Overall, our findings support the hypothesized
notion that variations in new politics factors account for more of the
variance in neoconservatism than variations in old politics factors.

Quite the opposite holds true for old conservatism, as shown in
Figure 5. This path model is derived from the same basic assumptions
as the previous one. However, after specifying the model union
membership and race were included since they could be expected to
have direct effects on old conservatism. On the other hand, religiosity

and value orientations were statistically insignificant with regard to old conservatism and could be omitted from the model. The fit of the model is slightly better than the one for neoconservatism since the selected variables of the old conservatism equation explain more than a quarter of the variance in the dependent variable. As we expected, party identification and social status account for most of the variance in old conservatism. The degree of the old politics orientations' class base is highlighted by the fact that the direct effect of social status on old conservatism is more than twice its effect on party identification and even amounts to a total effect of 0.35 after adding its indirect effect (0.04). In striking contrast to the determinants of neoconservatism, then, old conservatism clearly is the political ideology of the upper classes regardless of age or partisan attachment and the effects of status differences are even reinforced by party identification: Republican upper classes – and this is no surprise at all – are more conservative than Democratic or independent upper classes.

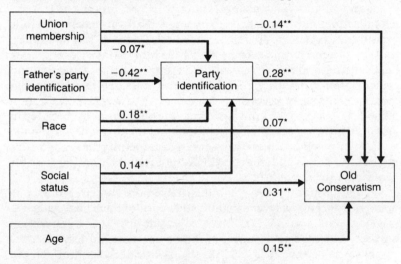

For equation 'Old Conservatism': $R^2 = 0.267$ $* p < 0.05$
                                   $N = 844$ $** p < 0.01$

Figure 5   *Path diagram old conservatism (standardized OLS estimate)*

Source: as Table 1

Conclusions: neoconservatism – a revolt against modernity?

The combined evidence provided by our analysis confirms our assumptions about neoconservatism as a sociocultural reaction to value change and cultural liberalization which cuts across traditional social class and party lines. Neoconservatives are predominantly religious people, have a high degree of materialist value orientations, are to be found among the working class and the lower and middle status groups rather than in the other social strata; they are bipartisan and relatively balanced in their generational structure. In all these aspects (but less so with regard to value orientation and age) they differ significantly from the old conservatives whose social and political profile reflects the old cleavage based on social class and party lines. Thus, the neoconservative public resembles those groups and movements which have protested against the consequences of the modernization process since its beginning with the national, democratic and industrial revolutions (Lipset, 1981: 488–503). In the context of the educational revolution and postindustrial society, the neoconservative revolt against modernity is the protest of those strata and groups displaced most severely by recent structural and cultural changes, i.e. occupational and value change and the related process of cultural liberalization. It should be remembered that our indexes include measures of high support for 'authorities', forces of law and order, tradition, hierarchy and even explicitly the Moral Majority on the one hand, and rejection of movements and groups of democratization and emancipation from discrimination on the other. To the degree that these latter forces represent the proponents of a 'selective radicalization of modern values' (Offe) and the former the opponents, both rooted in modernity, the new conflict does not divide the premodern from the modern or postmodern, but conservative modernity and progressive modernity. This is underlined by the support of the working class for neoconservatism.

As long as the process of industrialization had prohibited the workers from political participation and deprived them materially, the working class was on the progressive side of the modernization process. With the establishment of the welfare state, the historic 'class compromise' (Habermas, 1973), the political integration of the working class and finally with the structural and individual changes of postindustrialism and postmaterialism, the working class sees itself displaced by the modernization process in social, cultural and economic terms and on the side of other threatened groups, notably the religious old middle classes. Thus, the working class contributes to a constellation of forces which constitutes a strong neoconservative alliance.

Although leaders of the major left-wing parties in Western countries are working to create an alliance between working class and old left (notably in West Germany), the effort to combine ecology and economy so far has not succeeded and the tensions between old left and new left continue to exist, particularly with regard to the socio-cultural liberalism of the new left and the sociocultural conservatism of the workers who have transcended their traditonal working-class culture in the process of their 'embourgeoisement' (Goldthorpe et al., 1968). Our analysis has shown that the largest support group for the old liberalism – the working class – is at the same time the largest occupational component of neoconservatism. So it is plausible to assume that in the foreseeable future the neoconservative alliance between (materialist) old left and old right will dominate conflicts in the new politics dimension. However, one might argue that with the absolute or relative decline of the traditional working class and the old middle classes and with the increase of the new middle class, the prospects for a continuous powerful neoconservative alliance are limited. Moreover, generational replacement of older materialist cohorts by younger postmaterialist ones (Abramson and Inglehart, 1986) might contribute to the decline of neoconservatism.

But, as our findings suggest, a considerable part of the new middle classes themselves are neoconservative and recent generational changes have not (yet) produced a preponderance of sociocultural liberalism among the younger cohorts. As to now, the youngest generation, which has an equal share of liberals and conservatives in the old politics sense, is almost three times more conservative than liberal in the new politics sense. The question of a long-term trend towards postmaterialism and a new liberalism also depends on the effect of the latest economic crises on the subjective sense of deprivation or well-being of the youngest generation. It is possible that those who were socialized politically in the 1970s might react to the limited opportu-nities on the job market with a return to conservatism and materialism, since even the protest generation itself has reported a change towards conservatism on some issues during the 1970s (Jennings, 1987).

Notes

Research on this subject has been made possible in part by a grant from the Studienstiftung des deutschen Volkes and supplementary financial support through the Zentralarchiv für empirische Sozialforschung, Universität zu Köln. The data used for this contribution were made available by Ronald Inglehart; at the time of our analysis they had not yet been released.

1. For the connection between the rising national idea during the interwar period and the Democratic Party, see Beer (1966). The whole complex of the cross-cutting foreign policy and regional dimensions has been excluded, see for example Almond (1950), Shell (1986).

2. We have selected a recursive causal model with one-directional flow of effects although a non-recursive model would have been a more realistic approach which could have included the estimation of reciprocal influence especially between neoconservatism and party identification. Based on the assumption that issue orientations of a group

might cause a new partisan orientation of another party which is perceived to be a better representative of the group's concerns than the group's traditional party (Petrocik, 1981: 118), this procedure could have helped to answer the question to what degree the structural and individual changes outlined above are contributing to a realignment process *via* neoconservatism. However, efforts to construct instrumental variables for value orientation, party identification and neoconservatism which produced plausible second-stage least squares estimates failed with the data at hand.

3. These estimates are sample specific and cannot be compared directly across samples (King, 1986).

Appendix: Variable list and coding

Index issues and feeling thermometers
Income Equality:
  The government should sharply reduce income differences in our country
    1 Agree strongly   3 Disagree
    2 Agree   4 Disagree strongly
Industries:
  More private industries should be run by the government
    1 Agree strongly   3 Disagree
    2 Agree   4 Disagree strongly
Regulation:
  Government should play a larger role in regulating the economy
    1 Agree strongly   3 Disagree
    2 Agree   4 Disagree strongly
Inventions:
  No inventions should be put into use that increase the chance of unemployment
    1 Agree strongly   3 Disagree
    2 Agree   4 Disagree strongly
Equal opportunity for women:
  Stronger measures should be taken to give women opportunities equal to men
    1 Agree strongly   3 Disagree
    2 Agree   4 Disagree strongly
Abortion:
  Abortions should be made available to all women who want them
    1 Agree strongly   3 Disagree
    2 Agree   4 Disagree strongly
Feeling thermometers towards social and political groups:
  0 Very unfavourable
  100 Very favourable

Other variables
Party identification:
  1 Strong Democrat
  2 Democrat
  3 Independent Democrat
  4 Independent
  5 Independent Republican
  6 Republican
  7 Strong Republican

Levels of education:
1 Less than seventh grade completed
2 Less than tenth grade completed
3 Did not receive high school diploma
4 Completed high school and non-college training
5 Post-high school education (college, university)

Family income in 1980 before taxes:
1 None or less that $2,000
2 $2,000 – $3,999
3 $4,000 – $5,999
(...)
10 $18,000 – $20,999
11 $21,000 – $23,999
(...)
16 $36,000 – $39,999
17 $40,000 – $44,999
18 $45,000 – $49,999
19 $50,000 – $59,999
20 $60,000 – $69,999
21 $70,000 – $79,999
22 $80,000 and over

Social status:
Education + income/2 minus missing values
1 1 + (1–5)/2
2 2 + (6–9)/2
3 3 + (10–13)/2
4 4 + (14–17)/2
5 5 + (18–22)/2

Left–right self-placement:
1 Left
(...)
10 Right

Value orientation:
1 Materialist
2 Materialist (mixed)
3 Postmaterialist (mixed)
4 Postmaterialist
(For index construction see Barnes and Kaase, 1979)

Age of respondent:
16 years
(...)
91 years

Religiousness:
How often do you go to (church/synagogue)?
1 Never

2 A few times a year
3 Once or twice a month
4 Almost every week
5 Every week

Race:
  0 Non-white
  1 White

Respondent's union membership:
  0 No
  1 Yes

Party identification of respondent's father:
  0 Non-Democrat
  1 Democrat

Class:
  Coding based on 'Political Behaviour Two-Digit Occupation Code' from *Political Action Codebook*, pp. 479–82.
  Old middle class: 1, 2, 6, 8, 10, 21, 22, 23, 28, 30, 33, 34, 35, 36, 39, 41, 82, 89
  Working class: 42, 48, 49, 51, 65, 68, 71, 78
  New middle class: 3, 4, 5, 7, 9, 11, 12, 13, 19, 31, 32

References

Abramson, Paul and Inglehart, Ronald (1986) 'Generational Replacement and Value Change in Six West European Societies', *American Journal of Political Science*, 30 (Feb.): 1–25.
Achen, Christopher (1982) *Interpreting and Using Regression*. Beverly Hills: Sage.
Alford, Robert (1963) *Party and Society: the Anglo-American Democracies*. Chicago: Rand-McNally.
Almond, Gabriel A. (1950) *The American People and Foreign Policy*. New York: Harcourt, Brace.
Asher, Herbert B. (1976) *Causal Modeling*. Beverly Hills: Sage.
Barnes, Samuel and Kaase, Max (eds) (1979) *Political Action*. Beverly Hills: Sage.
Beer, Samuel (1966) 'Liberalism and the National Idea', *The Public Interest*, 2 (Fall): 70–82.
Bell, Daniel (1960) *The End of Ideology*. Glencoe, Ill.: Free Press.
Bell, Daniel (1973) *The Coming of Post-Industrial Society*. New York: Basic Books.
Bell, Daniel (1976) *The Cultural Contradictions of Capitalism*. New York: Basic Books.
Berry, William D. (1984) *Nonrecursive Causal Models*. Beverly Hills: Sage.
Bossle, Lothar (ed.) (1981) *Der Neokonservatismus – die Leitidee der achtziger Jahre?* Würzburg: Naumann.
Brand, Karl-Werner (ed.) (1985) *Neue soziale Bewegungen in Westeuropa und den USA*. Frankfurt am Main: Campus.
Bruce-Briggs, Barry (ed.) (1979) *The New Class?* New Brunswick: Transaction Books.
Bürklin, Wilhelm (1984) *Grüne Politik*. Opladen: Westdeutscher Verlag.
Campbell, A., Converse, P.E., Miller, W.E. and Stokes, D.E. (1960) *The American Voter*. Chicago: University of Chicago Press.

Chambers, William N. and Burnham, Walter D. (eds) (1967) *The American Party Systems*. New York: Oxford University Press.

Christadler, Marieluise (1983) 'Die "Nouvelle Droite" in Frankreich', pp. 163–216 in Fetscher (1983).

Converse, Philip E. (1964) 'The Nature of Belief Systems in Mass Publics', pp. 206–61 in David Apter (ed.), *Ideology and Discontent*. Glencoe, Ill.: Free Press.

Converse, Philip E. and Markus, Gregory (1979) ' "Plus ça change . . ." The New CPS Election Study Panel', *American Political Science Review*, 73 (Mar.): 32–49.

Crawford, Alan (1980) *Thunder on the Right*. New York: Pantheon.

Dalton, Russell J., Flanagan, Scott C. and Beck, Paul Allen (eds) (1984) *Electoral Change in Advanced Industrial Democracies*. Princeton: Princeton University Press.

Davis, James A. (1985) *The Logic of Causal Order*. Beverly Hills: Sage.

Dubiel, Helmut (1985) *Was ist Neokonservatismus?* Frankfurt am Main: Suhrkamp.

Epstein, Klaus (1966) *The Genesis of German Conservatism*. Princeton: Princeton University Press.

Fend, Helmut (1984) *Die Pädagogik des Neokonservatismus*. Frankfurt am Main: Suhrkamp.

Fetscher, Iring (ed.) (1983) *Neokonservative und 'Neue Rechte'*. München: Beck.

Flanagan, Scott C. (1982) 'Changing Values in Advanced Industrial Societies', *Comparative Political Studies*, 14 (Jan.): 403–44.

Goldthorpe, John H., Lockwood, David, Bechhofer, Frank and Platt, Jennifer (1968) *The Affluent Worker: Industrial Attitudes and Behaviour*. Cambridge: Cambridge University Press.

Goldwin, Robert A. (ed.) (1967) *Left, Right and Center: Essays on Liberalism and Conservatism in the United States*. Chicagao: Rand-McNally.

Grebing, Helga (1971) *Konservative gegen die Demokratie*. Frankfurt am Main: Europäische Verlagsanstalt.

Greiffenhagen, Martin (1971) *Das Dilemma des Konservatismus in Deutschland*. München: Piper.

Habermas, Jürgen (1973) *Legitimationsprobleme im Spätkapitalismus*. Frankfurt am Main: Suhrkamp.

Habermas, Jürgen (1982) 'Die Kulturkritik der Neokonservativen in den USA und in der Bundesrepublik: über eine Bewegung von Intellektuellen in zwei politischen Kulturen', *Merkur*, 36 (Nov.): 1047–61.

Habermas, Jürgen (1985) *Die Neue Unübersichtlichkeit*. Frankfurt am Main: Suhrkamp.

Harrington, Michael (1976) *The Twilight of Capitalism*. New York: Simon & Schuster.

Hill, Samuel and Owen, Dennis (1982) *The New Religious–Political Right in America*. Nashville: Abingdon.

Hughey, Michael W. (1982) 'The New Conservatism: Political Ideology and Class Structure in America', *Social Research*, 49 (Autumn): 791–829.

Huntington, Samuel P. (1957) 'Conservatism as an Ideology', *American Political Science Review*, 51 (June): 454–73.

Inglehart, Ronald (1977) *The Silent Revolution: Changing Values and Political Styles among Western Publics*. Princeton: Princeton University Press.

Inglehart, Ronald (1981) 'Post-materialism in an Environment of Insecurity', *American Political Science Review*, 75 (Dec.): 880–900.

Inglehart, Ronald (1983) 'Traditionelle politische Trennungslinien und die Entwicklung der neuen Politik in westlichen Gesellschaften', *Politische Vierteljahresschrift*, 24 (June): 139–65.

Inglehart, Ronald (1984) 'The Changing Structure of Political Cleavages in Western Society', pp. 25–60 in Dalton, Flanagan and Beck (1984).

Inglehart, Ronald (1985) 'New Perspectives on Value Change', *Comparative Political Studies*, 17 (Jan.): 485–532.

Inglehart, Ronald (1986) 'The Impact on Behaviour of Long-term Predispositions', paper prepared for the meetings of the International Society of Political Psychology, Amsterdam, June/July.

Inglehart, Ronald and Flanagan, Scott, C. (1987)'Value Change in Industrial Societies', *American Political Science Review*, 81 (Dec.): 1289–319.

Inglehart, Ronald and Klingemann, Hans D. (1976) 'Party Identification, Ideological Preference and the Left-Right Dimension among Western Publics', pp. 243–73 in Ian Budge, Ivor Crewe and Henry Fairlie (eds), *Party Identification and Beyond*. London and New York: Wiley.

Jennings, M. Kent (1987) 'Residues of a Movement: the Aging of the American Protest Generation', *American Political Science Review*, 81 (June): 367–82.

Kinder, Donald R. and Kiewit, D.R. (1981) 'Sociotropic Politics: the American Case', *British Journal of Political Science*, 11 (Apr.): 129–61.

King, Gary (1986) 'How Not to Lie with Statistics: Avoiding Common Mistakes in Quantitative Political Science', *American Journal of Political Science*, 30 (Aug.): 666–87.

Kristol, Irving (1972) *On the Democratic Idea in America*. New York: Harper & Row.

Kristol, Irving (1978) *Two Cheers for Capitalism*. New York: Basic Books.

Ladd, Everett C. and Hadley, Charles D. (1978) *Transformations of the American Party System*. 2nd ed. New York: Norton.

Lane, Robert E. (1962) *Political Ideology*. New York: Free Press.

Laponce, Jean A. (1981) *Left and Right: the Topography of Political Perceptions*. Toronto: University of Toronto Press.

Lederer, Robert (1979) *Neokonservative Theorie und Gessellschaftsanalyse*. Frankfurt am Main: Lang.

Lewis-Beck, Michael (1980) *Applied Regression*. Beverly Hills: Sage.

Lewis-Beck, Michael (1986) 'Comparative Economic Voting: Britain, France, Germany, Italy', *American Journal of Political Science*, 30 (May): 315–46.

Liebman, Robert C. and Wuthnow, Robert (eds) (1983) *The New Christian Right: Mobilization and Legitimation*. New York: Aldine.

Lipset, Seymour M. (1981) *Political Man*. Expanded and updated ed. Baltimore: Johns Hopkins University Press.

Lipset, Seymour M. (1985) *Consensus and Conflict*. New Brunswick: Transaction Books.

Lipset, Seymour M. and Rokkan, Stein (1967) 'Cleavage Structures, Party Systems, and Voter Alignments', pp. 1–64 in S.M. Lipset and S. Rokkan (eds), *Party Systems and Voter Alignments*. New York: Free Press.

Lipset, Seymour M. and Raab, Earl (1978) *The Politics of Unreason: Right-Wing Extremism in America, 1970–1977*. 2nd ed. Chicago: University of Chicago Press.

Lipset, Seymour M. and Schneider, William (1983) *The Confidence Gap*. New York: Free Press.

Luhmann, Niklas (1974) 'Der politische Code "konservativ" und "progressiv" in systemtheoretischer Sicht', *Zeitschrift für Politik*, 21 (3): 253–71.

Mannheim, Karl (1927) 'Das konservative Denken', *Archiv für Sozialwissenschaft und Sozialpolitik*, 57: 68–142, 470–95.

McClosky, Herbert and Brill, Alida (1983) *Dimensions of Tolerance*. New York: Russell Sage.

McClosky, Herbert, Hoffmann, Paul J. and O'Hara, Rosemary (1960) 'Issue Conflict and Consensus among Party Leaders and Followers', *American Political Science Review*, 54 (June): 406–27.

Middendorp, C.P. (1978) *Progressiveness and Conservatism: the Fundamental Dimension of Ideological Controversy and their Relationship to Social Class*. The Hague: Mouton.

Miller, Warren E. and Levitin, Teresa (1976) *Leadership and Change*. Cambridge, Mass.: Winthrop.

Moynihan, Daniel P. (1973) *The Politics of a Guaranteed Annual Income*. New York: Random House.

Müller-Rommel, Ferdinand (1983) 'Die Postmaterialismus-Diskussion in der empirischen Sozialforschung: Politisch und wissenschaftlich überlebt oder noch immer zukunftweisend?', *Politische Vierteljahresschrift*, 24 (June): 218–28.

Nie, Norman H., Verba, Sidney and Petrocik, John R. (1976) *The Changing American Voter*. Cambridge, Mass.: Harvard University Press.

Offe, Claus (ed.) (1984) *Arbeitsgesellschaft – Strukturprobleme und Zukunftsperspektiven*. Frankfurt am Main: Campus.

Offe, Claus (1985) 'New Social Movements: Challenging the Boundaries of Institutional Politics', *Social Research*, 52 (Winter): 817–68.

Peele, Gillian (1985) *Revival and Reaction: the Right in Contemporary America*. Oxford: Clarendon Press.

Petrocik, John R. (1981) *Party Coalitions*. Chicago: University of Chicago Press.

Podhoretz, Norman (1980) 'The Present Danger', *Commentary*, 69 (Mar.): 27–40.

Podhoretz, Norman (1981) 'The Future Danger', *Commentary*, 71 (Apr.) 29–47.

Rémond, René (1982) *Les Droites en France*. Paris: Aubier.

Rühle, Hans (ed.) (1982) *Der Neokonservatismus in den Vereinigten Staaten und seine Auswirkungen auf die Atlantische Allianz*. Melle: Knoth.

Schelsky, Helmut (1975) *Die Arbeit tun die anderen: Klassenkampf und Priesterherrschaft der Intellektuellen*. Opladen: Westdeutscher Verlag.

Schissler, Jakob (ed.) (1983) *Neokonservatismus in den USA*. Opladen: Westdeutscher Verlag.

Schumann, Hans-Gerd (1978) 'The Problem of Conservatism: Some Notes on Methodology', *Journal of Contemporary History*, 13 (Oct): 803–17.

Schumann, Hans-Gerd (1984) ' "Konservatismus" als analytischer Strukturbegriff', pp. 370–82 in Hans-Gerd Schumann (ed.), *Konservativismus*. Königstein: Athenäum.

Shafer, Byron (1983) *Quiet Revolution: the Struggle for the Democratic Party and the Shaping of Post-Reform Politics*. New York: Russell Sage.

Shell, Kurt L. (1986) *Der amerikanische Konservatismus*. Stuttgart: Kohlhammer.

Sorman, Guy (1983) *La révolution conservatrice américaine*. Paris: Fayard.

Steinfels, Peter (1979) *The Neoconservatives*. New York: Simon & Schuster.

Touraine, Alain (1969) *La société post-industrielle*. Paris: Denoël.

5

Postmodern Structures of Feeling: Values and Lifestyles in the Postmodern Age

Bo Reimer

We want the world and we want it now.

Jim Morrison

If one was to browse through the literature covering the concept of postmaterialism and do likewise for the more ambiguous concept of postmodernism, it is a safe bet that very few, if any, references would coincide. These are not concepts that belong to the same universe. Thus, at the outset, the idea of bringing them together in the same article seems almost absurd. On the other hand, this 'absurdity' may just be an indication that we live in postmodern times and that we should not be surprised by such an articulation. And despite their apparent incommensurability, they do have one aspect in common, making this articulation interesting: the will to analyse changes in contemporary society, changes occurring both in politics and in culture.

The question posed initially in my article will be: *What happens to materialist and postmaterialist values in postmodern times*? Are we still witnessing a major value change or is something else happening? Is the notion of postmaterialism at all relevant for Baudrillard's (1980) silent masses? I will argue that the value orientations of young people, being directed towards *immediacy*, cannot be contained inside a materialist/postmaterialist value construction. Further, I will argue that, in a postmodern consumer culture, a reconstruction of the value problematic, taking into consideration people's *lifestyles*, must be undertaken.

I have chosen an argumentative approach for this article. I will try to 'read' the concepts of postmaterialism and postmodernism. In order to add strength to my arguments, I will also interpret data collected in a Swedish national survey, dealing with the subjects outlined above.[1]

Perspectives on postmodernism

Describing the concept of postmodernism as ambiguous is understating the matter. Postmodernism may be characterized as: 'a space, a "condition" . . . where competing intentions, definitions, and effects, diverse social and intellectual tendencies and lines of force converge and clash' (Hebdige, 1986–7: 6–7).

Such a multidiscursive concept does not profit from one strict definition. What I will do in this chapter is use two different perspectives. First, I will treat postmodernism as the 'zeitgeist' or the *structures of feeling* of this age (cf. Williams, 1961). It is a perspective that emphasizes a *plurality of feelings*, impossible to contain under one concept or under one culture. This plurality, this movement from structure to structures, from culture to cultures, will serve as a preliminary distinction between postmodernism and modernism; a distinction that is not meant to imply a total break, but a 'restructuration of a certain number of elements already given' (Jameson, 1985: 123).[2] It is a perspective that positions the feelings of the age at a *microlevel*, to be created and recreated in social space, rather than as something possible to deduce, unmediated, from the socioeconomic system. Second, postmodernism will be treated as a way of theorizing; a theorizing 'without guarantees', that questions determinism, preferring a discussion on possible and probable sets of relations in historically specific contexts (cf. Hall, 1986a).[3]

With these perspectives in mind, we now move to a brief description of the postmaterialist hypothesis.

The theory and method of postmaterialism

According to Ronald Inglehart (1977a, 1985) the Western world is undergoing a period of value change; a change from materialist to postmaterialist values. The theoretical basis for this hypothesis is a combination of socialization theory and a Maslovian needs hierarchy theory. Basic values – per definition abstract, few in number and related to attitudes and behaviour (cf. Rosengren and Reimer, 1986) – are internalized at an early age and change very slowly. Furthermore, high priority is put on values high up on a value hierarchy. When physiological needs have been taken care of, other needs (intellectual, aesthetic, etc.) become more important. In the same way people tend to attach more importance to postmaterialist values than to materialist values, once the objective conditions for doing so occur. Thus, in comparison with older generations, post-Second World War generations that have never felt material insecurity put higher priorities on postmaterialist values, such as freedom of speech, than on traditional materialist values, such as economic growth. And, as long as prosperity continues, each new generation will be more postmaterialistic than the generation preceding it.

The empirical material used to support this hypothesis is collected in large-scale surveys where respondents rank order postmaterialist and materialist value items. Each respondent is ascribed the position of being either materialist, postmaterialist or mixed. The mixed group is the largest.

Over the last fifteen years, studies using the materialist/postmaterialist value scale have been undertaken in most West European countries, as well as in the United States, Canada and Japan (Inglehart, 1977a, 1984; Flanagan, 1982; Lafferty and Knutsen, 1985; Savage, 1985; Harding et al., 1986).

Postmaterialism in postmodern times

It is in the research area of quantitative political science that the value change hypothesis has attracted the most attention. This has led to a discussion conducted extensively on empirical/methodological grounds and directed towards (party) political change (Marsh, 1975, 1977; Van Deth, 1983; Böltken and Jagodszinski, 1985. Replies in Inglehart, 1977b, 1983, 1985).

The scope of the actual theory is, however, wider than that. It proclaims a general value change that reaches beyond traditional politics, that obfuscates the boundaries between the political, the social and the cultural. This is a grand statement, announcing (a) that these changes in social/cultural/political life actually have taken place, (b) that they may be traced back to a value change and *its* causes, and (c) that these changes are inevitable.

One of the cornerstones of postmodern thinking is the refusal of totalities, of all-encompassing grand theories subjecting every phenomenon under a single principle. This 'war on totality' (Lyotard, 1984: 82) substitutes discontinuities for continuities, spaces of dispersion for single centres.

'Inflicting' this perspective on the postmaterialist theory, it may be argued that the fallacy of this theory lies in its claim for universality and inevitability. It sets out on the task of trying to establish necessary, timeless relations. It treats historically and discursively constructed categories as solid, universal, forever fixed with one meaning. And it does not reflect upon its own chosen perspective.

The statements above do not imply a total rejection of the theory, however. I would like to argue for the merits of the postmaterialist theory as a fruitful *local theory*, helpful in understanding a post-World War II situation; as a theory that may be used to analyse, in the vocabulary of Laclau (1982), the 'articulation' between different social categories.[4]

In questioning the universality of the theory, a reasonable requirement is that I point to its shortcomings in a concrete way. I will try to show that the proposed value change may no longer be in process and that the prevailing structures of feeling in contemporary society cannot satisfactorily be grasped by the postmaterialist theory. In so doing, I will concentrate on young people. This does not mean that the tendencies here described are exclusive to youth. They are not. But these tendencies are stronger, more marked in this age group, and therefore easier to demonstrate.

Being young

Every generation has to undergo the experience of breaking away from its past and creating a life of its own. This is a process that can be traumatic. In previous times, young people could be expected to follow in the footsteps of their parents. Nowadays this is normally not the case. Instead, the responsibility of what to do with one's life is put more on oneself. This may cause worry and anguish. But it also means that one's life is not as automatically predetermined. A multitude of possibilities, undreamed of by older generations, opens up. Whole lifestyles may be tried, discarded and replaced, all in the search for 'the ultimate'.

A loosening of traditional bonds leads to an increasing individualization. This does not mean, however, that individual decisions are being made in a vacuum. Other socialization agents, besides the family, take on ever more important roles.

One of the characteristics of contemporary urban society, one of the components in the making of a postmodern society, is the proliferation of *signs and messages* surrounding us – rather contradictory in their nature, quite difficult to draw under a single intent. These signs and messages form, especially for youth, a natural part of the modern world:

> In this collage of sights and sounds we discover the immediate co-ordinates of the present: where existing meanings and views, ideas and opinions, are reproduced; where social practices are formed and experienced; where both consensus and rebellion is voiced; where dogma and innovation, prejudice and change, find expression. (Chambers, 1986: 185)

What distinguishes the situation for youth of today from that of older generations of youth is the combination of loose traditional family bonds and the life in a postmodern culture. In this modern world, where old structures erode, where 'All that is solid melts into air', old, traditional ways of living and thinking mix with new, sometimes opposing ways. Trying to contain these different structures of feeling under one master plan would seem, to say the least, difficult. In such an ephemeral environment, it would seem reasonable to assume that *change in itself* becomes the one common characteristic and that *immediacy* takes on primary importance.[5]

A prerequisite for the postmaterialist hypothesis is the generational value change. With the above interpretation of some key tendencies in contemporary society, I want to argue, however, that *despite* a higher level of education, *despite* living in a period of relative prosperity and peace, young people are *no* more likely to be postmaterialists than old people. Young people's value orientations, being directed towards immediate gratification rather than delayed gratification, do not fit into the postmaterialist/materialist value construction. They are, on the whole, *neither* materialists *nor* postmaterialists. As a result of a combination of cohort and age effects, they contain elements of both value orientations, making them something else altogether, something that calls for a different interpretation.[6]

As an empirical concretization of the preceding statements, Table 1 presents the twelve Inglehartian value items and their correlations with different background variables. The figures are taken from a Swedish national survey conducted in 1986, where the respondents rated all twelve societal goals on a seven-point scale, ranging from 'not at all important' to 'very important'.[7] The first six goals are the materialist items, the following six are the postmaterialist ones.[8]

A first impression gathered from Table 1 is that the correlations between the traditional background variables and the different value items are rather weak. Statistically, they do not 'explain' very much.[9] Furthermore, it seems that, instead of falling into distinct post-materialist/materialist groupings, the different background variables are either related in the same way to both postmaterialist and materialist goals or they only relate to some of the goals. Thus, people with lower levels of education tend to value all materialist and most postmaterialist goals higher than do people with higher levels of education. Females perceive all postmaterialist goals as more important than men do, *as well* as such materialist goals as 'the fight against crime' and 'fighting rising prices'. And when it comes to party preferences, only two goals correlate strongly: non-socialist sympathizers put great emphasis on 'making sure this country has strong military forces', whereas socialist sympathizers emphasized 'seeing that the people have more say in how things are decided at work and in their communities'.

When turning to the age variable, it has to be remembered that, according to the postmaterialist hypothesis, the proportion of postmaterialists should be the highest among young people. (The fact that we have switched from a ranking to a rating approach should not change this matter.) However, Table 1 shows that old people do indeed consider materialist goals to be more important than young people do,

Table 1   *Postmaterialist and materialist values, Sweden*
(*product moment correlations*)

Values	Gender[a]	Age[b]	Education	Household income	Party[c]	Class
Maintaining a high rate of economic growth	−0.11*	0.14*	−0.08*	0.02	0.04	0.01
Making sure this country has strong military forces	−0.04	0.15*	−0.09*	0.03	0.31*	0.11*
Maintaining order in the nation	0.06	0.20*	−0.20*	−0.05	0.04	−0.09*
Fighting rising prices	0.08*	0.19*	−0.21*	−0.05*	−0.15*	−0.16*
Maintaining a stable economy	0.00	0.11*	−0.17*	0.01	−0.07*	−0.08*
The fight against crime	0.09*	0.17*	−0.18*	−0.02	0.01	−0.09*
Seeing that the people have more say in how things are decided at work and in their communities	0.13*	−0.03	−0.06	−0.05	−0.29*	−0.20*
Trying to make our cities and country-side more beautiful	0.15*	0.03	−0.05	−0.08*	−0.03	−0.08*
Giving the people more say in important government decisions	0.10*	0.08*	−0.07*	0.00	0.00	−0.04
Protecting freedom of speech	0.05	0.03	0.00	0.05	−0.03	−0.01
Progressing toward a less impersonal, more humane society	0.16*	0.16*	−0.07*	−0.02	−0.07*	−0.06
Progressing toward a society where ideas are more important than money	0.20*	0.08*	−0.09*	−0.11*	−0.16*	−0.11*
N =	(1,503)	(1,503)	(1,500)	(1,513)	(1,240)	(1,332)

[a] A positive correlation means high female values on the variable in question.
[b] 15–75.
[c] Party is dichotomized between socialist and non-socialist parties.
* Significant at the 0.01 level.

Source: Swedish national study, 1986

but they *also* consider the postmaterialist goals to be more important. With the exception of the goal 'seeing that the people have more say in how things are decided at work and in their communities', *all* items correlate positively with age. If young people are more postmaterialistic than old people are, then it certainly does not show through here!

Table 1 does not paint a complete picture, of course. First, it opens up questions concerning its internal validity. Might it not be the case

that in surveys young people consider *everything* as less important than
old people do? And second, do the results imply that young people
have no values at all?

The latter question I have already touched upon. I have argued
that change and immediacy are at the centre of young people's
attention and that values encompassing such feelings are of primary
importance. Empirically, these two questions may now be addressed
simultaneously.

Included in the survey already presented was the set of values
compiled by the American sociologist Milton Rokeach (1973, 1979).
Whereas the Inglehart value items try to tap just one dimension, the
original Rokeach value survey is multidimensional. It mixes terminal
with instrumental values, personal with social. In the Swedish survey,
the Rokeach battery of eighteen terminal values was used. All values
were rated on a five-point scale.

Table 2 presents the correlations between the Rokeach value items
and those background variables used earlier. I will concentrate my
comments on the age variable and its relation to the different values. In

Table 2   *The Rokeach value survey (product moment correlations)*

Values	Gender[a]	Age[a]	Education	Household income	Party[a]	Class
A comfortable life	−0.02	−0.21*	−0.08*	0.02	−0.03	−0.07*
Family security	0.07*	−0.04	−0.03	0.07*	0.00	−0.03
Freedom	−0.06	−0.06	0.05	0.02	0.08*	0.01
Salvation	0.07*	0.22*	−0.14*	−0.14*	0.08*	−0.05*
Inner harmony	0.11*	0.10*	0.11*	0.09*	0.01	0.09*
Equality	0.16*	−0.01	−0.06	−0.10*	−0.25*	−0.15*
Wisdom	0.04	0.06	−0.02	0.01	0.05	0.06
Love	0.07*	−0.22*	0.07*	0.08*	0.03	0.03
Happiness	0.06	−0.21*	−0.03	0.02	−0.01	−0.04
Pleasure	−0.01	−0.35*	0.01	0.06	−0.03	−0.03
True friendship	0.10*	−0.14*	0.01	0.02	0.02	0.00
Self-respect	0.07*	0.05*	0.07*	0.07*	−0.03	0.06
A sense of accomplishment	0.01	−0.09*	0.01	0.04	−0.05	0.00
Social recognition	0.07*	0.07*	−0.11*	−0.05*	−0.04	−0.04
An exciting life	−0.04	−0.30*	0.06	0.02	0.03	−0.02
A world of beauty	0.08*	−0.04	−0.10*	−0.10*	−0.05	−0.04
National security	0.10*	0.14*	−0.14*	−0.04	0.03	−0.03
A world at peace	0.10*	0.04	−0.06	−0.03	−0.03	−0.03
N =	(1,528)	(1,528)	(1,527)	(1,535)	(1,253)	(1,500)

[a] See Table 1 for explanations.
* Significant at the 0.01 level.

Source: Swedish national study, 1986

so doing, it seems obvious that, even in surveys, young people *do* consider some values to be more important than their elders do. Indeed, more than half of the eighteen values are positively related to youth.

The pattern is rather distinct. It is personal, individual values, not social ones, that are important to young people. Two values stand out in particular: 'pleasure' and 'an exciting life'. This comes as no great surprise in relation to our previous discussion.

Thus far we have stayed on an 'inner' level, on the values and opinions of people. But looking at the values of young people, it is obvious that, in order to make sense of them, they must be related to the surrounding society, to the consumer culture, whose characteristics they in some sense reflect. And in trying to understand this relation, a useful starting point may be found in the work carried out by Pierre Bourdieu (1984, 1985).

Social space and the field of lifestyles

According to Bourdieu, every individual at an early age internalizes a system of dispositions that both serves as the generative principle of classifiable practices and as the system of classification (the capacity to differentiate practices and products). These two characteristics of what Bourdieu calls the *habitus* – the system of dispositions – constitute the lifestyle of the individual, i.e. his distinctive preferences or tastes. The habitus mediates between social structure and practices, functioning as a structuring structure, systematically organizing practices and the perception of practices.

The choice of a lifestyle is neither accidental, nor innocent. The field of lifestyles is a field of distinctions. It is a field *upholding* distinctions. Bourdieu constructs a social space where each person's position is based on his or her volume and proportion of economic and cultural capital. The social space is a

> multi-dimensional space, an open set of fields that are relatively autonomous, i.e., more or less strongly and directly subordinated, in their functioning and their transformations, to the field of economic production. Within each of these sub-spaces, the occupants of the dominated positions are constantly engaged in struggles of different forms. (Bourdieu, 1985: 736)

The field of lifestyles may be juxtaposed on the social space, and the different lifestyles deduced from the positions in this space. Thus, a high volume of cultural capital, as possessed, for instance, by artistic producers and higher-education teachers, means a high probability of a preference for avant-garde festivals and philosophical essays, whereas a high volume of economic capital (commercial employers, industrialists, etc.) means a high probability of a preference for auctions and business meals. A low total volume leads to a high probability of enjoying, among other pleasures, football and public dances (Bourdieu, 1984: 128-9).

This field of lifestyles functions as an upholder of distinctions by the way objectively classified practices are transformed into classifying practices, into symbolic expressions of class position. This is made possible by the ability of the dominating classes to define what are, in fact, totally arbitrary tastes as *the superior tastes*, available for enjoyment only to the chosen few.

No doubt the work of Pierre Bourdieu stands out as the most informed that has been carried out in the sociology of lifestyles, a fact that has also been acclaimed (cf. Garnham and Williams, 1980; Brubaker, 1985; Roe, 1987). Nevertheless, a critique has been raised against his treatment of cultural practices. John Frow argues that Bourdieu's theory of the aesthetic suggests that 'there is an intrinsic logic of cultural practices which matches the intrinsic logic of a unitary ruling-class structure' (1987: 62). The function of cultural practices becomes one of domination, and *solely* of that. By assigning such a single and static function to cultural practices, the theory has difficulty in accounting for differentiated, disruptive uses of both high and popular culture. The theory leaves no openings.

An opposing view of the possible functions of cultural practices can be found in what may loosely be called the 'cultural studies' tradition. Here, the interest is directed towards the appropriation of the components of the consumer culture in the creation of an identity, using what is available (cf. Hall and Jefferson, 1976; Hebdige, 1979). Both Bourdieu and the 'cultural studies' tradition would agree that, in a consumer culture, the field of lifestyles becomes an important battleground in the reproduction of society. They would disagree, however, on the necessity of the outcome of the processes going on in this field.

The work of Pierre Bourdieu has been applauded for its combination of theoretical and empirical sophistication. What is not always recognized, however, is that the empirical data in *Distinction* (Bourdieu, 1984) are quite old, collected in the 1960s, and often of an exemplificative character. The automatic correspondence between the position in social space and the choice of lifestyle that may or may not have existed in France twenty years ago is rendered as a valid statement for contemporary West European societies. But if it is the case that 'we are moving towards a society without fixed status groups in which the adoption of styles of life . . . which are fixed to specific groups have been surpassed' (Featherstone, 1987: 55), then the basis for the discussion on the 'meaning' of lifestyles is different. Thus, no examinations of lifestyles can take this correspondence as given.

Whether it exists or not is a question that has to be addressed at each specific occasion.

A similar discussion concerns the actual construction of social space, which, by being defined through total volume and proportions of economic and cultural capital, singles out two fractions of the dominant class. This overemphasis on two distinct fractions means that people distinguished by both maximum amount of cultural capital *and* maximum amount of economic capital are grouped with people distinguished by being in the intermediary position between these two fractions, two groups that neither theoretically nor empirically are identical. The *size* of these two groups in relation to Bourdieu's two pure groups of course depends on the historical and cultural setting.

Lifestyles of the young

How can we construct a field of lifestyles? We may start by locating it in the area of leisure.

> In the economies of late capitalism, leisure displaces labour, consumption displaces production, and commodities become the instruments of leisure, identity and social relations. (P)leisure lies at the centre of a low-employment, consumerist society. (Fiske, 1987: 118)

When it comes to leisure activities for Swedish youth, a number of 'spaces' of lifestyles, internally relatively homogeneous but externally heterogeneous, may be constructed. Theoretically, it makes sense to construct a couple of 'undistinguished' lifestyles, common to a majority of Swedish youth, and combine these with two 'distinguished' lifestyles, based on economic and cultural capital. Following Bourdieu, these lifestyles should correspond to the different amount and proportion of capital possessed by the young people involved.

Here, a construction of five lifestyles has been undertaken. They may be characterized as being directed towards 'domesticity', 'popular culture', 'the natural life', 'high culture' and 'economy'. The five lifestyles have been constructed with the help of ten leisure activities and interests. Two activities belong to each lifestyle. With the help of factor analysis, five factors – that may be interpreted as five lifestyles – were extracted.

Table 3 shows quite clearly five distinct lifestyles. The activities corresponding to each one – 'having your own home' and 'home decorating' to the 'domesticity' lifestyle, 'nutritious food' and 'exercise/jogging' to the 'natural life' lifestyle, 'listening to popular music' and 'going dancing' to the 'popular culture' lifestyle, 'stocks and bonds' and 'golf' to the 'economy' lifestyle, and 'reading fiction' and 'going to the theatre' to the 'high culture' lifestyle – load extremely

Table 3   Leisure activities and interests among Swedish youth
(15–29) (factor analysis [a] and product moment correlations)

	Factor 1	Factor 2	Factor 3	Factor 4	Factor 5	N
Activities and interests						
Having your own home	0.90	0.02	–0.03	–0.01	–0.06	
Home decorating	0.80	0.23	0.17	0.07	0.13	
Nutritious food	0.21	0.85	–0.07	–0.11	0.09	
Exercise/jogging	0.03	0.77	0.22	0.30	0.01	
Listening to popular music	0.08	0.00	0.83	0.00	0.08	
Going dancing	0.02	0.09	0.81	0.02	–0.02	
Stocks and bonds	–0.02	–0.02	–0.06	0.84	0.00	
Golf	0.06	0.12	0.07	0.79	0.03	
Reading fiction	0.00	–0.10	–0.02	0.00	0.86	
Going to the theatre	0.05	0.21	0.07	0.02	0.80	
Correlations [b]						
Gender	0.16*	0.15*	0.13*	–0.33*	0.32*	(454)
Age	0.16*	–0.02	–0.35*	–0.06	0.01	(454)
Education	0.02	–0.02	0.00	0.08	0.21*	(447)
Household income	0.04	–0.07	0.02	0.05	0.12*	(409)
Party	0.01	0.00	0.00	0.20*	0.04	(242)
Class	–0.12*	–0.10	0.10	0.09	0.10	(430)
Marital status	0.24*	0.01	–0.23*	–0.11*	0.03	(392)
Urbanization	0.02	0.03	–0.09	0.03	0.20*	(454)

[a] Principal Component Analysis, Rotation = Varimax.
[b] see Table 1.
* Significant at the 0.01 level.

Source: Swedish national study, 1986

high on each relevant factor and very low on all other factors. The
pattern could hardly have been more clear cut.

On the whole, gender is the background variable most strongly
correlated with the five lifestyles. Marital status and age (even in this
narrow age group) also show a strong correlation.

The ten items used here to capture five lifestyles are of course only
indicators of, and components in, a 'whole way of life'. People with
popular culture lifestyles also frequently watch entertainment on TV
and buy many records and tapes. The 'high culture' lifestyle includes
cinema-going and watching high cultural TV programmes. The
'domesticity' lifestyle is related to video-watching at home, etc.

The five lifestyles are not equally common. With the lifestyles being
built empirically on factor analysis, all respondents are included in
each factor. But, if belonging to a lifestyle is defined as having an

average of at least six on the seven-point scale on each relevant item, then roughly 50 percent would belong to the 'popular culture' and the 'domesticity' lifestyles, about 30 percent to 'the natural life' lifestyle, 15 percent to the 'high culture' lifestyle and almost 5 percent to the 'economy' lifestyle.

Theoretically, it is possible to belong to all lifestyles, and some people do belong to more than one. The most common combination is belonging to the 'popular culture' and 'domesticity' lifestyles (about 25 percent). All in all, about 30 percent belong to two lifestyles and almost 20 percent to three or more. No one belongs to all five lifestyles.

To sum up, it seems that, when constructing a Swedish field of lifestyles among youth, the spaces occupied are related to, but in no way determined by, one's position in social space (as defined by Bourdieu. Of course, gender, age and class may be used in other constructions of social space). The 'high culture' lifestyle is the one most related to structural background. A high level of education seems to be an almost necessary – but yet not sufficient – precondition for inclusion in this lifestyle. 'Economy', the other prestigious lifestyle, seems less closed off. The lower correlation with class background than with party sympathy indicates that the trajectory of this group seems to be one of upward motion.

The lack of total homology between the positions in social space and in the field of lifestyles indicates that the need for studying lifestyles may be a substantial one; not only are the classifying practices at work, but they work from a slightly different position than that presupposed by class position. One implication of this will be followed through when we now return to the postmaterialist and materialist value items (Table 4).

For young people, the importance assigned to the different value items are related to background variables in a pattern that is not dissimilar to the one presented for the whole sample. This means that females consider most values to be more important than men do, that people with a low level of education consider all goals to be more important than do people with a high level of education, and so on. If, out of this general pattern, we disentangle the different lifestyles, a more nuanced interpretation may be made. The two lifestyles consisting of a high volume of capital, 'high culture' and 'economy', are both characterized by a high level of education. Level of education in itself is negatively related to all values. But, by distinguishing between an economically and a culturally directed lifestyle, the pattern becomes different. An 'economy' lifestyle is positively related to most materialist goals and a 'high culture' lifestyle is positively related to all postmaterialist goals.

The discussion carried out here suggests that the value orientations

Table 4 *Postmaterialist and materialist values among Swedish youth (15–29) (product moment correlations)*

	Lifestyles[a]				
Values	Domesticity	Natural life	Popular culture	Economy	High culture
Maintaining a high rate of economic growth	–0.00	–0.06	0.12*	0.25*	–0.12*
Making sure this country has strong military forces	–0.04	–0.02	0.16*	0.14*	–0.17*
Maintaining order in the nation	0.08	0.09	0.04	0.05	–0.09
Fighting rising prices	0.13*	0.04	0.02	–0.08	0.03
Maintaining a stable economy	0.15*	0.07	0.11	0.01	0.03
The fight against crime	0.12*	0.07	0.09	0.03	–0.05
Seeing that the people have more say in how things are decided at work and in their communities	0.09	0.06	0.03	–0.16*	0.10
Trying to make our cities and countryside more beautiful	0.07	0.17*	–0.05	–0.01	0.07
Giving the people more say in important government decisions	0.07	0.08	0.03	–0.19*	0.12*
Protecting freedom of speech	0.06	0.06	0.03	–0.07	0.17*
Progressing toward a less impersonal, more humane society	0.09	0.03	–0.03	–0.12*	0.15*
Progressing toward a society where ideas are more important than money	0.07	0.09	0.02	–0.19*	0.19*

$N = 438$ [a] See Table 3.
* Significant at the 0.01 level.

Source: Swedish national study, 1986

of youth cannot simply be read through socioeconomic background. This background is not something static. It is contextually dependent. Thus, a high level of education 'means' something different in the context of an 'economy' lifestyle than it does in the context of a 'high culture' lifestyle. And it is in the concrete setting of daily life, in the encounter between the past and the present, that one's value orientations constantly are being formed and transformed.

The picture of the values of youth that has been presented here may seem negative. An increasing subjectivity seems to be spreading across all youth, and the only radical element to be traced seems to be the direction towards immediacy. But with this reconstruction of the value problematic using the notion of lifestyles, it seems that groups with similar background and upbringing but with differing lifestyles, stand for radically different value orientations. Indeed, the common direction towards individualization and immediacy may be separated into a radical and a conservative component.

In this context the move towards consumerism and lifestyles becomes important. As Mica Nava argues:

consumerism can be argued to exercise control through the incitement and proliferation of increasingly detailed and comprehensive discourses. Yet because of the diffuse nature of this control, because it operates from such a multiplicity of points and is not unitary, it is also vulnerable. If this is the case, then contemporary preoccupations with imagery and the buying of things can be understood not only as part of this new technology of power, but, as, variably (sometimes simultaneously), both a form of subjection to it and a form of resistance. (1987: 207)

A never fully closed system is, as Nava points out, a vulnerable one. The field of lifestyles is such a 'never fully closed' system. It is open to unexpected articulations, causing ruptures. It can temporarily encompass – but it can never fully contain – all structures of feeling.

Conclusions

Taking as its starting-point the conjunction between the two discourses of postmaterialism and postmodernism, I have tried to argue *against* the hypothesis concerning an automatic value change towards postmaterialism in Western European countries. My arguments have been based on the assumption that, in a pluralist consumer culture, where traditional family structures are eroding, young people's value orientations are also pluralist, too diverse to be contained inside a materialist/postmaterialist value conception. In this postmodern consumer culture, it seems we have to take into account *a different type of socialization* than that proposed by the Inglehartian model; a socialization that is *continuous*, forever faced with new, changing situations, leading to diverse value orientations.

The movements in contemporary society demand an openness on the part of the interpreters of contemporary events. Caution has to be raised against any certainty and automatic correspondence. The theoretical construction of social space and the field of lifestyles by Bourdieu is an excellent case in point. The framework may fruitfully be applied in different cultures and at different times, but the underlying assumptions, such as the correspondence between the two fields, must be treated precisely as that; as assumptions, not as something predetermined. Nothing is. Maybe this understanding is part of the postmodern condition we initially set out to identify.

Notes

1. The survey was conducted as part of the Internalized Culture research programme. This programme is a continuation of Cultural Indicators: the Swedish Symbol System

1945–75. Whereas the Cultural Indicators programme studied changing values in media over a thirty-year period, the aim of the new programme is to study values as internalized by individuals in the 1980s (Rosengren, 1985, 1986; Reimer, 1986; Rosengren and Reimer, 1986). The Internalized Culture programme is made possible by a grant from the Bank of Sweden Tercentenary Foundation.

2. In these definitions of postmodernism and modernism, I also include the cultural expressions of the arts, of both high culture and popular culture (cf. Schulte-Sasse, 1986–7).

3. The literature on postmodernism is now enormous. In this context relevant texts include Baudrillard (1980, 1985), Lyotard (1984), Foster (1985), Huyssen (1984), Jameson (1984), Eagleton (1985), Collins (1987), Hall (1986b) and Hutcheon (1987).

4. An analysis of this articulation is of course outside the scope of this chapter. See also Laclau and Mouffe (1985) and Hall (1986b).

5. The discussion on youth in contemporary society is based on the writings of the German socialization theorist Thomas Ziehe (Ziehe and Stubenrauch, 1982; Ziehe, 1986).

6. Differences in value orientations between young and old people in contemporary society may be separated into three effects: age effects, cohort effects and period effects. Empirically, it is impossible to separate between them in one study at one time. The argument here for a combination of age and cohort effects may thus only be made theoretically (cf. Glenn, 1977).

7. The data were collected through mail questionnaires, and simple random sampling was used. Response rate 68 percent.

8. The rating approach used in the survey is preferable to the more commonly used ranking approach. This is due partly to the statistical limitations of the ranking approach (Cattell, 1944; Hicks, 1970; Reimer, 1985), but mainly to a theoretical weakness: the ranking approach does not permit the respondents to be both postmaterialists and materialists, or, to be neither one nor the other.

9. The use of product moment correlations may be questioned when the variables included do not statistically meet an interval scale level criterion, or when the variables are dichotomized. However, in the context of the analyses made here, the problem may be considered to be relatively minor. The correlations between variables such as gender and the dichotomized party variable and the different value items are roughly the same using product moment correlations and Kendall's Tau, an ordinal scale level measure of association.

References

Baudrillard, Jean (1980) 'The Implosion of Meaning in the Media and the Implosion of the Social in the Masses', pp. 137–48 in Kathleen Woodward (ed.), *Technology and Postindustrial Culture*. London: Routledge & Kegan Paul.

Baudrillard, Jean (1985) 'The Ecstacy of Communication', pp. 126–34 in Foster (1985).

Böltken, Ferdinand and Jagodszinski, Wolfgang (1985) 'In an Environment of Insecurity: Postmaterialism in the European Community, 1970 to 1980', *Comparative Political Studies*, 17 (4): 453–84.

Bourdieu, Pierre (1984) *Distinction: a Social Critique of the Judgement of Taste*. Cambridge, Mass.: Harvard University Press.

Bourdieu, Pierre (1985) 'The Social Space and the Genesis of Groups', *Theory and Society*, 14: 723–44.

Brubaker, Rogers (1985) 'Rethinking Classical Theory: the Sociological Vision of Pierre Bourdieu', *Theory and Society*, 14: 745–75.

Cattell, Raymond B. (1944) 'Psychological Measurement: Normative, Ipsative, Interactive', *Psychological Review*, 51: 292–303.

Chambers, Iain (1986) *Popular Culture: the Metropolitan Experience*. London: Methuen.

Collins, James (1987) 'Postmodernism and Cultural Practice', *Screen*, 28 (2): 11–26.

Eagleton, Terry (1985) 'Capitalism, Modernism and Postmodernism', *New Left Review*, 152: 60–73.

Featherstone, Mike (1987) 'Lifestyle and Consumer Culture', *Theory, Culture and Society*, 4: 55–70.

Fiske, John (1987) 'Miami Vice, Miami Pleasure', *Cultural Studies*, 1 (1): 113–19.

Flanagan, Scott C. (1982) 'Changing Values in Advanced Industrial Society', *Comparative Political Studies*, 14: 403–44.

Foster, Hal (ed.) (1985) *Postmodern Culture*. London: Pluto Press.

Frow, John (1987) 'Accounting for Tastes: Some Problems in Bourdieu's Sociology of Culture', *Cultural Studies*, 1 (1): 59–73.

Garnham, Nicholas and Williams, Raymond (1980) 'Pierre Bourdieu and the Sociology of Culture: an Introduction', *Media, Culture and Society*, 2 (2): 209–23.

Glenn, Norval D. (1977) *Cohort Analysis*. Beverly Hills: Sage.

Hall, Stuart (1986a) 'The Problem of Ideology – Marxism without Guarantees', *Journal of Communication Inquiry*, 10 (2): 28–44.

Hall, Stuart (1986b) 'On Postmodernism and Articulation: an Interview with Stuart Hall', *Journal of Communication Inquiry*, 10 (2): 45–60.

Hall, Stuart and Jefferson, Tony, (eds) (1976) *Resistance through Rituals: Youth Subcultures in Post-war Britain*. London: Hutchinson.

Harding, Stephen and Philips, David with Fogarty, Michael (1986) *Contrasting Values in Western Europe*. London: Macmillan.

Hebdige, Dick (1979) *Subculture: the Meaning of Style*. London: Methuen.

Hebdige, Dick (1986–87) 'A Report on the Western Front: Postmodernism and the Politics of Style', *Block*, 12: 4–26.

Hicks, Lou E. (1970) 'Some Properties of Ipsative, Normative and Forced-Choice Normative Measures', *Psychological Bulletin*, 74: 393–6.

Hutcheon, Linda (1987) 'Beginning to Theorize Postmodernism', *Textual Practice* 1 (1): 10–31.

Huyssen, Andreas (1984) 'Mapping the Postmodern', *New German Critique*, 33: 5–52.

Inglehart, Ronald (1977a) *The Silent Revolution: Changing Values and Political Styles among Western Publics*. Princeton: Princeton University Press.

Inglehart, Ronald (1977b) 'Values, Objective Needs and Subjective Satisfaction among Western Publics', *Comparative Political Studies*, 9 (4): 429–58.

Inglehart, Ronald (1983) 'The Persistence of Materialist and Post-Materialist Value Orientations: Comments on Van Deth's Analysis', *European Journal of Political Research*, 11: 81–91.

Inglehart, Ronald (1984) 'The Changing Structure of Political Cleavages in Western Society', pp. 25–69 in R.J. Dalton, S.C. Flanagan and P.A. Beck (eds), *Electoral Change in Advanced Industrial Democracies: Realignment or Dealignment?* Princeton: Princeton University Press.

Inglehart, Ronald (1985) 'New Perspectives on Value Change: Response to Lafferty and Knutsen, Savage and Böltken and Jagodszinski', *Comparative Political Studies*, 17 (4): 485–532.

Jameson, Fredric (1984) 'Postmodernism, or the Cultural Logic of Late Capitalism', *New Left Review*, 146: 53–92.

Jameson, Fredric (1985) 'Postmodernism and Consumer Society', pp. 111–25 in H. Foster (ed.) *Postmodern Culture*. London: Pluto Press.

Laclau, Ernesto (1982) *Politics and Ideology in Marxist Theory*. London: Verso (first published 1977).

Laclau, Ernesto and Mouffe, Chantal (1985) *Hegemony and Socialist Strategy*. London: Verso.

Lafferty, William and Knutsen, Oddbjörn (1985) 'An Analysis of the Distinctness and Congruity of the Inglehart Value Syndrome in Norway', *Comparative Political Studies*, 17 (4): 411–30.

Lyotard, Jean-François (1984) *The Postmodern Condition: a Report on Knowledge*. Minneapolis: University of Minnesota Press.

Marsh, Alan (1975) 'The Silent Revolution, Value Priorities and the Quality of Life in Britain', *American Political Science Review*, 69: 21–30.

Marsh, Alan (1977) *Protest and Political Consciousness*. Beverly Hills: Sage.

Meddin, Jay (1975) 'Attitudes, Values and Related Concepts: a System of Classification', *Social Science Quarterly*, 55: 889–900.

Nava, Mica (1987) 'Consumerism and its Contradictions', *Cultural Studies*, 1 (2): 204–10.

Reimer, Bo (1985) 'Values and the Choice of Measurement Technique: the Rating and Ranking of Postmaterialism', Working Paper no. 8, Unit of Mass Communication, University of Gothenburg, Sweden.

Reimer, Bo (1986) 'Social Space and the Structuring of Communication Processes', Working Paper no. 19, Unit of Mass Communication, University of Gothenburg, Sweden.

Roe, Keith (1987) 'Culture, Media and the Intellectual: a Review of the Work of Pierre Bourdieu', pp. 17–27 in Ulla Carlsson (ed.), *Forskning om Populärkultur*. Gothenburg: Nordicom.

Rokeach, Milton (1973) *The Nature of Human Values*. New York: Free Press.

Rokeach, Milton (ed.) (1979) *Understanding Human Values*. New York: Free Press.

Rosengren, Karl Erik (1985) 'Culture, Media and Society', *Massa Communicatie*, 13: 126–42.

Rosengren, Karl Erik (1986) 'Media Linkages between Culture and Other Societal Systems', pp. 19–56 in Margaret L. McLaughlin (ed.), *Communication Yearbook 9*. Beverly Hills: Sage.

Rosengren, Karl Erik and Reimer, Bo (1986) 'The Cultivation of Values by Media', Lund Research Papers in the Sociology of Communication 6, Department of Sociology, University of Lund, Sweden.

Savage, James (1985) 'Postmaterialism of the Left and Right: Political Conflict in Postindustrial Society', *Comparative Political Studies*, 17 (4): 431–52.

Schulte-Sasse, Jochen (1986–87) 'Introduction – Modernity and Modernism, Postmodernity and Postmodernism: Framing the Issue', *Cultural Critique*, 5: 5–22.

Van Deth, Jan W. (1983) 'The Persistence of Materialist and Post-Materialist Value Orientations', *European Journal of Political Research*, 11: 63–79.

Williams, Raymond (1961) *The Long Revolution: an Analysis of the Democratic, Industrial and Cultural Changes Transforming our Society*. London: Chatto & Windus.

Ziehe, Thomas (1986) 'Inför avmystifieringen av världen: ungdom och kulturell modernisering', pp. 345–61 in M. Löfgren and A. Molander (eds.), *Postmoderna tider*. Stockholm: Norstedts.

Ziehe, Thomas and Stubenrauch, Herbert (1982) *Plädoyer für ungewöhnliches Lernen: Ideen zur Jugendsituation*. Reinbek bei Hamburg: Rowohlt.

6

Symbols and Politics as Culture in the Modern Situation: the Problem and Prospects of the 'New'

Kyösti Pekonen

The purpose of this essay is to study political culture from the viewpoint of the concept of politics. It is not self-evident if and in what respects the phenomena labelled culture and political behaviour are actually political. The problem concerns what aspects or sectors of culture are now political culture, and why. The political character of culture is researched here especially in regard to the concept of the 'new', because the 'new', specifically, is rendering the traditional and familiar problematic. This arises from the openness of the new situation and its many possibilities, conflicting interpretations and visions about what is happening, and the struggle over the direction of future action. However, these kinds of characteristics are considered as the preconditions of the political and of the political actualization of culture in the modern situation.

One supporting thesis, the idea developed especially by Max Weber, of politics as culture has been analysed in the essay. Weber's thesis rests on the supposition that the task of politics in modern society appears, in representative relationships between political leaders and citizens, almost exclusively to signify events and things.

The third level in the essay is to study, with a few Finnish examples, what kinds of change have been realized in the mode of making representative politics in the parliamentary political arena, when politics strives in the modern situation both to signify events and things and to situate the 'new'. The examples used reveal politics becoming more abstract, the personalization of politics, and the role of image, which all emphasize the growing importance of political imagery. A growing reliance upon political imagery suggests that the ability of electoral politics to continue giving meaning depends on political identities and identification where people make these symbolically, or imagine their future through symbols.

The place of culture and two aspects of culture

Culture in the broadest sense as used here means how we perceive the world. Marshall Sahlins has stated (1976: 142): 'Men begin as men . . . precisely when they experience the world as a concept (symbolically)'. Therefore: 'cultures are meaningful orders of persons and things' (Sahlins, 1976: x). This 'meaning' world created, revealed and described by language, words and symbols is as real as the objective world perceived through the senses. Moreover, the meaning world is more continuous and more stable than the sensuous world.[1] However, this account has its own problems, what is understood or conceived to be political or politics in this 'perceiving' of the world?

We can understand culture as a kind of implicit knowledge, where this implicit knowledge is stored especially in language. This side of the concept of culture may be seen, for example, in the way Jürgen Habermas determines his concept of life-world. The life-world is represented, for instance, as a 'culturally transmitted and linguistically organized stock of interpretive patterns' (Habermas, 1984). In the form of language and culture this reservoir of implicit knowledge supplies actors with unproblematic background convictions upon which they draw in the negotiation of common definitions of situations. In this viewpoint individuals cannot step out of their life-worlds. This kind of culture has, of course, some significance for political culture, but 'life-world' is also a culture based upon a consensus where 'everything' goes on without question. Therefore, one can question whether this significance is actually political at all. Does not 'to be political' rather mean struggle and conflict where the undiscussed is brought into discussion?

As a second approach from the viewpoint of the concept of culture we can use Max Weber. 'Culture', Weber declared, 'is a finite segment of the meaningless infinity of the world process, a segment on which human beings confer meaning and significance.' Humans impart significance by taking up 'a deliberate posture (Stellung) towards the world' (Weber, 1949: 81). 'Empirical reality becomes a culture to us because of and insofar as we relate it to values. It includes those segments of reality and only those segments of reality which have become significant to us because of this value-relevance' (Weber, 1949: 76). Thus, in the same way as our human reality can never be known 'without presuppositions' there are big differences in deliberate postures towards the world and how conflicting these postures are in society. If we agree that significance may be understood as the crucial concept in politics as action, then conferring meaning and significance, taking up 'a deliberate posture towards the world' may have the character of a political act. In this 'new taking up' some aspect of the former routines of everyday life may become questionable. Symbolic language (broadly understood) is the vehicle in declaring this new meaning.

When we are especially interested in that segment of the otherwise meaningless infinity of the world process, which is, for some reason, filled with meaning and, when we determine this 'new' giving of meaning to be a presupposition to political action, we can call this moment culture, which, again, in some situations is reflected in politics, that is, is political culture. If we do this, we cannot in advance decide the boundaries of political culture. Almost anything may become politicized in such a way that it becomes at least momentarily a part of political culture. But, of course, every giving of meaning is not political culture. Only those meaning-givings which are reflected in the political arena, in the arena of political forces and power relationships, may be understood as political culture.

If we approach the problem of political culture from the concept of politics we must discern, for example, apolitical, politicization, political, non-politicization and policy which affect differently the political characteristics of culture. But, the kind of attitudes, values, social problems and conflicts which are just now political and, or have become actualized as *political* culture, is not a problem of abstract determination, but depends on the actual sociopolitical situation in society.

Of course, there always exist power relationships, domination, conflicts and differences, but if they are not reflected in the political arena in any sense, they are not *political* problems in society *just now*. It is after all society and the power relationships and struggle about power in it which decide how political society is just now, what problems are politicized, or what kinds of problem have become politically significant for people, what aspects of common understanding have become problematic, questioned, politicized. And these kinds of questions explain the difference between political cultures in different societies and epochs.

'The modern situation' and the 'role' of politics: politics as culture

In determining the notion 'modern situation' I start with Max Weber and with his concepts of 'rationalization' and 'disenchantment of the world' and the 'contradictions' which these produce both for modernity and politics. As is known, Weber meant by 'rationalization' the process by which explicit, abstract, intellectually calculable rules and procedures are increasingly substituted for sentiment, tradition, and rule-of-thumb in all spheres of activity. Rationalization demystifies and instrumentalizes life. 'It means that . . . there are no mysterious incalculable forces that come into play, but rather that one can, in principle, master all things by calculation. This means that the world is disenchanted' (Weber, 1964a: 139).

The starting-point for 'contradictions' is that, rationalization and the disenchantment of the world gradually dissolve traditional super-stitions, prejudices and errors; but this disenchantment of the world does not replace, for example, traditional religious world-views with anything that could fulfil the functions of giving meaning and unity to life. Rather, the disenchanted world is stripped of all ethical meaning. The gain in control is paid for with a loss of meaning. However, Weber believed that 'for nothing has any value for man as a man which he cannot do with passion' (Loewith, 1970: 122).

Weber, however, also supposed that the triumph of reason as rationalization and as the disenchantment of the world brings with it the dominion of *impersonal* economic necessities and also *impersonal* bureaucratically organized administrations. From this viewpoint he describes the spirit of capitalism as a 'vast and mighty cosmos' that 'determines with irresistible force the lifestyles of all the individuals who are born into it' (Weber, 1958: 180).

These blind forces working in society behind the backs of actors raise questions concerning the real possibilities of politics in modern society: how far these blind forces extend; how automatically they function and how binding they are. When thinking about modern politics the problem is, how much and what kind of scope the blind forces working in society leave for politics. These 'contradictions' are built deep inside modern politics and their 'traces' may be easily seen in the empirical level of everyday routine politics.

In high capitalism, in a highly rationalized and disenchanted world, the 'real enemy' of meaning is the 'dominion of the "orders", "instal-lations", and "establishments" of modern life which came into being through rationalization' (Loewith, 1970: 108). Impersonal, routine-like orders threaten to make a modern man merely an object, which again raises the question of the meaninglessness of human existence in contemporary culture.

The paradox of rationalization there is that it also signifies the status of human action in a world whose structures imprison action in routines and require it to be calculating, instrumentalist and predictable. Therefore, one can say that in the (post)modern situation 'meaninglessness was no longer an aesthetic experience of the few, but a contagion' (Wolin, 1984: 84). Sheldon S. Wolin expounds the leitmotif of Weber's analysis of modern politics to be the striving to answer the challenge posed by 'the meaninglessness of human existence' (Wolin, 1984: 74). The specific problem in the modern situation is the surfeit of and the binding nature of order. Against this possibility of meaninglessness Weber 'longed for' the individual who could be the 'human hero' in relation to the dominion of orders. On the other hand, Weber lays a heavy emphasis on modern politics as a possible means of bringing about new meanings in this otherwise impersonal and reified world. Politics has this possibility just because the substance of real modern politics is values which mean more than the rationalizing and routinizing forces, and because the 'mean' of this modern politics is emotions. Weber states:

> As a separate structure, a political community can be said to exist only if and in so far as, a community constitutes more than an 'economic group'; or, in other words, in so far as it possesses value systems ordering matters other than the directly economic disposition of goods and services. (1968: 902)

Weber thought that only charismatic politics – which means in the arena of parliamentary politics rivalry and struggle about leadership, where legitimacy based on emotions is the active force of persuasive ability – can rescue politics as subjective action; action where subjective values, meanings and will may still function. With his concept of charismatic politics Weber wanted to rescue politics from the fate which is continually threatening it even in parliamentary politics. The fate is that politics may be reduced to a part of a routine-like domination of people, that politics may be identified with the rational-legal state, that politics may be withering to rational impersonal administration, that politics may no longer have the possibility of becoming political culture. In the concept of politics used by Weber, one is searching for meaning in a world otherwise so meaningless. Politics is an ability and possibility of creating subjective meaning consisting of a relationship to the world which reveals social forces and necessities. In politics the process of rationalization is punctured by certain discontinuities of history, of which one of the most important is the concept of charisma, which in modern times is the basis of real politics. Weber thought that everything which is connected to the transcendence of everyday routines presupposes charisma.

What conclusions may we draw, thinking about the concept of political culture in the modern situation from Weber's analysis? Charismatic politics as the transcendence of everyday routines is the politics of 'the new', which is characterized by an intensive giving of meaning, so that it is conceived to be in some way political. From the concentration upon 'the new' follows several important issues. The first problem is how to talk about this 'new'. It needs new politics which is embodied in the new language which again is in conflict with the language of the 'past', and this new language must in charismatic politics become personified either in charismatic leaders or movements. At any rate, every new situation is a possible crisis of the representational relationship, persons, parties, or movements, and the language spoken by them. Therefore, the new situation brings with it at least momentarily the abstraction and personalization of politics. This personalization involves both political leaders and spectators of politics. The trend in the modernizing process has been that the individual has to stand more and more on his or her own feet; he or she must decode for him- or herself what is taking place. It is ever more difficult to resort to some traditional narrative. Of course, a very interesting and very important problem is what it exactly means when political leaders try to represent in their persons some 'new', and how the followers judge this 'new', and how political judgement functions. I think there are good reasons for speaking about the role of political imagery and about charismatic politics as a struggle about people's political imaginations.

Language, speech and politics

Max Weber has stated in his essay 'Politics as a Vocation' (1964a: 95): 'To an outstanding degree, politics today is in fact conducted in public by means of the spoken or written word.' I try to study only the specific consequences which follow from the fact that politics comes true through words, what it means to the 'way' of making representative politics between politicians and citizens in the parliamentary political arena. This conducting through words is a precondition for viewing politics as culture.

It is especially language which mediates between idiosyncratic interpretations of the situation and the conventional symbols of society. Language provides the opportunity for engaging in social interaction, and serves as the main agent of man's integration into culture. An individual or group cannot oppose this integration since there is no choice but to acquire the language of the culture in which one hopes to be understood. Jointly shared symbolic expressions which are articulated through language are the means of socialization and create a social bond between individuals and groups, since the roles and social relations available in society are transmitted and internalized through language (Mueller, 1975: 18). It is also worth noting that this function of language often realizes itself unconsciously: language is a part of our unconsciousness.

But language becomes real only when it is used, that is, in speech. Language, its 'approving', is a condition of speech, but from another direction its existence and, above all, its transformation, presuppose speech. In speech a priori conventional concepts are used in concrete situations; concepts are brought into relation with external objects; the present is compared with yesterday's concepts, and these may generate conflicts, for example between the subjective and the objective, the past and the present. The substance of this possible conflict between language and speech is that some unforeseen changes may result in signification, and the changing of meanings by which people judge subject matters is the substance of variation. I think there are good reasons for arguing that politics in the modern situation is nearer to speech than language.

We must also take into account how this kind of politics comes true empirically, how it realizes itself, how we know politics. It is clear that politics is not just any material commodity like a bicycle, car, or meal. Politics is talk. Consider, for example, how important talk is in the daily lives of politicians, how most of us know politics only through the talk of others (politicians, newspapers, TV news, etc.).[2]

The aim of this talk is to define the situation. Defining is much more than stating facts which would be the same to everyone. The question may be one of 'naming' the facts so that these facts become such a part of a story or narrative that they have some sense, and, along with this 'naming', give meaning (inside this story or narrative). In the definition of the situation 'language is . . . not simply an instrument for describing events but itself a part of events, shaping their meaning' (Edelman, 1977: 4). 'It is language about political events rather than the events themselves that everyone experiences' (Edelman, 1977: 142). Therefore, when there is talk about politics, people mostly respond to symbols (Edelman, 1964: 172).

We may say that modern democracy differs from earlier political systems in that nowadays the political system presupposes and leans on the concept of legitimacy perhaps more than ever before – remembering that this legitimacy in a way presupposes and comes from talk. However, this talk may be 'talk' with people's political imagery, where 'everything' is not said aloud. Now there seems to be an unresolved dilemma: on the one hand we say that legitimacy presupposes speech, but, on the other hand, in a way silence is *also* the ideal type of legitimacy. Everything goes on without question (Lukes, 1974: 36–45). Then the function of the critique is to bring the undiscussed into discussion. On the other hand, there is no need for a critique, to break the immediate fit between the subjective structures and the objective structures, if there is no objective crisis which forces new experiences, to see how conventional concepts and symbols fail to describe new experiences correctly. But when something new has happened, one has to find new words for this new situation; these new words and new language name the situation, and by this naming say what all this is about. The critique as new experience and as new language destroys self-evidence practically. The question now is of a crisis situation which calls for extraordinary discourse, and the speaking subject who is capable of giving expression to these extraordinary experiences acquires the image of charisma (Bourdieu, 1977: 170). From this viewpoint, and when we take into account the fact that because any language that can command attention is an 'authorized language' (Bourdieu, 1977: 171) invested with the authority of a group, the things it designates are not simply expressed, but also authorized and legitimized, political leadership is the ability of a new language in a new situation.

Charismatic politics as politics which transcends everyday routines means then the language and speech which in one way or another makes problematic 'the before', 'the general', 'the automatic', 'the legitimate', 'the univocal word', etc. In other words, charismatic politics is the way in politicizing some elements in deliberate postures to the world.

How to talk about the 'new': the concept of the symbol

In the concept of symbol, in one of its many meanings, the question is also of experiences which transcend the finite province of the meaning of the world of everyday life, referring to other finite provinces of meaning, to other 'realities'. With the help of symbols man tries to comprehend these transcendent phenomena in a way analogous to our perceptible world (Schütz, 1973: 297, 331).

These 'other realities' and ideas are spheres of both language and existential experience. This means that with the help of symbols and through symbolization the members of society can experience society, country, state, politics, political leaders, etc., as more than an accident, and in this experience can participate in a whole which transcends particular existence. One can experience life – at least momentarily – as significant.

A symbol hints at something which does not exist as a thing or matter immediately perceptible to the senses. Rather, a symbol is a means by which that which is not immediately perceived is made sensible. With symbolization we give things, events and actions meanings which mean more than things, events and actions themselves, as such. In symbolization 'immediate reality' and the experiences coming from it are not expressed as such, but are sublimated with crystallized symbolic expressions for the definition of the deeper essence of reality. The symbol is then the crystallization of a linguistic or image-like description; a summary which expresses and is a vehicle in the transition from the private to the public sphere. Here, reality is not only described, but also valued; what reality truly is like and what is important in it is defined. Although a symbolically expressed idea of reality is not in the beginning empirical reality immediately perceptible to the senses, symbolic consciousness of reality becomes, as far as reality is actually defined here, more significant than everyday life and its routines.

In his book *Semiotics and the Philosophy of Language* (1984), Umberto Eco tries to define in a more accurate way 'a "hard core" sense of symbol', understood as 'a specific semantico-pragmatic phenomenon', which he labels 'as symbolic mode'. Some of the main characteristics of the symbolic mode are: first, Eco states that 'although symbol is some form of external existence immediately present to the senses, symbol is not accepted for its own worth, as it lies before us in its immediacy, but for the wider and more general significance which it offers to our reflection' (Eco, 1984: 143). Secondly, symbols are ambiguous and multivocal; they have the capacity to resonate among many meanings at once. Symbols are vague, open, ineffective to express a 'final' meaning, and in the last resort inexhaustible, so that with symbols and by symbols one indicates what is always beyond one's reach. Therefore 'in "genuine symbolism", the forms do not signify themselves; rather, they "allude to" or hint at a wider meaning' (Eco, 1984: 144). Thirdly, this also means that there are no correct interpretations of symbols. A symbol has no authorized interpreter. Rather, a symbol leaves the interpreter face to face with the uncoded. Therefore the same symbol can have multiple meanings; what matters is that this symbol undoubtedly means something to people. That is why 'the power consists in possessing the key to the right interpretation, or (which is the same) in being acknowledged by the community as the one who possesses the key' (Eco, 1984: 152).

Likewise, symbols have two aspects. On the one hand, symbols may function as a sedimented language which functions in a non-politicizing way. Here, the content of symbol is generally unquestioned, widely taught, and believed. The form of legitimacy is silence. This kind of symbol has effects on politics, but effects come true 'unconsciously', or at least they are not considered to be political. On the other hand, symbols may be a mean in a politicizing process. Here, symbols may be a mean in making sensible that which is not yet known; symbols may tell about some other reality; symbols may be a vehicle in aiming at some 'new'. In this respect symbols may be understood as a form of political speech which tries to talk about that which does not, precisely speaking, exist (immediately to the senses), which one cannot attain, which one cannot express exhaustively, but which one is obliged to 'try to grapple with', which one consciously and/or unconsciously wants, is longing for, and to which one is making an allusion. Political symbols, and especially their potential for manipulation, are more evident in transitional or crisis periods than in periods of relative peace. These transitional periods are politicized through the struggle between symbols which again try to tell what reality truly is.

The abstraction of politics in the modern situation

Max Weber thought that the basic 'contradictions' of modern politics exist between the dominion of impersonal economic necessities and the need for meaning. The level of the dominion of impersonal economic necessities may be seen in the language of everyday routine politics. In Finland this may be seen in parliamentary politics especially by the hegemony of language and way of speaking which I have called 'non-political necessity language and speech' (Pekonen, 1985, 1987).[3] There is no talk about what 'new' thing must and could be done; this has been replaced by consensus speech. The purpose of this language of necessity is to say that there exist no other possibilities in policy-making than those realized in the government's policy which is the same as consensus. I have described this kind of consensus politics as politics which strives to non-politicization, to restoring apolitical consensus.

In necessity language and speech we have been told that economic necessities are the primus motor of the decision-making called political. Economy is something primary, determining and politics only secondary, something which must follow the laws of economy. This way of speaking reveals a conception according to which economic necessity unites even perhaps differing interests in a necessity to act in the same way, that is, consensuously. The problem, however, is as follows. Is there anything political in the necessity which is said to bind everybody and to presuppose from everybody uniform action? Is this not rather a question of non-politicization and of furthering passivity? This kind of non-political uniform action is not a very favourable ground for the emergence of a new meaning-giving politics. I think that this image of 'economism' may be one of the reasons for the decreasing appreciation of parliamentary politics in Finland (this decreasing appreciation being the increasing passivity in elections, especially of younger generations and of less well-to-do people, cf. Martikainen [1988]).

If the policy of 'economism' strives to non-politicization, what then has been the 'real scope' for politics in the day-to-day political situation. Weber's thesis was that in the modern situation politics lives especially as politicization: politics lives in politicized situations. The specific meaning of politics is heightened in a changing situation of society where political leadership is an ability to create and use a new language presupposed by a new situation. Max Weber thought that almost exclusively here politics may become significant for modern man. Otherwise, politics is near to ritual and administration. We can say this with better reason when we remember the deep cleavage existing in modern mass politics between a few political actors and the great mass of citizens whose active role is only as spectators: they are active only when they are interested in their role as spectators.

So, in principle, if politics is talk, therefore, especially in the new situation, it is all the more an abstract thing which must always be spoken out. In this respect this speaking out says and determines what is happening; what is problematic and political in what is happening. The concept of politics, what politics is just now, the 'area' of politics, who makes politics in this situation, etc., no longer have self-evident answers. By this I mean that in a way this new as such has become the target of modern politics because to represent some new is a condition to be political and to differentiate oneself from others, etc. However, this representing the 'new' may be realized in many ways. Here I try briefly to describe how this challenge of 'new' has been answered in Finland in the 1980s in the phase of a political cycle where politicized situations are missing.

In modern society we must also take into account the growing importance of the mass media in this speaking out of politics. The mass media is the most important, sometimes the only source of political information. What is known about politics comes mainly via political speech in the mass media, and therefore the mass media has a very important role as the means whereby modern politics tries to bind people's political imaginations.

Politics dependent on and carried through the mass media, where the news has the important role in the construction of political spectacles, often means rapidly changing political scenes in the modern situation, with changed roles for the spectator. If the 'new' is the constitutive element there is no single horizon, single story or narrative where one can easily locate oneself and what is happening. Rather the spectator conflates many horizons.

Now, if the 'new' is what every political actor is searching for and if politics must always be spoken out, and when the only 'common' horizon for interpretation has been the impersonal economic necessities which, on the other hand, have not been real vehicles in politicizing something or in striving to something politically new, this has meant *the shortening of the time dimension of politics*. Day-to-day political problems and disputed questions come to the fore and their relevance to the whole of parliamentary politics becomes all the more important. The aim of parliamentary politics in this situation, when political actors try to answer the challenge posed by the modern situation, seems to be *the 'electrifying' of situations* (the phrase is Fredric Jameson's). When the present moment and situations are continually changing, all that is left is the 'electrification' of always new, repetitive and differing kinds of situation. The continuance of time has the tendency to be interrupted or to split. There exist only situations and the politics of these situations. It seems that even politics has run across the experience that time does not necessarily have continuance.

Even modern parliamentary politics must live continually renewing the present moment and in continuous change. In the mass media this means that communication does not in itself help us to remember, but rather that it serves forgetting in that communication, in its news-making, continually tries to produce the explicitly *new*. Reality here is no longer progress in history, rather, reality is changed into images depending on a situation, and time is split into a series of present moments. In parliamentary politics this splitting of the time dimension may be seen, for example, in connection with elections in Finland in the 1980s. *Elections always seem to be a new situation which needs new political posters with new political slogans.* That is the reason why parties have changed their slogans in every election in Finland in the 1980s. The slogans change so rapidly that it is very difficult to remember the party political slogans in earlier elections. Slogans are not intended to represent the long-term ideological interests and aims of the parties. Once slogans have been discovered and used they may be forgotten (Pekonen, 1984).

The personalization of politics and the role of image in the modern situation

In the modern situation where, according to Max Weber, the role of politics is to signify deliberate postures to the world, and where the spontaneous way of parliamentary politics in answering this challenge has been, for example in Finland, the electrification of situations before spectators, these trends again have produced the personalization of politics. In principle, of course, this personalization has two possibilities: either it may function as a way of making culture political in some respects, politicizing by new meaning-giving (e.g. Max Weber's charismatic politics), or it may function as a way of non-politicizing politics.

The transcendence of everyday routines, and the ability to give new meanings presupposes charisma, and succeeding here brings charisma. In charismatic politics person, image and issues are complementary, not opposites. In and through images fundamental political problems may be posed and argued. This is the case with both Ronald Reagan in the United States and Margaret Thatcher in Britain.

The personalization of politics may, however, function as a non-politicizing mechanism. In this case the symbolic dimensions of the image do not strive towards the transcendence of everyday routines, rather the symbols arise from and affirm the necessities of everyday life. This kind of personalization may be seen in many areas of the Finnish parliamentary political system in the 1980s. For example, in parliamentary elections the trend has been such that rivalry in elections – the rivalry of parties about voters, and candidates' rivalry about seats in parliament – takes place increasingly through the individual candidate's public image when the substance of the advertising campaign is the candidate him/herself. This public image has again increasingly been reduced to the candidate's picture and short slogans which tell voters how good, energetic and honest he/she is – and that is all. This hints at the fact that traditional ideologies, social problems and their resolution are replaced by a candidate's persona; 'ideology' is synonymous with the candidate's image (Pekonen, 1984).

The candidate's personal campaign does not so much project political plans as a public image: what he/she looks like, his/her family, and, most of all, his/her intellectual and emotional life. By their self-praise they try to show that they are the best possible representatives. But representing what? Because every candidate must try to make him/herself necessary – at least in the citizen's political imagination – and because big political questions seem not to be forthcoming, the only alternative would seem to be self-praise and artificial, manufactured images.

I have described the historical change in creating images in campaign advertising in the following way (Pekonen, 1986: 50):

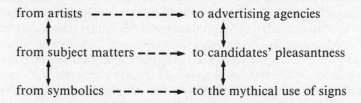

In Finland candidates' pleasantness has become the ideal type of image in elections in the 1980s. This means that in creating images candidates try to associate themselves with signifiers which, on average, reflect pleasantness in society. 'Image' is understood here as 'likeness'; a candidate's election advertisement is like a speech of 'idealized likeness'. But has politics which strives to a political 'new' anything to do with pleasantness? Not very much, because 'political politics' is about breaking routines and the pleasantness that mostly comes with that. Pleasantness produces the atmosphere of general affirmativeness. A political reality which is characteristic of missing politics, the disappearance of politics in the sense of 'collective struggle' and 'changing the situation' is constructed by this kind of image.

The 'objective' task in this kind of personalization of politics is to anchor the signified, that is, the principle of representation by binding representation to the question of persons. In this sense we can speak about a special 'image-discourse' where the discourse of some politicians' images may be compared to the discourse of car models; the question is of a hierarchy between signs. In other words, discourse concerning politics may be replaced by discourse concerning signs. This 'shift' in the object of discourse means that while in public discourse best images for the situation are searched for and created at the same time, it has also been proved that the best are representing and leading us.

Politics as personal advertisement – as a picture and short text of the idea that says, 'I will take care of your interests' – is the construction of impersonal 'personal connection' between two people (political actor and spectator) who in general do not personally meet each other. The special significance of politics in this sense is to emphasize personal connections, the social status of subjectivity just because society in its other sectors of domination is so impersonal.

This trend towards the personalization of politics has meant that *image has become an increasingly important concept in Finnish politics* (Pekonen, 1986). But here image must be understood as a signifier which does not have any necessary relationship to the signified, that is to issues, policies and a person's real subjectivity. In other words, the question may be of an artificial image. That an image can become familiar as a natural way of making this kind of politics, presupposes the same types of change in everyday life: to become acquainted with a given kind of publicity and consumption as 'the philosophy of life' are two conditions of this kind. On the other hand, only when objects become automatized as signs, and become systematized and exchangeable as a result, can one speak about the consumption and consuming objects (Baudrillard, 1981: 66). In other words, quick, broad, and omnipresent publicity based on central mass media and acquaintance with consuming signs – the generalization of sign value as the philosophy of consumption, the 'independence' of the signifier, and the way of speaking of this philosophy being that everything is in principle exchangeable – are the conditions upon which politics and politicians as images are consumed.

However, when politics and politicians are 'consumed', the consuming may bring with it changes in political culture. One change may be within the reference of image. One could hypothesize according to which – for example, in charismatic politics, which is based on a vocation (see Weber, 1964a) – image must as a rule be like a linguistic sign, this sign being a unit in a 'closed language system', in a 'closed narrative'. The vocation in a way 'closes' the language and narrative and locates the horizon for interpretation. The iconic nature of an artificial image again strives to replace ideology which is 'closed' and linguistic especially because *image as an iconic sign is more open*: 'it is a mental concept' (Lowe, 1982: 134).

Conclusion: the problem of political culture in the modern situation – the case of Finland

Generally speaking we may say that the opportunities of the new situation always lie in its openness. The new situation may open up opportunities and scope for real politics: many new visions and interpretations of reality are in principle available; there exist many chances for group expression; the old disenchanted politics may be replaced by the new politics; the new public space may be opened up, etc.

However, it seems as if in Finland we are now living in an epoch characterized by 'political' symbolism which arises more from everyday life and its necessities than symbols which would transcend the routines of everyday life: these kinds of symbol are now missing from parliamentary politics. Politics in this situation is in a way realistic, but all the same very tightly bound up with social necessities; politics is more order and routine than breaking routines. One could also say that there are no strongly politicized problems, consensus is high and, therefore, political culture lives a 'quiet life'. As a result politics as meaning-giving plays no penetrating role in what is happening: politics has little to do with how people imagine their future and make their identifications. It is not politics which binds peoples' social imagery, and the symbols of the future do not come from politics. From this viewpoint one could also say that doing politics to represent a 'new' is a problem. The problem is in the difficulty of situating our own present moment, especially in respect to the future. However, this is necessary in politics. In order to extricate ourselves from this there has to be a satisfaction with substitutes; politics must be concluded from the external features of a politician's personality. The understanding of the time and history of politics has become implicit: it is after all within, but only as signs which an individual reader must himself decode and interpret. In a way – and this is really very ironic – this kind of politics is very 'symbolic', but at the same the 'symbolic' has very little to do with political culture as meaning-giving.

Notes

1. The actual meaning again arises from the collision between the past and the specificity of a concrete event. Therefore meaning is dependent both on the structure inside which an event comes true, and on the effect of an event; or a significant event is a relationship between an episodic event and a given symbolic system. Therefore one can also say that culture is the organization of the current situation in terms of a past (Sahlins, 1983).

2. 'In a larger sense the "words" of politics extend beyond spoken and written utterances to drawings, paintings, photographs, film (the picture's allegedly worth a thousand words); and to gestures, facial expressions, and all manner of other actions (actions that proverbially speak louder than words). These other kinds of political "words" are *symbols*. In short, political talk is symbolic activity' (Nimmo, 1978: 66).

3. An example of this way of speaking is the Social Democratic Prime Minister Kalevi Sorsa's statement in a newspaper interview: 'To the low profile effect also changes in other sectors of society with the diminishing of economic expansion. One *must* act in a narrower scope within which there are not many chances to raise the profile. The latest party which tried to deny *the validity of the facts approved by others* was . . . Now, even this party *has been compelled* to confess those facts. *In the pressure of reality* there remain few possibilities for imagination. One cause is now . . . a deeper knowledge of the *lawfulness* in society and economy than before which *causes* the policies of parties to become all the time of the same kind' (*Helsingin Sanomat*, 19 Feb. 1984). In another newspaper interview, now Foreign Minister, Kalevi Sorsa stated: 'When making political decisions parties *are compelled* in the future to harmonize the decisions to the *frames dictated by the economic necessities*. And it is better that the situation is understood clearly. It is vain to imagine politics to be in some way higher than economy' (*Uusi Suomi*, 13 Feb. 1988).

References

Baudrillard, Jean (1981) *For a Critique of the Political Economy of the Sign*. St Louis: Telos Press.

Bourdieu, Pierre (1977) *Outline of a Theory of Practice*. Cambridge: Cambridge University Press.

Eco, Umberto (1984) *Semiotics and the Philosophy of Language*. London: Macmillan.

Edelman, Murray (1964) *The Symbolic Uses of Politics*. Urbana: University of Illinois Press.

Edelman, Murray (1977) *Political Language: Words that Succeed and Policies that Fail*. New York: Academic Press.

Habermas, Jürgen (1984) *The Theory of Communicative Action*. Vol. 1: *Reason and the Rationalization of Society*. Boston: Beacon Press.

Loewith, Karl (1970) 'Weber's Interpretation of the Bourgeois–Capitalistic World in Terms of the Guiding Principle of "Rationalization"', pp. 101–22 in D. Wrong (ed.), *Max Weber*. Englewood Cliffs, NJ: Prentice-Hall.

Lowe, D.M. (1982) *History of Bourgeois Perception*. Chicago: University of Chicago Press.

Lukes, Steven (1974) *Power: a Radical View*. London: Macmillan.

Martikainen, Tuomo (1988) *Puuttuva punainen viiva: äänestäminen vuoden 1987 eduskuntavaalissa*. Helsinki: Tilastokeskus.

Mueller, C. (1975) *The Politics of Communication: a Study in the Political Sociology of Language, Socialization and Legitimation.* New York: Oxford University Press.

Nimmo, Dan (1978) *Political Communication and Public Opinion in America.* Santa Monica: Goodyear.

Pekonen, Kyösti (1984) 'Moderni politiikka ja vaalimainokset' [Modern politics and election campaign advertisement], *Politiikka,* 2: 190–9.

Pekonen, Kyösti (1985) 'Policy-making and the Relationship between Politics and Bureaucracy', *International Review of Administrative Sciences,* 51 (3): 207–20.

Pekonen, Kyösti (1986) 'Imagon merkitys modernissa parlamentaarisessa politiikassa' [The role of image in modern parliamentary politics], pp. 36–60 in J. Nousiainen and M. Wiberg (eds), *Kansalaiset ja politiikka 1980-luvun Suomessa.* Turku: Turun yliopisto.

Pekonen, Kyösti (1987) 'Poliittinen puhe ja parlamentaarinen politiikka kysynnän kontrollina' [Political speech and parliamentary politics as the way to control 'the demand'], *Paradoksi,* 7: 41–59.

Sahlins, Marshall (1976) *Culture and Practical Reason.* Chicago: University of Chicago Press.

Sahlins, Marshall (1983) 'History and Structure'. *Suomen Antropologi,* 3: 118–27.

Schutz, Alfred (1973) *Collected Papers.* Vol. 1: *The Problem of Social Reality.* Hague: Martinus Nijhoff.

Weber, Max (1949) *The Methodology of the Social Sciences.* Glencoe, Ill.: Free Press.

Weber, Max (1958) *The Protestant Ethic and the Spirit of Capitalism.* New York: Scribners.

Weber, Max (1964a) 'Politics as a Vocation', pp. 77–128 in H.H. Gerth and C. Wright Mills (eds), *From Max Weber: Essays in Sociology.* New York: Oxford University Press.

Weber, Max (1964b) 'Science as a Vocation', pp. 129–58 in H.H. Gerth and C. Wright Mills (eds), *From Max Weber: Essays in Sociology.* New York: Oxford University Press.

Weber, Max (1968) *Economy and Society.* Vol. 2. New York: Bedminster Press.

Wolin, Sheldon S. (1984) 'Max Weber: Legitimation, Method, and the Politics of Theory', pp. 63–87 in W. Connolly (ed.), *Legitimacy and the State.* Oxford: Basil Blackwell.

7

Changes in the Political Culture – Challenges to the Trade Union Movement: the Debate on Nuclear Energy in Swedish and German Trade Unions

Detlef Jahn

Structural changes among employees are a major explanatory variable in the literature on social change in the social sciences. The increase in female employment, the number of white-collar workers and the expansion of the (social) service and public sector all lead to the analysis of the feature of postindustrial society (Bell, 1973, 1976). This development affects the labour movement fundamentally because the increase in these categories of workers, accompanied by the diminishing in number of 'classical' manual workers, results in a dissolving of the coherence of the traditional working class. I will argue that these changes in the occupational structure go together with cultural changes which lead to a new social conflict in society that challenges the normative resources of the trade unions and creates antagonism among employees. For trade unions this development affects their relationship with their membership (the unions' role as interest organizing associations).

Trade unions, however, are more than just dependent on a membership which can identify itself with the aims of the organization and which can be mobilized to fight for the unions' goals; they are also entrenched in a system of associations (the unions' role as political pressure groups). The integration of trade unions into the political system makes unions an influential political power, especially in countries where the trade union movement is centralized and co-ordinated. The status of trade unions in society is decisively determined by the evolution of their policies, which is defined by the process of modernization and the values of modernism.

I shall consider here the Swedish and German unions as examples of both politically influential and corporatist unions. I shall use the issue of nuclear energy in order to identify the conflicting dimensions and groups and to demonstrate the impact of the changes in the political culture on trade union organizations. We shall see that the union structure and environment are crucial variables in explaining organizational involvement and response.

Changes in the political culture

The concept of 'political culture' as put forward by Almond and Verba (1963) refers to individual political orientations and attitudes towards the political system, institutions and behaviour patterns on the one hand, and the individual self-placement within this political framework, on the other. The analysis of change in the political culture either builds upon Almond and Verba's work or focuses on value change as put forward by Inglehart and by Barnes et al. (Almond, 1987: 31; Inglehart, 1977; Barnes and Kaase, 1979). The latter approach in particular emphasizes a new cleavage structure in society. The left versus right conflict between labour and capital, so the argument goes, is no longer the sole cause of disagreement, 'postmaterial' and 'material' values are increasingly becoming responsible for social dispute. In particular, 'Green parties', new social movements and protest against nuclear power, peace policy and the role of women in society are the expressions of demands which go beyond material satisfaction. Research on value change and new social movements indicates that the protagonists of new values have a common structural base: young, highly educated employees in the human service sector (Inglehart, 1977; Cotgrove and Duff, 1980). This group, however, is not identical with the middle class, but cuts across this category (Kriesi, 1987: 317–18). Peter L. Berger considers two elements within the middle class as the main actors of social conflict in current Western societies:

> Contemporary Western societies are characterized by a protracted conflict between two classes, the old middle class (occupied in the production and distribution of material goods and services) and a new middle class (occupied in the production and distribution of symbolic knowledge).
> ... one's attention is drawn to both political and cultural aspects of the matter. Class conflict is always about interests, in the hard material sense. But classes also develop a specific culture or subculture (or, if one prefers, a specific class consciousness). (P.L. Berger, 1986: 67–8)

Monique Dagnaud and Dominique Mehl (1983) take account of this fact when they distinguish between elite, sub-elite and counter-elite. The elite are the established decision-makers who put decisions into effect. Sub-elites and counter-elites are relevant social actors because they possess cultural capital (e.g. education) and social capital (e.g. occupations) (Bourdieu, 1983) just like the elite. The counter-elite – mostly employed in the service sector, above all teachers – sympathize with social change, whereas the sub-elite – mostly employed in highly skilled jobs in administration and industry – are more motivated to oppose the economic and political establishment in order to gain their own place in the existing power structure. In this sense the counter-elite or new middle class '. . . tends to be politically and ideologically to the left of the old middle class, and it is ipso facto anticapitalist in overall orientation' (P.L. Berger, 1986: 68).

Although the counter-elite express left ideals, they are not always attracted to left-wing parties and trade unions. One reason may lie in the evolution and historical development of trade unionism, to which I will turn in the next section. At this point, however, I wish to integrate the changes of values explained within the analytical framework of modernity. As I will outline in the next section, trade unionism has developed closely according to the values of modernity. However, trends have emerged in advanced industrial societies which have questioned whether the process of modernization is right. Berger et al. (1973) point out that modernization creates a 'homeless mind' that tries to escape anomy by self-reference. The result is a pluralization of diverse lifestyles.

The semantic field of modernism consists of *functional rationality* and is expressed empirically by the belief in progress and economic growth. In practice this principle prevails and penetrates in more and more life areas and is inherent in both bourgeois and socialist ideology. Jürgen Habermas (1981) describes in detail this dynamic process as the colonization of the 'life-world' by the 'system' which in turn alters culture, politics and economy (Offe, 1986; Habermas, 1985).

These developments have coincided with the process of individualization in the last two decades. Individualization has often been conceptualized as a consequence of social change, for example during the inner-worldly asceticism of Protestantism (Max Weber), the 'free worker' in capitalism (Karl Marx), or during the process of the division of labour (Emil Durkheim). The new aspect of individualization, however, consists of an ambiguous development (Beck, 1986: 205–19): the separation from traditions and the loss of security, on the one hand, and simultaneously a new social integration, on the other. Social mobility, competition, urbanization, etc., erode traditional links but at the same time common experiences are conveyed by mass media and the (labour) market.[1] The process of individualization is accompanied by both: an opening of opportunities and a standardization of lifestyles.

The process of de- and remodernization is accompanied by social structural changes, such as the increase in non-manual work and the integration of women in the labour market, but also with the results of the process of modernization (expansion of the public, education and welfare sectors, shortening of working hours, public consumption, etc.). So the term 'postmodernity' may refer to the cultural resources of society, as does 'postindustrial society'. Both concepts refer to the above-mentioned social structural changes (Vester, 1985): 'Theoretical, like ascetical, postmodernity has meant a break with formalisms' (Lash, 1985: 3).[2]

Although the concept of 'postmodernity' cannot be applied to a concrete society it might, as Habermas suggests, be used as a theoretical construction. He points out that the term has a useful purpose because it allows us to take our distance from the present society and also allows for the analysis of social developments under a wider perspective (Habermas, 1986). In this sense 'postmodernity' may serve as a working hypothesis with which to describe a vague and unclear modification of culture in modern society (Jameson, 1984).

The social conflict which emerges out of the competing lifestyles is not so much a struggle between materialist and postmaterialist values as about whether some values can survive at all within the dominant value structure of society. Yet the process of modernization creates by-products which increasingly limit the opportunity of different lifestyles. Ulrich Beck (1986) points to the present society as a 'risk society' (*Risikogesellschaft*). Social progress, once a means of obtaining social consensus, begins to threaten part of the population – and this in the abstract postmodern sense of subjective involvement. Another group of society considers precisely this progress of modernization as their fulfilment in life. Only in this sense is the new social conflict a 'conflict around the questions of the grammar of lifestyles' (Habermas, 1981: vol. 2, 576). Claus Offe gives the following example:

> For instance, personal autonomy is by no means a 'new' value; what is new is the doubt that this value will be furthered as a more or less automatic by-product or covariant of dominant institutions such as property and market mechanisms, democratic mass politics, the nuclear family, or the institutions of mass culture and mass communications. What is at issue is not the value but the mode of implementation of values, and the presupposed links between the satisfaction of different values (e.g., between income and intrinsic satisfaction in work, or the link between control over elites and personal development of judgement and understanding in democratic mass politics). (Offe, 1985c: 849; see also Kriesi, 1987)

The attitudes of citizens towards nuclear power may reveal the (post)modern conflict in society on an empirical level. This issue is at the centre of environmental questions and the struggle against nuclear power plants has resulted in new social movements which, in the eyes of some social scientists, are the avant-garde of social change (Touraine et al., 1982). Cotgrove and Duff identify two competing paradigms in society which coincide more or less with modern and postmodern values. They point out:

Nuclear power stations in particular have come to have a deep symbolic significance: centralized, technologically complex and hazardous, and reinforcing all those trends in society which environmentalists most fear and dislike – the increasing domination of experts, threatening the freedom of the individual, and reinforcing totalitarian tendencies. Opposition to nuclear power is seen for many as a key issue on which to take a stand against the further advance of an alliance between state power and commercial interests. (Cotgrove and Duff, 1980: 338)

Survey data from Sweden and the Federal Republic of Germany support the theoretical implication of the diversity of the middle class. In Sweden, however, the data were collected at the time when the referendum on nuclear power was held in 1980. Here the population had three possibilities on which to vote: one for further nuclear power development until substitutes were available (line 1); another for further development, with an intended stop in the next century (line 2) – this alternative was called the working-class line because it was promoted by the Social Democratic Party and the blue-collar trade union confederation LO – and yet another line which opposed nuclear power completely (line 3). For Germany, only a comparison between a pro and con attitude is possible, but the data indicate, in addition, the situation before and after Chernobyl. Figure 1 and Table 1 reflect the expected picture of employees in the welfare and social service sector being the most strongly opposed to nuclear power in both countries.

The data show that skilled workers mostly favour nuclear energy. White-collar workers oppose it, but among higher ranks a rather positive attitude is common. These results are valid both for Germany and Sweden. Obviously, as can be seen from Figure 1, the change in opinion is among high-ranking white-collar workers after Chernobyl. This is probably so because the number of indifferent answers decreased strongly in this group. Blue-collar workers, on the other hand, are still quite indifferent to the nuclear power issue. Table 1 reveals that workers, especially industrial workers, show the most loyal behaviour to the 'working-class line' while the white-collar workers present a very incoherent picture. Himmelstrand et al. reflect upon the incoherence between industrial workers and service workers:

> Unemployment is seen as the greatest threat by more industrial workers than service workers; for environmental problems it is just the opposite. As we have already pointed out the trade union movement has traditionally emphasized problems of employment and production more than external environmental problems – a position which now must be reassessed in a manner which provides the responsiveness of the labour movement to new issues arising. (1981: 209)

But we see from the data of the Swedish referendum that service workers simply do not harbour coherent attitudes when they emphasize

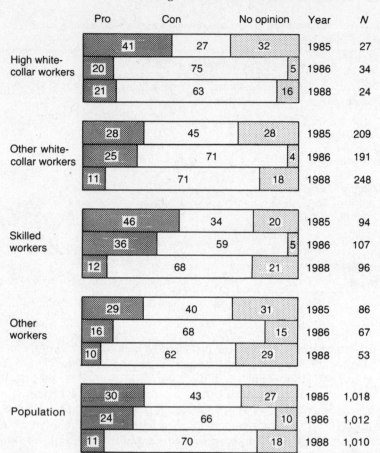

Figure 1   *Occupational groups and attitudes towards nuclear power in West Germany (percent: not always 100 percent because of rounding)*

Source: *Emnid-Information*, No. 3/4, 1985; No. 5/6, 1986 and No. 2/3, 1988

the importance of new issues. More precisely, there are two rival groups: on the one hand, *skilled workers and higher white-collar workers* (in Germany the change since Chernobyl seems to be most dramatic within these occupation groups) favour nuclear energy. In the terms of Berger et al. (1973) they are the primary bearers of functional rationality in technological production and bureaucracy. In a Dutch survey Hanspeter Kriesi (1989) points out that managers, protective services employees (police, firemen, army personnel, etc.), technical services employees (computer specialists, technicians and natural scientists) and unskilled workers are the least likely to

Table 1   *Occupational groups and referendum choice on nuclear power in Sweden, 1980 (percent)*

Occupational group	Develop nuclear power until substitutes available (line 1)	Develop nuclear power but stop next century (line 2)	Oppose nuclear power (line 3)	No response	N
Industrial workers	9	58	30	3	(434)
Other workers	10	47	39	4	(621)
Low white-collar workers	21	38	39	2	(303)
Middle white-collar workers	20	35	40	5	(571)
High white-collar workers	45	23	29	3	(336)
Small self-employed	37	21	38	4	(131)
Farmer	19	5	72	4	(101)
Students	18	17	60	5	(144)
Population	19	39	39	3	(3,839)

Source: Holmberg and Asp, 1984: 348, Table 9.6

participate in the antinuclear power movement (apart from the petit bourgeoisie). On the other hand, it is *low and middle white-collar workers* who oppose nuclear power most frequently. More specifically, it is those in traditional professions, the administrative and commercial services but above all those in social and cultural services (social workers, medical services personnel, teachers, librarians, the clergy, journalists, artists, architects, academics, etc.) who supply the antinuclear power movement (but also other new social movements, see Kriesi [1989]) with its supporters. The traditional workers, however, form a third group. *Blue-collar workers at the middle and lower level* are relatively unaffected by or even indifferent to the nuclear energy issue. This is reflected by the high number of blanks among these groups, even shortly after Chernobyl. In Sweden this pattern is less obvious since the issue was highly politicized during the referendum campaign where the Social Democrats were able to translate the issue into the terms of left and right (Micheletti, 1985: 128; see also Sifo, 1987). With some reservations and modifications we may conclude that the groups which are the least penetrated by '. . . the "new" paradigm are exactly the "principal" classes of capitalist societies, namely, the industrial working class and the holders and agents of economic and administrative power' (Offe, 1985c: 835).

To sum up: the process of modernization creates a conflict between different lifestyles which leads to changes within the political culture of advanced industrial societies. It is not the change of the political culture but rather the change of segments which results in a (often latent) conflict between the dominant pattern of functional rationality and its countervailing powers. What consequences will this have for trade unions?

The challenge for the trade union movement

In order to understand the challenge for the trade union movement we must consider two interwoven developments: first, the involvement of trade union members in the new values and, second, the development of trade union organizations and policies.

The nuclear power issue and trade union involvement

In order to gain insight into the trade unions' involvement in the nuclear power issue I should like to present some survey data which, however, do not allow a comparison between countries without fundamental restrictions. Figure 2 and Table 2 both reflect the tendencies discussed above on the organizational membership level.

The German survey (Figure 2) shows that trade union members are

	Pro	Con	No opinion	Year	N
Trade union members	51	23	26	1981	124
	23	70	7	1986	182
	10	63	27	1988	155
Non-members	39	33	28	1981	826
	25	65	10	1986	885
	11	70	18	1988	842
Population	41	31	28	1981	1,026
	24	66	9	1986	1,017
	11	70	18	1988	1,010

Figure 2 *Attitudes towards nuclear power and trade union membership in West Germany (percent: not always 100 percent because of rounding)*

Source: *Emnid-Information*, No. 5, 1981; No. 5/6, 1986 and No. 2/3, 1988

Table 2   *Trade unions and referendum choice in Sweden, 1980 (percent)*

Trade union membership	Develop nuclear power until substitutes available (line 1)	Develop nuclear power but stop next century (line 2)	Oppose nuclear power (line 3)	No response	N
Members in general	15	45	35	4	(581)
LO members	8	53	34	5	(328)
TCO members	25	35	36	4	(253)
Population	19	39	39	3	(3,839)

Source: Data made available by Sören Holmberg, Department of Political Science, University of Gothenburg

slightly more decided in the nuclear power issue than the general public and, as in the case of the general public, the pro-majority switched over to a strong con-majority after Chernobyl. This pattern changed, however, when in May 1986 the trade union congress of the German DGB (Deutscher Gewerkschaftsbund) decided to take a stand against nuclear energy. This decision, however, was and is challenged by influential membership groups (some single unions, work councils in the energy sector, etc.). The decrease in positive statements towards nuclear energy in 1988 and the simultaneous increase in indifferent attitudes may reflect the unsureness of union members towards this issue.

The Swedish data (Table 3) allow some further interpretations. In Sweden there are two dominating trade union peak organizations. The LO (Landsorganisationen i Sverige), which organizes blue-collar workers, and the TCO (Tjänstemännens Centralorganisation), which organizes white-collar workers. The referendum choices on nuclear power show that blue-collar workers stick substantially to the 'working class' line 2 promoted by the Social Democrats and the LO. TCO members tend much more towards the extreme choices 1 and 3. The TCO board, however, officially took a neutral stand but in fact supported line 2 (Micheletti, 1985: 118–22).

A closer look at the distribution between the private and public sectors shows the TCO's problem more clearly – a problem which exists in the LO as well, but not to such an extent. A majority of employees in the public sector voted for line 3, while employees in the private sector to a significant degree chose line 1, as Table 3 shows.

What we can see from the data is that the white-collar workers' problem is not resolved by the integration of these occupational groups into trade unions, rather they polarize the working class around new issues. Blue-collar workers seem to be more or less loyal to

Table 3 *Trade unions' involvement in the private and public sectors and referendum choice in Sweden, 1980 (percent)*

Trade union and sector of work	Develop nuclear power until substitutes available (line 1)	Develop nuclear power but stop next century (line 2)	Oppose nuclear power (line 3)	No response	N
LO					
Public sector	6	49	40	6	(138)
Private Sector	10	56	29	4	(190)
TCO					
Public sector	18	31	46	2	(118)
Private sector	30	39	28	2	(135)
Total					
Public sector	12	40	43	5	(256)
Private sector	18	49	30	3	(325)

Source: Data made available by Sören Holmberg, Department of Political Science, University of Gothenburg

social democratic policy. However, there is still another occupational group which deserves special attention: skilled workers. This group of workers is to a large extent in favour of nuclear energy. Furthermore, they represent the core group of trade union membership and traditionally have a strong influence on their organization's policy.

The channels through which new (and also established) elements find their ways into trade union policy might be roughly classified as follows: information; parties; interest groups; the national degree of politicization of production; persons; and new social movements. Although there may be overlapping within the categories, it makes sense to distinguish them here and to relate them to trade unions in both countries.

1 *Information*. It is obvious that trade unions often took a stand quite late in the nuclear power debate. Most of the information had been prepared in advance by the pro-nuclear groups (Nelkin and Pollak, 1977; Micheletti, 1985: 53–74 for Sweden; Grumbach, 1986 for Germany). Later, especially in Germany, 'alternative' scientists and institutions diffused antinuclear power material.

2 *Parties*. Trade unions' orientation towards social democratic parties was obvious in both countries (Pollak, 1981). Social Democratic parties favoured nuclear power in the beginning. Here again national differences emerge. In Germany, the Greens and later a reorientation of the Social Democrats (SPD) weakened the pro-nuclear power influence. In Sweden, however, the Social Democrats (SAP) retain

positive attitudes towards nuclear power and the antinuclear power forces were integrated into established parties, where new issues have to compete with traditional ideology and play only a minor role (Centre party: agrarian and classical naturalistic views; Communist party: traditional left orientation and loyal to SAP).

3 *Interest groups.* The collaboration of interest groups, as often described and analysed in the neocorporatist debate, worked as a pro-nuclear power force in both countries. With reference to democratic corporatism, as in Germany but even more so in Sweden, Peter Katzenstein notes: 'Politics is of great importance, but it is important within interest groups, determining which issues get on the public agenda and setting the parameters of political choice' (1985: 33). This was certainly true in both countries when guideline decisions on nuclear power were taken and the term 'economic growth coalition' was coined (Alemann, 1983). It is still valid for the thinking patterns in society even when the consensus between capital and labour seems to have been interrupted in both countries (Lash, 1985; Esser, 1982). Especially after the referendum in Sweden the nuclear energy issue could not gain headline priority on the daily agenda, apart from a short period after the Chernobyl accident. In Germany, on the contrary, the issue was never out of the news.

4 *Politicization.* In Sweden the nuclear power issue was hotly debated at the time of the 1976 and 1979 parliamentary elections and of course in the context of the 1980 referendum on nuclear power. The loss of the Social Democratic party in these elections was often explained by its stance in the nuclear power issue (Vedung, 1979; Gahrton, 1981). Particularly when the issue could be translated into one of personal involvement, did the Social Democrats run into trouble and, in the aftermath of the referendum, politics in Sweden resumed its earlier mode (Holmberg and Asp, 1984: 437–70; Jahn, 1988a).

The Federal Republic of Germany, on the other hand, has never had as homogeneous a political culture as Sweden. But the success of new social actors in the political and other spheres has made Germany interesting as a case in point concerning new politics (Jahn and Müller-Rommel, 1987). Since the mid-1970s, the nuclear power issue has remained in the public debate in Germany and has increased in intensity. This is not only due to the Green party, which came to constitute a potential coalition partner for the Social Democratic party, but also because of the higher sensitivity of the public to environmental issues. Länder (Regional) governments (Hamburg and Hessen) encountered difficulties because of this issue.

An analysis of two dailies, *Dagens Nyheter* (*DN*) in Sweden and *Frankfurter Allgemeine Zeitung* (*FAZ*) in Germany following the accidents at the nuclear power plants in Harrisburg and Chernobyl reveals that this issue was treated to a more or less equal extent in 1979–80 but that in 1986–87 the number of articles was significantly greater in Germany.[3] It is not true that Chernobyl was considered less relevant than Harrisburg in Sweden, quite the contrary, but in Germany, Chernobyl had an enormous public resonance. The issue was more frequently discussed and sustained a longer period in *FAZ* than in *DN* in 1986–87.

5 *Personal influences.* The role of persons involved in trade unions and industry, parties, or other interest groups at the beginning certainly supported the pro-nuclear power policy, too (Radkau, 1983: 430–4). Here again, especially in the case of Germany, a change is visible. Activists from new social movements are often involved in trade union politics as well (see for example in a Dutch survey: Kriesi and von Praag, 1987: 335–6) and confront trade unions with anti-nuclear power attitudes. The same is true of members of the Green party. The same tendencies are valid for the Swedish labour movement. TCO, in particular, was influenced by environmental groups, whereas LO rejected and excluded those influences from the very beginning (Micheletti, 1985; Jahn, 1988b).

6 *New social movements.* Finally, one must make mention of the co-operation between new social movements and the unions. Especially in Germany the relationship between new social movements and the trade unions was quite conflictual in the 1970s but became more constructive in the 1980s. In Sweden the demands of new social movements were embodied in the established political channels which made the movements partly unnecessary (Rubert, 1985).

All of these influences have to be transformed into the inner-organization language before processes of learning and re-evaluation can be said to take place. This process, however, is dependent on traditional factors and ideological orientations.

Trade unions in the process of modernization
In order to understand the policy and problems of trade unions within the framework of changes in the political culture it is helpful to analyse their historical development. For that I will place trade unions within the conceptual framework of 'old' and 'new' politics or paradigms.

'Old politics' and 'old paradigm' are terms which describe the established mode of political performance. The former term emphasizes the social cleavage of established politics, the antagonism of working class and bourgeoisie or the left/right dimension (Barnes and Kaase, 1979). The latter term refers to a comprehensive model of what politics is about: the social base of actors, issues, concerns, values and modes of action such as power and distribution relations (Raschke, 1980;

Offe, 1985c). 'New politics' emphasizes the cleavage which occurs between materialist and postmaterialist values. The new paradigm consists of ecological issues and lifestyle questions.

'Old politics' and trade union policy: from antagonism to consensus

There are two periods within the framework of old politics (Sabel, 1981). The first apparently extends from about the middle of the nineteenth century to the middle of the twentieth. This was the time of the formation of the trade unions' 'new collective identity' (Pizzorno, 1978):

> During this early period of capitalism, the division of labour was such that work relations bound together on the job and fused their relations at work with their lives at home. Work thus gave rise to an all-embracing community. Implicit in the idea of community is the idea of solidarity; and the institutional face of solidarity in a working community was the trade union. In this period, membership in trade unions was thus more a sign of a particular social identity than the result of a calculation of expected economic benefits. The leaders of these organizations were not plagued by the free-rider problem, because paying dues was a moral obligation, not an investment. (Sabel, 1981: 224)

In this first period of old politics there was a well-defined antagonism between the social actors, capital and labour. However, both classes believed in social progress through technical progress. 'Class conscious workers', Alain Touraine (1986: 152) notes, 'accept the basic cultural values of an industrial society (such as belief in progress through improved industrial productivity) but see themselves as victims of the social control of economic activities.' This conviction, which was shaped as early as the 1930s and 1940s in most of the corporatist countries (Katzenstein, 1985: 210), constituted the normative ground of the postwar consensus, the second period of old politics.

Economic progress subverted the workers' commitment to the union in particular. The normative ties of the membership to the organization were replaced by instrumental ones and the gap opened between specific organizational self-interests and membership interests (Pizzorno, 1978). This development was determined by sociostructural changes such as geographical and social mobility, which resulted in the dissolving of the traditional working-class milieu (Mooser, 1984; P.A. Berger, 1986; Lindhagen and Nilsson, 1970). One measurement of the trade unions' ability to ensure organizational strength and survival in this situation was the formation of alliances with capital. In this period consensus politics and economic growth obtained an ideological status (Sabel, 1981: 209). This was the unquestioned prerequisite for social welfare. Capital and labour formed an alliance whereby '... capitalism as a growth machine was completed by organized labor as a distribution and security machine' (Offe, 1985c: 822).

In his theoretical reflections on the development of trade unions Walther Müller-Jentsch traces the historical lines of the evolution from 'classical' to 'intermediary' unions. The classical unionism emphasizes the role of unions as social movement and expression of the socioeconomic interests of their members. The struggle within the wage system and against the capitalist order were the main points of reference (Müller-Jentsch, 1986: 49–67). To consider trade unions as intermediary organizations takes account of changes which took place in the second period of old politics. Unions' '. . . politics are the result of the pragmatic resolution of differences between interests of capital on the one hand and labour on the other' (Müller-Jentsch, 1985: 4; for Sweden see Fulcher, 1988: 131; for Germany see Esser, 1982: 261). This pragmatic resolution of differences between the interests of capital and labour had fundamental consequences for trade unions as organizations. The formulation of interest shifted from antagonistic class interests towards (a) general and compatible interests with the capitalist system (general welfare expectations and growth of profits through economic growth politics), and (b) 'sectional interests'. Sectional interests are not identical for all workers, but vary according to different markets and working conditions. They may become almost antagonistic in character if they obstruct or hinder the process of capital accumulation. The result was that capital's role as the opponent of labour weakened in the minds of the members. This development was reinforced by intra-organizational rationalization, which was initiated to guarantee survival of the organization. That again constituted a further factor for the replacement of 'normative' ties, which are especially important for the involvement of active union members by instrumental ones (Streeck, 1981). Alain Touraine summarizes this development with the words:

> Unions may remain important, but what appears to have declined permanently is the 'labor movement' as such – the capacity of organized labor to challenge the system of social and economic organization. Trade unionism was, at a given time, a social movement; it is now a political force that is necessarily subordinated to political parties and to governments because it tends to defend specific interests . . . Gone is the link between unions and alternative images of a reconstructed society. (1986: 172–3)

Since solidarity faded, latent interest diversity among the members could not be counteracted by an appeal on common normative grounds. In this way the decoupling of industrial values from the ideology of class antagonism and class struggle during the consensus policy made the heterogeneity of the working class become acute. The heterogeneity consists of sectorial, industrial, even non-work oriented interests and resulted in organizational weakness:

> Under the influence of growing heterogeneity, or even antagonism between the interests of particular, increasingly differentiated groups of employees (resulting from cultural, economic and organizational processes of differentiation), the chances of realizing employee interests will lessen to the degree that the level of effective solidarity among the membership base shrinks, that is, in so far as these tendencies toward differentiation and division cannot be successfully counteracted. (Offe, 1985b: 164)

The replacement of normative ties by instrumental ties makes the labour movement and its organizations vulnerable, on the one hand, to social developments which challenge the economic growth consensus and on the other, to movements and developments which are able to activate 'normative' resources. Both conditions are present in the period of new politics.

'New politics' and trade union policy: the challenge of economic growth consensus

Empirical studies demonstrate that unions have more difficulty in organizing employees in the service occupations, which often hold post-material values (Schacht, 1987: 278). 'Postmaterialists' are significantly more dissatisfied with democracy and – important for unions – with their job situation (Marsh, 1975: 24; Jahn, 1985: 59–97). In order to clarify the relation between 'postmaterialism' and trade unionism we shall again refer to the work of Stephen Cotgrove and Andrew Duff, who compare the attitudes of industrialists, trade unionists, the public and members of environmentalist groups in a British survey.[4] They find a high 'postmaterial score for trade union officials' (Cotgrove and Duff, 1981: 96). A deeper look at the Inglehart index, however, reveals conflicting dimensions. On questions of participation both groups agree, but on the basic question of 'maintaining a high rate of economic growth' they sharply disagree. Two percent of the environmentalists give high priority to economic growth as opposed to 44 percent of trade unionists (46 percent of the public).[5]

Intermediary organizations such as unions, however, are not independent of their membership. They are caught between a 'logic of influence' and a 'logic of membership' (Schmitter and Streeck, 1985; Streeck, 1987). The former demands that unions act according to the economic growth policy in order to play the rules of corporatist society. In concrete terms this means that they support nuclear energy. The latter logic, however, renders unions dependent on the compliance of their membership. Increasing heterogeneity deprives unions (and all other intermediary organizations) of the resources for a 'mechanic solidarity' upon which ground it is only possible to reach 'organic solidarity' for the organization (Streeck, 1987: 477, 'the extinction of the regular' as Streeck puts it [1987: 474]). With the erosion of solidarity the latent conflict among employees becomes acute, particularly in situations where issues are politicized which represent the conflict of new and old values.

The debate on nuclear energy in trade union organizations

In this secion I look at the impact the above-mentioned developments have on trade union policy. On the one hand, I am interested in the evaluation of nuclear power by trade unions. This may indicate where unions stand on a pro–con nuclear energy continuum. On the other hand, of special interest is how far the polarization of political culture leads to fragmentations of the trade union movement.

In order to investigate the internal union debate on nuclear power I will use the method of content analysis of the Union congresses before and after the accidents of Harrisburg and Chernobyl. The analytical material consists of the motions of the trade union congresses of the German trade union confederation (DGB) in May 1978 and May 1986 and the Swedish blue-collar trade union confederation (LO) in October 1976 and 1986. Furthermore, the data of the Swedish white-collar confederation (TCO) in 1979 are reported. For the latter, no comparison over time was possible since there had not been a congress after the Chernobyl accident before this essay was written.

In analysing the perception of nuclear power of trade unions I shall apply two different kinds of content analysis. First, the evaluative assertion analysis developed by Osgood et al. (1956). This method makes it possible to measure intensity of attitudes with a high degree of reliability (Holsti, 1969). Intensity ranges from –3 absolute disapproval to +3 absolute approval. With this method it should be possible to identify the stands trade unions take on the nuclear power issue. Secondly, I have constructed analytical dimensions to which the debate on nuclear power refers. For that I have considered the dimensional categories of existing content analyses about the debate on nuclear power (above all Braczyk et al., 1985; Früh, 1981; Holmberg and Asp, 1984; Kitschelt, 1984). Herbert Kitschelt points out that the choices of energy technology cannot be explained on the grounds of technological aspects alone and that the background of social value preferences and the interpretation of reality are also relevant. Because of this the debate on energy technology and especially nuclear power reveals independent sociopolitical orientations which can be summarized in different dimensions (Kitschelt, 1984: 11). Kitschelt's approach in particular allows for extracting the pro and con attitudes in the individual dimensions in an ideal-typical way. He deduces these ideal-typical evaluations from the huge body of literature on nuclear energy mainly from the USA and West Germany, but also from France and to a minor extent Sweden. For my analysis I have modified the categories and the operationalization of Kitschelt's pro–con evaluations to render them appropriate for the analysis of trade unions.

The dimensional categories and some examples of their ideal-typical evaluations are outlined in the following.

The *technology dimension* summarizes all technological evaluations. Positive and negative evaluations of nuclear energy on these dimensions go along with pro and con evaluations on the other dimensions. The *ecology dimension* covers the assessment of the consequences of radiation, nuclear power plant accidents, etc. The pro statements argue that nuclear energy is safe and that consequences of radiation are acceptable. Con statements argue in the reverse direction. The *need dimension* considers ethical questions, needs and production and desired social structure. Pro arguments emphasize the importance of continuity and large-scale production. Fear of nuclear energy is considered irrational and economic growth and technical progress are desirable. Con arguments, in contrast, stress that people's fear should be taken seriously and that energy production should be changed in accordance with social aspects rather than with economic imperatives. The *economy dimension* focuses on the mode of calculation of the nuclear power plants, effects on the labour market, and political economic aspects such as property rights, etc. Pro arguments favour business accounts and postulate a direct relation between energy supply, nuclear energy and employment. The investment should be decided by the owners of energy companies. Con statements question pure business accounts and like to replace them with accounts which take societal and social aspects into consideration. Furthermore, they deny a direct relationship between employment and the way energy is produced in society and they ask for state intervention or state ownership of energy companies. Finally, the *political dimension* illuminates the sociopolitical consequences of nuclear power, for example the effect on democracy, the perception of political parties and administrations. Pro arguments see no political harm in the use of nuclear energy. New social movements, Green parties and other opponents of nuclear energy are considered with suspicion. Referenda and other forms of 'direct democracy' are seen as (if at all) a last resort and should be avoided. The con arguments question the procedures of established decision-making processes within representative democracy. They stress the importance of new social movements, etc., and see the danger of terrorist and military misuse of nuclear energy.

Now we are able to relate the theoretical interpretations of the changes within political culture to the empirical data. The following assumptions can be made:

The 'classical' trade unions' policy favours nuclear energy because it is a technology which stands for technical progress and economic growth. This may find its empirical expression in a positive evaluation of nuclear power and the stress of technological and economic arguments.

Influences on new politics may be expressed by a negative evaluation of nuclear energy, at least in relative terms, when we compare the results of the 1970s with those of the 1980s and the stronger (negative) pressure from dimensions such as need and ecology.

We may expect that blue-collar trade unions are less subject to the influences of new politics than white-collar unions, that is, they face less internal diversity because their membership is more homogeneous than the membership of white-collar unions. Furthermore, we may expect that blue-collar unions have a more positive attitude towards nuclear energy as an expression of their 'classic' politics than their white-collar counterpart.

The findings

Table 4 reflects the result of the evaluation of nuclear energy by the different trade union peak organizations and the frequencies of the individual dimensions. The upper part of the Table gives the evaluation of nuclear energy by the different national confederations.[6] We see that LO and the DGB evaluated nuclear energy more negatively in 1986 than in the 1970s but that LO retained its positive stand. At the LO Congress in 1976 two motions were proposed. One evaluated nuclear energy negatively (the Wood Industry Workers' Union) and another judged it positively (the Federation of Electricians). The LO board took a compromise stand, but tended to be more positive than negative. As the statistics demonstrate, the degree of diversity was quite high at this congress. The picture did not fundamentally change at the LO Congress in the autumn of 1986. A motion from the Paper Industry Union, the Federation of Electricians and the Construction Workers' Union evaluated nuclear power fairly positively. No negative opinions about nuclear energy were voiced. That the democratic process was pro nuclear power biased I have shown elsewhere (Jahn, 1988b; see also Micheletti, 1985: 115).

In TCO, as well, the pro nuclear bias is present even when the evaluation of all motions is clearly negative. Of nineteen motions seventeen were rejected, of which only one judged nuclear energy positively. The average of the evaluative assertion (EA) index was,

Table 4   *The results of the content analysis of trade union congress motions, Sweden and West Germany*

	TCO[a]	LO		DGB	
	1979	1976	1986[a]	1978[a]	1986
Evaluative assertion (EA) index					
of all motions	−1.18	0.35	0.17	1.47	−1.01
$\bar{x}$	−0.90	0.29		2.12	−0.68
Variance	3.90	3.57		0.53	1.64
Minimum	−2.60	−2.00		1.09	−2.10
Maximum	2.63	2.63		2.67	2.40
Range	4.89	4.63		1.58	4.50
N (evaluations)	(60)	(15)	(3)	(23)	(31)
Frequencies (percent):					
Dimension					
Technology	39.5	28.6	25	31.5	44.4
Ecology	7.8	10.7	0	19.1	22.5
Need	19.4	10.7	12.5	4.5	8.6
Economy	25.6	46.4	62.5	24.7	8.6
Politics	7.8	3.6	0	20.2	15.9
N (statements)	(129)	(28)	(16)	(89)	(151)
Number of motions	21	3	1	6	8

[a] The statistics consider only statements with more than three evaluations (total index sums up all evaluations of the congress).

nevertheless, −1.79. The two motions which were approved scored +2.15. The boards of two TCO member unions advised rejection of the critical motions put forward by their members and submitted to the Congress the two motions which were then accepted. However, the TCO debated the issue very diversely. Motions from the Federation of Salaried Employees in Hospital and Public Health Service (SHSTF), the Union of Municipal Government Officers (SKTF), the Federation of Civil Servants (ST) and the Union of Teachers (SL) opposed nuclear energy, whereas the TCO union SALF (Swedish Union of Supervisors and Foremen) took a positive stand in its nuclear power motions.

In Germany the DGB faced a much stronger diversity in the 1980s than in the 1970s, although the fronts remained the same. The Postal Workers' Union, the Youth Department, the Commerce, Banking and Insurance Workers' Union (HBV) and the Education and Science Union (GEW) most strongly opposed nuclear energy. The influential unions (the DGB Board, Metalworkers' Union [IGM], the Public

Service and Transport Union [ÖTV], the Chemical, Paper and Ceramics Workers' Union [IGCPK] and the Mineworkers' Union [IGBE]) were most positive towards nuclear energy. Even when the DGB shifted towards a slightly negative attitude to nuclear power in 1986 the proportions remained the same. When the DGB opposed nuclear energy at its Congress of 1986, it decided in favour of the weakest antinuclear power position with respect to other attitudes presented at the Congress. The shift from pro to con can best be explained by the Chernobyl shock (the Congress took place just one month later).

The bottom part of Table 4 shows clearly that the LO most frequently refers to economic arguments. It is striking, however that the LO, at its Congress in September 1986, was able to maintain – or even increase – its emphasis on economic arguments at the expense of ecological and security aspects shortly after the accident at the nuclear power plant in Chernobyl. The German DGB represents a reverse case. In 1986 the economic arguments in the DGB diminished by two-thirds compared with 1978, the need dimension nearly doubling at the same time. TCO, for which no comparison over time is possible, shows the highest proportion of need-oriented arguments.

If we summarize the results so far we see that the shift of evaluations of nuclear energy from the 1970s to the 1980s seems to be slightly in the direction of a more critical attitude. How can we interpret this shift? For that I wish to consider the other dimensions.

Figure 3 reflects the shift of attitudes on each individual dimension in its aggregated form for all congress motions of the single congresses (for TCO only the 1979 Congress is considered). As we can see, the LO shifted mostly on the technology dimension. Ecological and political statements which scored either slightly or extremely positively were not mentioned at all at the 1986 Congress. Much more stress was given to economic arguments, which even shifted towards the pro pole of the ideal-typical continuum in 1986. It is highly significant that the LO completely neglected all security and ecological aspects after the accident at Chernobyl and instead concentrated on economic aspects. This pattern indeed argues against an increasing influence of new politics on the LO (Czada, 1988: 86–9). Striking, however, is the clear stand the LO took on the need dimension. In both years the LO scored clearly in favour of the con arguments. This is due to statements which prefer changes in the organization of energy supply, the promotion of more efficient and energy saving technologies and the acceptance of the fears of the population about nuclear power. All these statements, nevertheless, remain more or less in the tradition of the 'old' left ideology. Economic growth, etc., was never questioned.

The DGB shifted on all dimensions towards the con position,

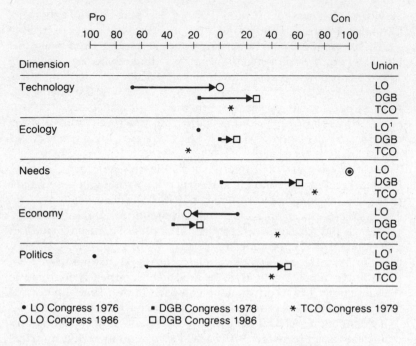

* LO Congress 1976   ▪ DGB Congress 1978   ✳ TCO Congress 1979
O LO Congress 1986   ☐ DGB Congress 1986

[1] The motions of LO Congress in 1986 do not mention this dimension

Figure 3   *Changes of trade unions' attitudes towards nuclear energy on a pro/con continuum in the 1970s and 1980s, Sweden and West Germany (percent of evaluations)*

especially on the political and need dimensions. Here we may speak of a very moderate adoption of elements of new politics by the DGB. The first fact, however, may be partly explained by the change from a social democratic to a conservative government in Germany. The second fact probably shows more clearly the influence of new politics.

The TCO shows a more critical attitude towards nuclear energy than the LO and also the DGB. It seems that the TCO is more affected by environmental issues than the other trade union organizations. The reasons for this are most likely its membership (white-collar workers) and union character (pluralistic, no ideological bounds).

In order to identify the competing dimensions I dichotomize the motions according to their respective pro and con evaluations on the technology dimension. We can see that these evaluations correspond to the pro and con assessments on the other dimensions. Figure 4 summarizes this fact. The further the distance between p and c or P and C the bigger the disagreement in this dimension.

Dimension	Pro 100	80	60	40	20	0	Con 20	40	60	80	100	Union
Technology	p				N				c			LO
				p	**P**		**C**	c				DGB
	p								c			TCO
Ecology	p								c			LO[1]
				p	**C**	**P**			c			DGB
	p								c			TCO
Needs									pcN			LO
				p		**P**			c**C**			DGB
		p							c			TCO
Economy				N			c					LO
			p	**P**		c	p **C**					DGB
		p							c			TCO
Politics	p											LO[2]
			p				c	**P**		**C**		DGB
	p									c		TCO

p pro nuclear energy on the ideal-typical scale 1970s
P pro nuclear energy on the ideal-typical scale 1980s

c con nuclear energy on the ideal-typical scale 1970s
C con nuclear energy on the ideal-typical scale 1980s

N neutral motion of LO 1986

[1] The motions of LO Congress in 1986 do not mention this dimension
[2] The motions of LO Congress in 1986 and con motion in 1976 do not mention this dimension

Figure 4 *Evaluations of individual dimensions after pro/con dichotomization*

For the DGB, Figure 4 shows that the need dimension remains dominant for disagreement but that the economy dimension also polarizes positions. The trade-off between needs and economy reveals the conflict between lifestyle oriented new politics and material reward oriented old politics. The development of this trade-off Andrei Markovits describes when he points out:

Although the activist unions are hostile to the greens' cruder forms of no-growth ecologism as their accommodationist colleagues, one can nevertheless detect a growing eco-consciousness among certain unions belonging to the former group. This in no way implies that the activists have resolved the contradictions inherent in the dichotomy between economy and ecology. Rather, one could argue that reformers within the unions have been forced to begin a lengthy process of reflection with regard to ecology and 'new social movements'. (1986: 446)

For the LO and the TCO we can identify the same patterns. The exception is the LO's con evaluation on the need dimension and the increase in economic statements with simultaneous decrease in security and political arguments in the motions in 1986 compared with 1976 (see above). For the TCO the ideal-typical polarization is particularly clear in all dimensions.

All these data make it doubtful that the shift from extreme pro to moderate pro or con attitudes will be long lasting. But as we can see from the 1970s' data an opposition of unions and groups which oppose nuclear power exists. These unions are mainly in the public sector and organize service workers. Also the youth organizations oppose nuclear power, so we again find the same cleavage line on the organizational level as on the individual level. It seems very likely that the same groups which participate in new social movements, Green parties, or have internalized postmaterial values, make new demands on their trade union organizations. The unions which tend to take a more positive stand on nuclear power are the traditional unions, above all the 'energy unions', but also engineers' unions and the metal workers' unions. The white-collar unions, however, seem to be in the centre of the postmodern conflict.

Conclusion

From the empirical data we can conclude that the new aspects of social conflict in society that are triggered off by changes in the political culture have an effect on the trade union organization. However, the union structure and ideology, and the sociopolitical environment are crucial variables for the degree to which elements of new politics find their way into union policy.

The LO is most reluctant to deal with new values. Probably one reason for this is the strong commitment of Swedish dominant agents – to which the LO certainly belongs – to economic growth as a means of solving social problems (Meidner and Hedborg, 1984: 104–12). The strong social democratic commitment seems to be another main factor in explaining the difficulties of new issues becoming implemented in Swedish blue-collar unions. The white-collar unions in Sweden, on the other hand, ran into considerable difficulty because of the new issues. This is certainly because their ideological commitment is less defined than it is in the blue-collar unions. A further factor which may calm the political discussion of nuclear energy is the referendum. Through this procedure a decision was taken, and the public and the organizations therefore stopped dealing with the issue. Moreover, to change a decision once agreed upon or enacted by democratic measures such as the referendum is very difficult (Anton, 1980: 159).

In Germany the politicizaton of new issues is fairly strong. New social movements and the Green party in parliament raise their issues over and over again. These debates also have effects on the German trade unions.

The crucial sector in both countries, however, is the (social) service sector where conflicts arise between different attitudes and lifestyles *within* white-collar groups and *between* them and blue-collar groups, above all skilled workers in technological occupations. This conflict does not halt for trade unions. As I could demonstrate, they have to deal with the diverse and often antagonistic demands of their members.

Little has been said about the prospects of unions. Claus Offe (1985a) discusses three alternatives: first, a pessimistic one, that of industrial trade unions and white-collar workers drifting apart. This development is more likely in Anglo-Saxon countries. In the two countries being discussed, the other two alternatives seem more likely. The second is the non-polarized existence and action of blue-collar and white-collar unions. This situation may remain peaceful until serious economic and social problems reveal the contradiction between these unions. The third, and rather more optimistic alternative, is that the more progressive white-collar workers form an alliance with changed blue-collar workers unions. In this scenario unions would keep the progressive elements, but would suffer internal conflicts. Furthermore, it would imply that unions – and the labour movement as a whole – would form an alliance with elements from new social movements (Offe, 1985c: 864–8; Martens, 1986; Jahn, 1989) and thus broaden their policy concerns to encompass non-workplace issues and non-work issues such as consumer questions, living conditions, etc. (Negt, 1984). In this case the labour movement could revitalize its dying normative sources (Habermas, 1986) by means of a 'transfusion of fresh blood' from new social movements.

Essential for the unions' internal debate and also for their politics in relation to other organizations is the decision-making process. As the concept of postmodernity suggests, there are diffuse needs and interests in current society which cannot be resolved by instrumental-rational decisions oriented towards economic determinism. Habermas's concept of communicative action, which presupposes non-coercive and non-distortive argumentation (*herrschaftsfreier Diskurs*), may lead towards integrating other rationales within the decision-making process. This concept, however, remains too abstract to be applied in real decision processes. Tom Burns and Reinhard

Ueberhorst (1988) try to develop a concept for 'systematic conflict resolution and policy-making in a world of high science and technology'. This research, however, is in its early stages and further theoretical (hypothesis of postmodernity), empirical (value change), and procedural (decision-making) research on the societal and organizational level is necessary. For the analysis of trade unions we can conclude for now that changes in the political culture – and in structural conditions – lead to a redefinition of the normative resources of trade unions and of their role in society. Trade unions are at the crossroads between political abstinence and retreat on economic issues and an expansion of their policy concerns into new areas which could bring about many unforeseeable consequences.

Notes

This chapter reflects the first results of an ongoing research project which is being conducted by the author at the European University Institute in Florence (EUI). For helpful comments I wish to express my gratitude to Michael Huber, Angela Liberatore and Giandomenico Majone (EUI). Furthermore, Mike Laver and Claus Offe (University of Bielefeld) made invaluable comments on the essay. On a former version of the article I received criticism and encouragement from Colin Crouch (Oxford), Bob Blackburn (Cambridge), Gösta Esping-Andersen, Wilfried Gotsch (EUI) and Roar Hagen (EUI and University of Tromsö). I alone, however, am responsible for the interpretation of the article. I am also indebted to Gale Strom for her help in editing the essay.

1. The importance of the labour market is stressed in the concept of work society. Changes in the quality and quantity and transitions of individual perception and the political status of work are summarized in this concept (Berger et al., 1973; Offe, 1985b; Jahn, 1986; Aho, 1986).
2. The concept of modernity and postmodernity cannot be discussed here in detail. For that, see for example the special issue on postmodernism in *Theory, Culture and Society*, 5, (2–3) (1988). In particular, see Mike Featherstone's essay for conceptual definitions and Douglas Kellner's article for a conclusive overview.
3. The content analysis was conducted 90 weeks and 40 weeks after the reactor accidents at Harrisburg and Chernobyl, respectively. The frequencies of four areas were surveyed: front page, editorial, foreign and home news. I wish to express my gratitude to Eva Berndtsson who helped in collecting the data.
4. Cotgrove and Duff criticize Inglehart's (1977) narrow concept of 'postmaterialism'. Their concept of the 'utopian environmentalists', i.e. those who are members of environmental groups and want fundamental changes of society in order to protect the environment, includes four main dimensions: wealth creation versus limits of growth, authority versus participation, markets versus non-markets, individual versus collective. Environmentalists and trade unionists more or less go along with the authority/ participation and market/non-market dimension.

The fundamental differences, however, are on the wealth creation/limits of growth dimension, especially concerning economic growth, and on the individual/collective dimension. The authors summarize: 'Environmentalists are opposed not simply to the way industrial society goes about achieving the goal of wealth creation: they are opposed to its central and dominant economic and material values. Utopian environmentalists want a different kind of society from other members of their society . . . Post-material values are the values which they want to see made real in some future utopia' (Cotgrove and Duff, 1981: 99).

5. It answered to the statement: 'There is a need for nuclear power' on a 7-item scale in Britain and the USA: 25.5 percent (USA: 30.7 percent) of the public agreed to this statement (only item 7) and 11.2 percent (9.3 percent) disagreed (item 1); 6.3 percent (10.3 percent) of the environmentalists agreed and 26.7 percent (34.5 percent) disagreed; 50.6 percent (70.2 percent) of the industrialists agreed and 1.5 percent (1.3 percent) disagreed; 27.9 percent (44.7 percent) of the trade unionists agreed and 10.1 percent (14.1 percent) disagreed (Kessel and Tischler, 1981; Fietkau et al., 1982).

6. For a deeper analysis, where I have analysed the individual motions in more detail, see Jahn (1989).

References

Aho, S. (1986) 'Labour Society and its Crisis as Sociological Conception – a Reply to Detlef Jahn', *Acta Sociologica*, 29 (1): 69–72.

Alemann, U. von (1983) 'Krisen der Arbeitsgesellschaft – Katharsis der Interessensvermittlung? Parteiensysteme und soziale Bewegungen im ökonomisch-ökologischen Umbruch', in J. Matthes (ed.), *Krise der Arbeitsgesellschaft? Verhandlungen des 21. Deutschen Soziologentages in Bamberg 1982*. Frankfurt am Main: Campus.

Almond, G.A. (1987) 'Politische Kultur-Forschung – Rückblick und Ausblick', pp. 27–38 in Berg-Schlosser and Schissler (1987).

Almond, G.A. and Verba, S. (1963) *The Civic Culture: Political Attitudes and Democracy in Five Nations*. Princeton: Princeton University Press.

Anton, T.J. (1980) *Administrated Politics – Elite Political Culture in Sweden*. Boston: Nijhoff.

Barnes, S. and Kaase, M. (eds) (1979) *Political Action – Mass Participation in Five Western Democracies*. Beverly Hills: Sage.

Beck, U. (1986) *Risikogesellschaft – auf dem Weg in eine andere Moderne*. Frankfurt am Main: Suhrkamp.

Bell, Daniel (1973) *The Coming of Post-Industrial Society*. New York: Basic Books.

Bell, Daniel (1976) *The Cultural Contradictions of Capitalism*. London: Heinemann.

Berg-Schlosser D. and Schissler, J. (eds) (1987) *Politische Kultur in Deutschland – Bilanz und Perspektiven der Forschung*. Opladen: Westdeutscher Verlag.

Berger, P.A. (1986) *Entstrukturierte Klassengesellschaft? Klassenbildung und Strukturen sozialer Ungleichheit im historischen Wandel*. Opladen: Westdeutscher Verlag.

Berger, P.L (1986) *The Capitalist Revolution: Fifty Propositions about Prosperity, Equality, and Liberty*. New York: Basic Books.

Berger, P.L, Berger, B. and Kellner, H. (1973) *The Homeless Mind: Modernization and Consciousness*. New York: Random House.

Bourdieu, P. (1983) 'Ökonomisches Kapital, Kulturelles Kapital, Soziales Kapital', pp. 183–91 in R. Kreckel (ed.), *Soziale Ungleichheit*. Göttingen: Otto Schwartz.

Braczyk, H.-J., Hengstenberg, H., Mill, U., Jahn, D., Schmidt, G. and Stodiek, F. (1985) *Synopse der Erfahrung über Planung, Bau und Betrieb von WAA – Medienanalyse*. ASIF-Bielefeld: Zwischenbericht.

Burns, T.R. and Ueberhorst, R. (1988) *Creative Democracy: Systemic Conflict Resolution and Policymaking in a World of High Science and Technology*. New York: Praeger.

Cotgrove, S. and Duff, A. (1980) 'Environmentalism, Middle-Class Radicalism and Politics', *Sociological Review*, 28 (2): 333–51.

Cotgrove, S. and Duff, A. (1981) 'Environmentalism, Values and Social Change', *British Journal of Sociology*, 32 (1): 92–110.

Czada, Roland (1988) 'Auf den Weg zur Produktionspolitik: zur Entwicklungslogik neokorporatistischer Gewerkschaftseinbindung in Schweden', pp. 70–90 in Walther Müller-Jentsch (ed.), *Zukunft der Gewerkschaften: ein internationaler Vergleich*. Frankfurt am Main: Campus.

Dagnaud, M. and Mehl, D. (1983) 'Elite, Sub-Elite, Counter-Elite', *Social Science Information*, 22 (6): 817–65.

Esser, J. (1982) *Gewerkschaften in der Krise – die Anpassung der deutschen Gewerkschaften an neue Weltmarkt Bedingungen*. Frankfurt am Main: Suhrkamp.

Featherstone, M. (1988) 'In Pursuit of the Postmodern: an Introduction', *Theory, Culture and Society*, 5 (23): 195–216.

Fietkau, H.-J., Kessel, H. and Tischler, W. (1982) *Umwelt im Spiegel der öffentlichen Meinung*. Frankfurt am Main: Campus.

Früh, W. (1981) *Inhaltsanalyse: Theorie und Praxis*. München: Verlag Ölschläger.

Fulcher, J. (1988) 'Trade Unionism in Sweden', *Economic and Industrial Democracy*, 9 (2): 129–40.

Gahrton, P. (1981) 'Vist finns en ny politisk dimension i Sverige', *Sociologisk Forskning*, 18 (3): 51–8.

Grumbach, J. (1986) *Energieforschung und Arbeitnehmerinteressen – Zielfindungsprobleme gewerkschaftlicher Forschungs- und Technologiepolitik*. Frankfurt am Main: Campus.

Habermas, J. (1981) *Theorie des kommunikativen Handelns*, 2 vols. Frankfurt am Main: Suhrkamp.

Habermas, J. (1985) 'Exkurs zum Verhältnis des Produktionsparadimas', pp. 9–33 in *Der philosophische Diskurs der Moderne: Zwölf Vorlesungen*. Frankfurt am Main: Suhrkamp.

Habermas, J. (1986) 'The New Obscurity – the Crisis of the Welfare-State and the Exhaustion of Utopian Energies', *Philosophy and Social Criticism*, 11 (2): 1–18.

Himmelstrand, U., Ahrne, G., Lundberg, L. and Lundberg, L. (1981) *Beyond Welfare Capitalism – Issues, Actors, and Forces in Societal Change*. London: Heinemann.

Holmberg, S. and Asp, K. (1984) *Kampen om kärnkraften – en bok om väljare, massmedier och folkomröstningen 1980*. Stockholm: Publica.

Holsti, O.R. (1969) *Content Analysis for the Social Sciences and Humanities*. Reading, Mass.: Addison-Wesley.

Inglehart, R. (1977) *The Silent Revolution: Changing Values and Political Styles among Western Publics*. Princeton: Princeton University Press.

Jahn, D. (1985) 'Arbeit als Schlüsselkategorie der ökonischen und sozialen Entwicklung – Gesellschaftstheoretische und sozialtheoretische Aspekte eines Bedeutungswandels der Erwerbsarbeit', unpublished master's thesis, University of Bielefeld.

Jahn, D. (1986) 'Some Remarks on the Notion of Labour Society – a Reply to Simo Aho', *Acta Sociologica*, 29 (1): 61–8.

Jahn, D. (1988a) 'Tschernobyl und die schwedische Energiepolitik', *Österreichische Zeitschrift für Politikwissenschaft*, 17 (1): 43–51.

Jahn, D. (1988b) ' "Two Logics of Collective Action" and Trade Union Democracy: Organizational Democracy and "New" Politics in German and Swedish Unions', *Economic and Industrial Democracy*, 9 (3): 319–43.

Jahn, D. (1989) 'The Greening of the Red? New Social Issues and Trade Unionism', in M. Friberg (ed.), *New Social Movements in Europe*. London: Cassell Tycoll.

Jahn, D. and Müller-Rommel, F. (1987) ' "Krise der Arbeitsgesellschaft" und "Politische Kultur": zur Verbindung von zwei globalen Konzepten', pp. 344–55 in Berg-Schlosser and Schissler (1987).

Jameson, F. (1984) 'The Politics of Theory: Ideological Positions in the Postmodernism Debate', *New German Critique*, 33 (4): 53–65.

Katzenstein, P.J. (1985) *Small States in World Markets – Industrial Policy in Europe*. Ithaca: Cornell University Press.

Kellner, D. (1988) 'Postmodernism as Social Theory: some Challenges and Problems', *Theory, Culture and Society*, 5 (2–3): 239–70.

Kessel, H. and Tischler, W. (1981) 'International Environment Survey – Umweltbewusstsein im internationalen Vergleich, Ergebnisse einer Umfrage', Science Center Berlin, International Institute for Environment and Society, discussion paper IIUG/dp 81–8.

Kitschelt, H. (1984) *Der ökologische Diskurs – eine Analyse von Gesellshaftskonzeptionen in der Energiedebatte*. Frankfurt am Main: Campus.

Kriesi, H. (1987) 'Neue soziale Bewegungen: auf der Suche nach ihrem gemeinsamen Nenner', *Politische Vierteljahresschrift*, 29 (4): 315–34.

Kriesi, H. (1989) 'New Social Movements and the New Middle Class: the Class Base of New Social Movements', in M. Friberg (ed.), *New Social Movements in Europe*. London: Cassell Tycoll.

Kriesi, H. and von Praag, Jr, P. (1987) 'Old and New Politics: the Dutch Peace Movement and the Traditional Political Organizations', *European Journal of Political Research*, 15 (3): 319–46.

Lash, S. (1985) 'The End of Neo-Corporatism?: the Breakdown of Centralized Bargaining in Sweden', *British Journal of Industrial Relations*, 23 (2): 215–39.

Lindhagen, J. and Nilsson, M. (1970) *Hotet mot arbetarrörelsen*. Stockholm: Tiden.

Markovits, A.S. 1986: *The Politics of the West German Trade Unions – Strategies of Class and Interest Representation in Growth and Crisis*. Cambridge: Cambridge University Press.

Marsh, A. (1975) 'The "Silent Revolution", Value Priorities, and Quality of Life in Britain', *American Political Science Review*, 64 (1): 21–30.

Martens, H. (1986) *Krise der Gewerkschaften oder Krise der Gewerkschaftsforschung*. Sozialforschungsstelle Dortmund, Dortmund.

Meidner, R. and Hedborg, A. (1984) *Modell Schweden – Erfahrungen einer Wohlfahrtsgesellschaft*. Frankfurt am Main: Campus.

Micheletti, M. (1985) *Organizing Interest and Organized Protest – Difficulties of Member Representation for the Swedish Central Organization of Salaried Employees (TCO)*. Stockholm: Department of Political Sciences.

Mooser, J. (1984) *Arbeiterleben in Deutschland 1900–1970*. Frankfurt am Main: Suhrkamp.

Müller-Jentsch, W. (1985) 'Trade Unions as Intermediary Organizations', *Economic and Industrial Democracy*, 6 (1): 3–33.

Müller-Jentsch, W. (1986) *Soziologie der industriellen Beziehungen: eine Einführung*. Frankfurt am Main: Campus.

Müller-Rommel, F. (1985) 'The Greens in Western Europe – Similar but Different',

International Political Science Review, 6 (4): 483–99.

Negt, O. (1984) *Lebendige Arbeit, enteignete Zeit: Politische und kulturelle Dimensionen des Kampfes um die Arbeitszeit*, Frankfurt am Main: Campus.

Nelkin, D. and Pollak, M. (1977) 'The Politics of Participation and the Nuclear Debate in Sweden, the Netherlands, and Austria', *Public Policy*, 25, (3): 333–57.

Offe, C. (1985a) 'Angestellte – die "anderen" Arbeitnehmer', *Gewerkschaftliche Monatshefte*, 36 (10): 583–97.

Offe, C. (1985b) 'Interest Diversity and Trade Union Unity', pp. 151–69 in C. Offe, *Disorganized Capitalism: Contemporary Transformations of Work and Politics*. Cambridge: Polity Press.

Offe, C. (1985c) 'New Social Movements: Challenging the Boundaries of Institutional Politics', *Social Research*, 52 (4): 817–68.

Offe, C. (1986) 'Die Utopie der Null-Option: Modernität und Modernisierung als politische Gütekriterien', pp. 143–72 in P. Koslowski, R. Spaemann and R. Löw (eds), *Moderne oder Postmoderne? Zur Signatur des gegenwärtigen Zeitalters.* (CIVITAS Resultate Band 10, Acta humaniorae VCH.) Verlagsgesellschaft Weinheim, Pappellee.

Osgood, C.E., Saporta, S. and Nunnally, J. (1956) 'Evaluative Assertion Analysis', *Litera*, 3, 47–102.

Pizzorno, A. (1978) 'Political Exchange and Collective Identity in Industrial Conflict', in C. Crouch and A. Pizzorno (eds), *The Resurgence of Class Conflict in Western Europe since 1968.* Vol. 2. New York: Holmes & Meier.

Pollak, M. (1981) 'Die westeuropäischen Gewerkschaften im Spannungsfeld technologiepolitischer Entscheidungen – das Beispiel der Auseinandersetzung um die Atomenergie', *Journal für Sozialforschung*, 21 (2): 123–40.

Radkau, J. (1983) *Aufstieg und Krise der deutschen Atomwirtschaft 1945–1975: Verdrängte Alternativen in der Kerntechnik und der Ursprung der nuklearen Kontroverse.* Reinbek bei Hamburg: Rowohlt (rororo).

Raschke, J. (1980) 'Politik und Wertwandel in den westlichen Demokratien', *Aus Politik und Zeitgeschichte*, B 36/80, 23–45.

Rubart, F. (1985) 'Neue soziale Bewegungen und alte Parteien in Schweden: Politischer Protest zwischen Autonomie und Integration', pp. 200–247 in K.-W. Brand (ed.) *Neue soziale Bewegungen in Westeuropa und den USA: ein internationaler Vergleich.* Frankfurt am Main: Campus.

Sabel, C.F. (1981) 'The Internal Politics of Trade Unions', in S. Berger (ed.), *Organizing Interests in Western Europe.* Cambridge: Cambridge University Press.

Schacht, K. (1987) 'Politische Kultur, sozialer Wandel und Wahlverhalten im Dienstleistungszentrum Frankfurt', pp. 275–81 in Berg-Schlosser and Schissler (1987).

Schmitter, P. and Streeck, W. (1985) 'The Organization of Business Interests' (working-title). Manuscript, European University Institute, Florence.

Siegmann, H. (1985) *The Conflict between Labor and Environmentalism in the Federal Republic of Germany and the United States.* Aldershot: Gower.

Sifo (1987) *Ett År efter Tjernobyl.* Stockholm: Sifo.

Streeck, W. (1981) *Gewerkschaftliche Organisationsprobleme in der sozialstaatlichen Demokratie.* Königstein: Athenäum.

Streeck, W. (1987) 'Vielfalt und Interdependenz: Überlegungen zur Rolle von intermediären Organisationen in sich ändernden Umwelten', *Kölner Zeitschrift für Soziologie und Sozialpsychologie*, 39 (4): 471–95.

Touraine, A. (1986) 'Unionism as a Social Movement', pp. 151–73 in S.M. Lipset (ed.), *Unions in Transition – Entering the Second Century.* San Francisco: ICS Press.

Touraine, A., Hegedus, Z., Dubet, F. and Wieviorka, M. (1982) *Die antinukleare Prophetie: Zukunftentwurfe einer sozialen Bewegung.* Frankfurt am Main: Campus.
Vedung, E. (1979) 'Kärnkraften ger ny blockbildning i politiken', *Tvärsnitt*, 1: 42–8.
Vester, H.-G. (1985) 'Modernismus und Postmodernismus – Intellektuelle Spielerei?', *Soziale Welt*, 36 (1): 3–26.

8

From 'Old Politics' to 'New Politics': Three Decades of Peace Protest in West Germany

Rüdiger Schmitt

Peace protest in a changing culture of participation

This chapter deals with the mobilization of protest movements at differing stages of political-cultural development. Various waves of protest may at first sight seem very similar and may suggest a basic continuity through time; however, an analytical perspective may well reveal an essential discontinuity in them. The present focus is upon the phenomenon of peace protest in West Germany. During the past three decades four periods of peace protest in West Germany can be distinguished: the anti-rearmament protest between 1950 and 1955; the 'Fight Nuclear Death' (Kampf dem Atomtod) movement of 1957–8; the Easter marches of the 1960s; and the peace movement of the 1980s.

In styling itself the '*new* peace movement' the contemporary protest movement seeks to identify with this tradition of historical predecessors. Also a number of analysts have interpreted today's peace protest in terms of such an historical continuity (Buro, 1977, 1983; von Bredow, 1982, 1985; Mushaben, 1985; Wasmuht, 1987). The present essay questions this perspective. In contrast to the 'continuity hypothesis' this analysis proposes that peace protest in the 1980s can more adequately be grasped against the background of major changes which have been taking place in the West German political culture over the past twenty years. Thus the view taken here is that the peace movement of the 1980s can be understood as a manifestation of a more general 'participatory revolution' (Kaase, 1984) which has been taking place in the context of an emerging 'new politics' (Baker et al., 1981) rather than as a new rise of a constant tendency in West Germany to challenge political elites on peace issues by means of mass mobilization. The ultimate aim is to make a contribution to the analysis of continuity and change in the development of political culture of Western democracies, with particular emphasis on the conditions of political mobilization.

The attitudes of West Germans toward political participation have doubtless undergone major changes during the past three decades. The classic study by Almond and Verba on *The Civic Culture* (1963) characterized West Germans of the late 1950s with a high degree of passive and formal political participation and at the same time a very low level of active participation in the political process. Voting was found to be normatively well anchored in the context of civic responsibility, while 'norms favoring active political participation are not well developed' (Almond and Verba, 1963: 429). In the collection of follow-up studies, *The Civic Culture Revisited*, David Conradt (1980) reported an increase in positive evaluations of active participation and a heightened level of political self-esteem. West Germany seemed to have adapted to the 'normality' of Western democracies.

But for many of today's citizens it is no longer sufficient to restrict themselves to the political role of the 'subject competent', that is, to 'be aware of [their] rights under the rule', or even to 'participate in the making of the rules' relying on the means provided by the institutional order of the political system as characterizes the 'citizen-competent' type (Almond and Verba, 1963: 214). These normative key concepts of the civic culture study are now in the process of being transcended empirically by an extension of the 'political repertory' of significant segments of the public. Supplementary to institutionalized forms of political participation 'unconventional' forms have gained importance, 'which do not correspond to the norms of law and custom that regulate political participation under a particular regime' (Barnes and Kaase, 1979: 41). These include 'the use of such tactics as petitions, demonstrations, boycotts, rent or tax strikes, unofficial industrial strikes, occupation of buildings, blocking of traffic, damage to property, and personal violence' (Barnes and Kaase, 1979: 59).

Attitudes towards interest organizations and political parties have also undergone changes. The West German party system of the 1950s was, in its principal features, an organizational reflection of social-structural conflict dimensions which date from the past century. The most important of these conflict dimensions were the class cleavage and the religious cleavage. The working class had formed an enduring affiliation with the Social Democratic party (SPD), one which was further solidified by trade-union membership. Catholics, on the other hand, tended toward the Christian Democratic Union (CDU). Still more important in structuring the religious conflict dimension is the division between the religiously oriented and the secularized segments of the population (Klingemann, 1985: 244f.). Political parties represented traditionally the value orientations acquired by their supporters through group-specific political socialization and served as principal agents of political mobilization (Hofrichter, 1985: 12). Their major function lay in the generation of political meaning, providing a framework for interpreting political events. Party elites were 'able to define and structure situations for the masses and the measures of policies appropriate for them' (Wildenmann, 1975: 280). Both the mass media and the party organizations served as channels to communicate these interpretations of reality to society at large. Further agents for the generation of such cultural and political meaning were the unions and churches (Hofrichter, 1985: 13f.).

A correlate of the 'participatory revolution' at the level of inter-mediate political actors is an 'increasing tendency for citizens with particular demands to organize themselves outside the established political institutions in general and outside the existing parties in particular' (Barnes and Kaase, 1979: 40f.). The further intermediary organizations are likewise losing influence in particular segments of society. New collective actors are entering the political arena, to which some scholars ascribe the properties of social movements (Brand, 1982; Brand et al., 1983; Brand, 1985; Roth and Rucht, 1987; Kaase, 1989). In West Germany, moreover, the Green party as 'parliamentary arm' of these movements has entered party competition with considerable success (Bürklin, 1984).

Political science has not hitherto been successful in establishing a coherent theory of these multilevelled processes of change. The state of empirical research appears particularly deficient (Kaase, 1989). One finds the concept of value change becoming prominent in most of the research on this question, in particular that of postmaterialist value change as developed by Inglehart (1977). Based on his considerations Baker et al. (1981) conceptualize the phenomenon as the emergence of a new type of political orientation which has begun to compete with the so-called 'old politics'. The latter stems from the basic interest conflict in industrial society and includes high evaluation of security as a goal of politics in a material sense as well as in other decision areas, such as international politics (Baker et al., 1981: 139ff.). The 'new politics' is conceptualized as being in part nationally specific, depending on the particular structure of social and political conflict in the respective country. As a constant feature it may, furthermore,

> develop around questions common to most highly industrialized societies, such as environmental pollution, the dangers of nuclear energy, the questions of women's equality and human rights, and the need for peaceful international co-existence and for helping the third world. . . . Regardless of which particular *ends* are championed, the New Politics stresses the importance of open access to political *means* and resources. Freedom of speech for minorities, access to the decision-making machinery of the state, the ability to participate in politics, and, if necessary, to resort to demonstrations and other forms of elite-challenging behavior are not only necessary instruments of the New Politics but are also *ends in themselves*. (Baker et al., 1981: 141; emphasis added)

Thus this view proposes a normatively anchored demand for increased possibilities for political participation as the ideological core of the 'new politics'. It should be noted that in terms of a conceptual distinction introduced by Brand (1982), this understanding of the phenomenon can be characterized as a 'rising-demands' approach, as opposed to 'need-defence' approaches. The latter interprets the 'participatory revolution' as being a *reaction* to serious political problems which the established elites leave unsolved.

However, empirical studies have consistently found a number of sociodemographic correlates of the newly developing political orientations. At present the matter remains open as to whether these findings indicate the durable establishment of a new cleavage (Kaase, 1989). Based on these empirical findings a variety of considerations on the social origins of 'new politics' and 'participatory revolution' has been developed. Inglehart (1977) proposes an effect of the socialization experiences of the postwar generation which have been characterized by affluence and material security. Theories based on the presumed consequences of educational expansion stress the dominance of the higher educated among the supporters of the 'new politics' (Bürklin, 1984; Alber, 1985). Other studies propose effects of occupational status or situs and see an important social basis in (at least segments of) the new middle class (Baker et al., 1981; Pappi and Terwey, 1982; Raschke, 1985: 411ff.). Meulemann (1983) proposes value change to be a consequence of social secularization.

We can summarize those aspects of *old politics*[1] relevant in the context of this study as the following:

A central role as generators of political meaning lies with political parties and other organizations of interest mediation.

Political orientations can, by mediation through party preferences, be traced back to the traditional cleavage structure of society, that is, the conflict dimensions of religion and social class.

Proposed features of the *new politics*, on the other hand, are the following:

The decreasing importance of traditional intermediate organizations, such as the established political parties, and the increasing importance of self-organized forms of mobilization.

The predominant importance of participation norms.

The predominance of the postwar generation, the higher educated, the new middle class and the secularized among those with 'new' political orientations.

From this perspective which juxtaposes the old and the new politics we should expect *attitudes toward peace protest in the 1950s*:

to be strongly related to the main dimension of party-political conflict,
to reflect the social-structural basis and organizational backing of this
  party-political conflict.

In the 1980s, however, these attitudes should:

be only very weakly related to the main party-political conflict and
  strongly related to attitudes toward political participation,
reflect the characteristic social basis of the new politics rather than the
  traditional cleavage structure.

Data

The present analysis examines dimensions of continuity and discontinuity in the mobilization basis of various waves of peace protest in West German society. Survey data are available for the protest against West German rearmament and the 'Fight Nuclear Death' movement of the 1950s and the peace movement of the 1980s. Due to lack of suitable data the Easter marches of the 1960s cannot be included in this analysis. All analyses are based on representative surveys of the West German population. Because of its particular geopolitical setting West Berlin is excluded from this study. For the 1950s two surveys are used which were conducted by the DIVO Institute under the direction of American authorities.[2] The first was carried out in January 1955 and included questions on the protests against West German rearmament. The second survey, in April 1958, questioned attitudes towards plans to equip the Bundeswehr with nuclear weapons as well as towards protests against it. Data are also utilized from several surveys carried out by the Forschungsgruppe Wahlen, which include questions on the peace movement of the 1980s. These are the Politbarometer surveys of October 1981, May 1982 and May 1983, and the first wave of the panel study for the 1983 general election, collected in November 1982. As the overall distributions of attitudes toward the peace movement proved very stable over time these four surveys have also been cumulated into a single data set for some of the analyses presented here. All data sources are referred to in the tables by the date of the respective survey; the cumulated data set is referred to as '1981–3'.[3]

Contours of peace protest in the 1950s and the 1980s: an overview

This section describes the three phases of peace protest in West Germany with particular attention to the goals of protest, the respective protest movement's alignments with political and social organizations, and its dominant type of activities. By way of introduction Table 1 presents the univariate distributions of attitudes among the West German population over the respective points of political controversy; here we see that these security-policy controversies have, indeed, deeply divided public opinion. Table 2 below provides the corresponding distribution of attitudes toward the protest movements themselves.

Table 1 *Attitudes towards security-policy plannings in the 1950s and the 1980s (percent)*

In general are you for or against the participation of West Germany in the military defence of Western Europe?

	Very much for	Somewhat for	Somewhat against	Very much against	No opinion	N
January 1955	17.6	27.0	14.1	22.9	18.3	(1,867)

As you know there is much discussion at present about questions of nuclear energy. In your opinion, should our military be equipped with nuclear weapons?

	Yes	No	No opinion	N
April 1958	20.4	67.1	12.5	(927)

Here is a list of political demands. Please tell us for each of these if you are more for or more against it:
– No new missiles in West Germany regardless of what the East bloc does.

	More for	More against	No opinion	N
November 1982	55.1	42.9	2.0	(1,622)

The idea of rearming the Western part of demilitarized Germany can, on the part of the Western powers, be traced as far back as 1948. The basic policy decision that a West German defence contribution should close a perceived gap in Western defence capability dates from 1950. Despite the small range of options genuinely open to the 'penetrated system' of postwar West Germany (Hanrieder, 1967) this issue became a major source of internal conflict of the newly founded German Federal Republic. (On the political background and history of the rearmament debate, cf. Wildenmann, 1963; Sommer, 1974; Jacobsen, 1975; von Schubert, 1970, 1978; Albrecht, 1980; Otto, 1981; Militärgeschichtliches Forschungsamt, 1982; Foschepoth, 1985; Dietzfelbinger, 1984.) Although the important decisions were taken abroad, the interests of the Western powers in the question of West German rearmament and NATO membership converged with the political strategy of the first West German chancellor, Konrad Adenauer, and his government dominated by the CDU. The debate over this issue was essentially one between the government and the parliamentary opposition. Among the principal opponents was the major opposition party *SPD*. The West German Trade Union Confederation (Deutscher Gewerkschaftsbund) remained generally in the background of the debate and lent only at a rather late date active support to the policy of its political ally SPD. Of the two churches the Catholic Church stood solidly by the government while important groups of the Protestant Church categorically opposed rearmament. Campaigns against rearmament were also waged by secular-bourgeois pacifists and by the Communist party, however with less success due to the small support base of these organizations.

The protest against rearmament and NATO membership largely took the form of mass demonstrations. There was also a campaign calling for a referendum on the subject which failed. The protest events reached their peak with the proclamation of a German Manifesto (Deutsches Manifest) in January 1955 which was accompanied by mass protest activities. The distribution of attitudes of West Germans towards these demonstrations is presented in Table 2. Some 9 percent of those surveyed supported these protest activities, while 70 percent expressed no awareness of them. As the existence of the Bundeswehr and its integration into NATO today demonstrates, the movement failed. After the ratification of the rearmament and NATO treaty by the government majority in parliament in February 1955 the protest quickly faded away.

The goal of the next wave of peace protest which arose in 1957 was to prevent the deployment of (US-controlled) tactical nuclear weapons on West German territory (see Rupp, 1980, for a comprehensive portrayal of this protest wave). Again the SPD played a leading role, as it initiated a campaign to oppose nuclear armament, labelled 'Fight Nuclear Death'. This campaign enjoyed official support from the unions and from Protestant groups. Again there were mass rallies, and again the idea of a referendum was put forward. This time the SPD announced plans for conducting a referendum, but this failed as the Constitutional Court forbade it. A number of opponents of nuclear armament even called for a general strike as a last resort for halting the implementation of nuclear armament. As Table 2 indicates, popular

Table 2   *Attitudes towards peace protest in the 1950s and the 1980s (percent)*

Have you perhaps heard of demonstrations against military rearmament which have taken place recently in West Germany? Do you agree in general with these demonstrations or do you disagree?

	Never heard about it	Agree with the demonstrations	Disagree with the demonstrations	No opinion	N
January 1955	70.1	8.8	18.4	2.8	(1,867)

In discussions about nuclear armament the following opinions are sometimes expressed:
– The parliament elected by the people has decided about nuclear armament of the Bundeswehr; we must accept this decision.
– In a question of such importance as nuclear armament a referendum should be held.
– If all other means fail to prevent nuclear armament, a general strike should be called.

	Accept the decision	Hold referendum	General strike	No opinion	N
April 1958	22.2	57.4	7.4	12.9	(927)

In West Germany a peace movement has existed for some time [following additional text in sentence only October 1981 and May 1982] which expresses opinions as to the best policy for preserving peace differing to some extent from those held by the government and by the parties in parliament. Do you think this peace movement is necessary, superfluous, dangerous, or is it a matter of indifference to you?
[Filter question to all respondents answering 'necessary':] Would you be ready to participate in a peaceful demonstration of the peace movement or not?

	Necessary, ready to participate	Necessary, not ready to participate	Superfluous	Dangerous	Indifferent	N
October 1981	24.8	19.9	23.5	12.6	19.3	(1,001)
May 1982	24.4	20.6	22.2	9.5	23.3	(1,038)
November 1982	23.2	18.1	25.0	7.9	25.7	(1,613)
May 1983	21.7	25.4	22.8	6.7	23.4	(1,014)

opinion clearly favoured the holding of a referendum; if we add to those favouring the referendum those supporting a general strike, we can conclude that in this case peace protest was evaluated positively by some two-thirds of the West German public. The protest movement against nuclear armament came to an end in the summer of 1958 as an immediate consequence of the failure of the SPD campaign both within parliament and among voters, as well as, from a more general perspective, as a consequence of the fundamental programmatic reorientation taking place within the SPD in the late 1950s (Hütter, 1975).

In parallel to similar developments in most Western democracies the 'new' peace movement emerged in the early 1980s, bringing to an end a decade of relative quiet in the field of security-policy decision-making. This protest wave was soon to eclipse all its predecessors in its resource-mobilization capacity (cf. Jenkins, 1983, on the general resource-mobilization perspective), not only with respect to mass mobilization, but also to the building of an effective organization, utilizing mass media, and developing a multifaceted strategy of counteracting the government's policy (for overviews see Brand et al., 1983; Kielmansegg, 1985; Leif, 1985; Mushaben, 1985, 1986; Janning et al., 1987; Wasmuht, 1987). The object of protest here was the NATO 'double-track' decision of 1979 (Holm and Petersen, 1983), and its expressed goal was to prevent the implementation of the second component of this, the deployment of new American medium-range nuclear weapons on the territory of West Germany.

A significant difference to the instance of the 1950s is that peace protest in the 1980s was not initiated by a politically established organization. This time it was not part of a strategy by the SPD's party elites to complement their parliamentary policies by extra-parliamentary means, but, with the roles reversed, intense discussion in the rank and file of the SPD and the party's security-policy reorientation at the elite level came about only as a reaction to the mobilization of the peace movement. Groups and organizations contributing resources to the peace movement include: religious groups, most of them of Protestant denomination; organizations affiliated with the ecology movement, including the Green party; orthodox Communist groups; and, although on the whole ambivalent and distanced, occasionally also Social Democratic and trade union organizations. Protest activities range from large-scale demonstrations over manifold activities of local peace groups and the self-organized holding of a referendum to actions of civil disobedience. The present analysis of the contemporary peace movement will make use of survey data collected between October 1981 and May 1983, thus covering its major mobilization period. As Table 2 shows, public support for the peace movement was constantly at a level of some 45 percent over this time.

Empirical analyses

Issue-relatedness of peace protest in the 1950s and 1980s
Peace protest is directed against security policy plans or measures of the government in office. In an instrumental view, it can be interpreted as a means employed by those opposed to these policies to attain their modification or revocation. It was proposed above that peace protest in the 1980s cannot sufficiently be explained in terms of its relation to a particular political issue but only with respect to a general increase in the positive evaluation of active and direct political participation among certain population groups. The analysis of stability and change of mobilization conditions for peace protest therefore begins with an assessment of its actual issue-relatedness, both in the 1950s and the 1980s. If support for peace protest is to be conceived of as a policy-specific phenomenon, the attitude towards peace protest must show a strong correlation to attitude positions towards the security-policy plans, the implementation of which the protest aims to prevent. Table 3 shows the joint distribution of attitudes towards peace protest and towards security-policy issues for 1955, 1958 and 1982, respectively.

Table 3 *Attitudes towards peace protest and towards security policy issues in the 1950s and the 1980s: bivariate relationships (percent)*

	For peace protest		Against peace protest				
	Against security-policy plan	For security-policy plan	Against security-policy plan	For security-policy plan	*N*	$\frac{\text{Phi}}{\text{Phi}_{max}}$	Chi-square
January 1955	27.0	4.9	17.6	50.5	(471)	0.72	246.64
April 1958	70.9	5.1	4.5	19.4	(756)	0.75	426.2
November 1982	26.8	14.7	29.4	29.1	(1,582)	0.19	57.3

For question texts, see Tables 1 and 2. Recodes as described in Appendix, except for treatment of missing values which are excluded here.

For the 1950s attitudes cluster clearly into consistent attitude types: those which are against the security-policy plans and for peace protest, on the one hand, and those which are for the security-policy plans and consequently against peace protest, on the other. While distributions in the 1950s show clear 'peaks' at these attitude types, the distribution in 1982 appears much more 'even'. Opposition to missile deployment does not necessarily lead to support for the peace movement. This marked degree of attitude inconsistency in terms of issue-relatedness of protest suggests that behind support for peace protest in the 1980s is a considerably furthering component which has no direct relation to the expressed goals of the protest movement. This may be the above proposed unspecific positive orientation towards direct political participation. The bivariate correlation coefficients[4] between attitudes towards security policy and those towards peace protest substantiate the observed differences. In 1955 and in 1958 this association was very strong, thus indicating a high degree of issue-specific instrumentality in peace protest. In the 1980s the strength of the association has decreased considerably. This indicates that the relationship between attitudes towards peace protest and towards security policy in the 1980s is no longer as straightforward as it was in the 1950s.

Peace protest and sociopolitical cleavages in the
1950s and 1980s
The aim of this section is to examine continuity and change in the relationship of attitudes towards peace protest to the main dimensions of sociopolitical cleavage between the 1950s and the 1980s. The traditional cleavage structure of West German society is represented by the variables of occupational status and religious denomination, indicating group-specific socialization experiences (Kaase and Klingemann, 1979: 534), and by variables indicating the degree to which social-structural interest conflicts are culturally founded by organizational loyalties (union membership and church attendance).[5] As an additional indicator for the importance of old politics in structuring attitudes towards peace protest, the traditional party-political main conflict dimension (CDU/CSU versus SPD) is used. The hypothesized increased importance of the 'new politics' for peace protest will be indicated by associations with its sociodemographic correlates, as measured by the variables of age and education. It is supposed that contemporary peace protest enjoys most of its support among the younger and the better educated. Bivariate association coefficients for 1955, 1958 and 1981–3 are shown in Table 4.

Religious denomination shows only very weak associations with attitudes towards peace protest. The associations which do appear are for 1958 and for the 1980s in line with the religious alignment of significant sectors of the respective 'movement elites'. It is the Protestants who are on average slightly more in favour of peace protest than Catholics. In operationalizing the religious cleavage in West Germany church attendance is generally more effective than religious denomination. This proves the case in our analysis as well. Each wave of peace protest could win more support of those with low loyalties to either of the churches. This could suggest a relationship of peace protest to social secularization. But the alternative interpretation that

Table 4   *Attitudes towards peace protest and sociopolitical cleavages: bivariate relationships*

	January 1955	April 1958	1981–3
Religious denomination	0.09 (4.1)*	−0.12 (12.6)**	−0.05 (13.2)**
	(*N* = 481)	(*N* = 889)	(*N* = 4,333)
Church attendance	0.24 (28.7)**	0.21 (42.6)**	0.21 (205.3)**
	(*N* = 507)	(*N* = 916)	(*N* = 4,658)
Occupational status	0.24 (15.7)**	0.16 (15.6)**	−0.13 (61.1)**
	(*N* = 265)	(*N* = 585)	(*N* = 3,666)
Trade-union membership	0.06 (1.9)	—	0.09 (38.6)**
	(*N* = 507)		(*N* = 4,535)
Party preference	0.58 (91.1)**	0.75 (342.4)**	0.21 (176.6)**
	(*N* = 270)	(*N* = 601)	(*N* = 3,800)
Age	0.01 (0.1)	0.14 (17.2)**	0.28 (372.2)**
	(*N* = 505)	(*N* = 926)	(*N* = 4,666)
Level of education	0.20 (21.3)**	0.15 (20.6)**	−0.44 (891.8)**
	(*N* = 507)	(*N* = 927)	(*N* = 4,666)

Entries are $\text{phi}/\text{phi}_{max}$ (chi-square).
'Minus' signs are introduced arbitrarily to indicate inversion of relationships with reference to column 1.
* = significant at 5 percent level.
** = significant at 1 percent level.

in the peace movement a new type of religiousness without strong ties to a church institution is evidencing itself cannot be ruled out on the basis of our findings.

It has been shown elsewhere already that the peace movement obtains particular support in the new middle class, that is, among civil servants and white-collar employees (Schmitt, 1987). This status group, with its rather unclear position with respect to traditional class conflict, has replaced the working class as the largest status group in West German society with passage to the 'postindustrial society' (Bell, 1973) over the last thirty years. Our results show that in this period an inversion of orientations towards peace protest between working class and new middle class has occurred. In 1955 and 1958 the new middle class was rather conservative in its orientations while the social basis of peace protest lay with the workers. Workers' attitudinal orientations toward peace protest today, however, are no less distant than the position of the old middle class (Schmitt, 1987). Rather, the new middle class is now more in favour of peace protest. Another positive association can be found with union membership. This appears constantly, but rather weakly, in the 1950s and the 1980s (for a more detailed analysis, cf. Armingeon and Schmitt, 1986).

We find the highest relationships in 1955 and in 1958 with party preference. More than any other factor the party-political conflict between CDU/CSU and SPD has structured attitudes towards peace protest. Today it has lost most of its earlier importance although it has not disappeared completely. In particular its predominance compared with the other observed relationships has faded away. More detailed analyses of the party political anchoring of the peace movement reveal that its core supporters are oriented towards the Green party. Among partisans of the SPD the peace movement enjoys more support than other new social movements. But those among SPD partisans who support the peace movement, on the other hand, are also characterized by some sympathy for the Greens (Schmitt, 1987).

The variable of age was dichotomized with those below the age of 35 distinguished from those above. Dichotomization at this point has proved to be of importance in several empirical studies on the peace movement (Küchler, 1984, 1985; Schmitt, 1987). In general the variable age indicates a particular position in the life cycle, on the one hand, and on the other, a specific historical-generational context of political socialization. If support for peace protest were due to a life-cycle effect it should manifest itself in both the 1950s and the 1980s. Empirical evidence suggests that general life-cycle explanations would be misleading. In 1955 peace protest was unrelated to age. For 1958 we find a weak relationship, but a very strong one in the 1980s: people are more inclined to support the peace movement the younger they are. There is no evidence for a generally (that is, independently of the historical setting) increased tendency to support peace protest among the younger. Baker et al. (1981: 21f.) define the age of 15 as the 'point of maximal environmental impact'. By this criterion we can identify those who have experienced their political socialization in the politically 'mature' and economically affluent West Germany after 1962 as the major supporters of peace protest, with respect to the variable of age.

Education is a variable which with respect to our considerations should be influential on attitudes toward peace protest only in the 1980s: the higher educated should be more supportive towards the peace movement. Indeed there appears a very strong relationship of educational level to the attitude towards the peace movement. While unexpectedly there is also a relationship of some degree in the 1950s, this was of an inverse nature: the higher educated then were less inclined to support peace protest than were those with lower levels of education.

Determination of support for peace protest in the 1950s and 1980s: causal models
We shall now analyse jointly all factors which have proven important in structuring attitudes towards peace protest in the 1950s and the 1980s; the principle of comparability between these two periods which

guided the analyses in the previous section will not be pursued here. The aim of this section is to uncover the typical interrelations among determinants of support for peace protest in the 1950s and 1980s, respectively, in integrated causal models. As the distribution of attitudes towards the protest against rearmament is very skewed this analysis will not be performed for 1955. This suggests itself also for reasons of research economy as the results reported for 1955 and 1958 have proven similar in all important aspects.

Figure 1 presents a hypothetical explanatory model for support of peace protest in the 1950s. It is proposed that party-preference should be the core variable of the model. It is referred thereby to the dominant role of the SPD in initiating peace protest in the 1950s in particular, as well as to the political parties' general importance as agents for generating political meaning at that time, which was discussed above. It is suggested that the general preference for the SPD induces support of its policies on particular issues, as, for instance, a negative attitude towards nuclear armament for the West German military. This attitude in turn affects that towards peace protest which in the 1950s can be interpreted as a direct reaction to the security-policy attitude. The relationships to social-structural variables measured in the bivariate analyses can be interpreted such that the social basis of peace protest in the 1950s was identical with that of the SPD. It can be assumed therefore that these relationships only reflect indirect linkages with social-structural factors which are mediated by party preference.

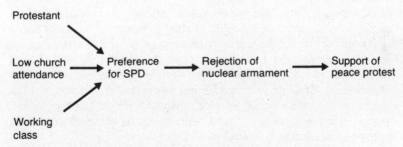

Figure 1   *Determination of support of peace protest in the 1950s: a hypothetical model*

When estimated as path analysis[6] this hypothetical model achieves a good fit. It accounts alreay for 38 percent of the variance in the dichotomized attitude towards peace protest. Inspection of residual covariances suggests some additional paths whose incorporation could improve the model. Including these paths results in the empirically fitted path model of Figure 2, which has a very good fit of $R^2 = 0.43$.

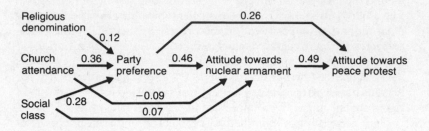

Entries are beta coefficients ($R^2 = 0.43$)

Figure 2   *Determination of support of peace protest in April 1958: a path model*

Thus the hypothetical model for 1958 turns out as a suitable conceptualization of the determination of support for peace protest in the 1950s. All hypothesized effects are indeed represented in the model as paths of substantial strength. Deviations occur insofar as the effect of party preference is not only mediated by the attitude towards security policy. There is also a direct effect on the attitude towards peace protest. Apparently the mere leadership of the SPD in the protest campaign of 1958 was sufficient to generate a positive attitude towards it with all those holding an SPD preference, even if it was not – as a direct instrumental response – mediated by rejection of nuclear armament.

Furthermore, we find weak direct effects of social-structural variables on the attitude towards nuclear armament. Workers had a slight tendency to reject nuclear armament even if it was not mediated by preference for the SPD. To expose the impact of low church attendance on the security policy attitude required attitudinal mediation by SPD preference. If this was not the case low church attendance resulted in a slightly more positive attitude. In other words, among partisans of the CDU/CSU the religiously oriented were more opposed to nuclear armament.

In an analogous approach to that taken for the protest campaign of 1958, a hypothetical model for support of the 1980s peace movement was developed and tested. Again a three-step model for explaining political attitudes is utilized (cf. Pappi and Laumann, 1974). It is assumed that the attitude towards the peace movement can be traced back to sociodemographic variables by mediation of general political values. In the 1950s party-political loyalties predominated in structuring these general political orientations. They could therefore be represented in our model by party preferences. As mentioned above, most approaches to explaining 'new politics' refer to processes of value change. It has been shown elsewhere that Inglehart's postmaterialism index is indeed strongly associated with attitudes towards the peace movement (Inglehart, 1984; Schmitt, 1987). Therefore this analysis will not be repeated here. Instead the hypothesized core value of the new politics, that is, the normative importance of increased political participation as assumed by Baker et al. (1981), is taken into account for an alternative operationalization of the value basis of support of the peace movement.

For this purpose, data on the subjectively felt importance of increased citizens' influence on political decisions are used. The hypothetical causal model for support of peace protest in the 1980s is presented in Figure 3. The model proposes that support of the peace movement depends on positive evaluation of political participation and on rejection of NATO's planned missile deployment. The attitude towards this security-policy issue is also conceptualized as a component

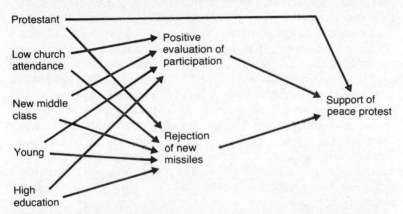

Figure 3 *Determination of support of peace protest in the 1980s: a hypothetical model*

of the new-politics syndrome in accordance with its definition as quoted above. It is furthermore assumed that these two intervening variables are related to sociodemographic variables. Participation should be evaluated most positively and missile deployment rejected most among the young, among the higher educated, among members of the new middle class, and among the secularized. Additionally for the security policy variable an influence of religious denomination can be hypothesized: Protestants should be more ready to reject the missile deployment due to the tradition of pacifism in this Church. As Protestant groups also play a major part in the 'movement elite' a direct path of religious denomination on the attitude towards the peace movement is included in the model.

While the hypothetical model for 1958 produced quite a good fit the hypothetical model for 1982 proves very unsatisfactory when tested empirically. It shows only a poor fit of $R^2 = 0.03$. It is clear therefore that this model contains very serious specification deficiencies. Hints for missing important paths can be derived again from the analysis of residual covariances. Furthermore, an attempt to improve the model may be made by including an additional intervening variable. To improve the model a 'need-defence' perspective is applied by taking into account the defensive nature of much of the peace movement's argumentation. In the view of those in the movement, participating in it represents an act of resistance to political elites who are seen as acting irresponsibly in a matter as far-reaching as the question of peace and war (cf., for example, Krippendorff, 1985). The newly included variable thus operationalizes the general evaluation of West German elites.

By including this variable as a third intervening variable, and by allowing a number of direct paths from sociodemographic variables to the attitude towards the peace movement, the model's fit can be improved considerably, although it still does not approach the result for 1958 in its magnitude. The relationship of the participation variable initially incorporated for theoretical reasons is very weak. Its contribution to the explanatory power of the model is, in fact, so low that it can be omitted without a reduction of explained variance. Since we are interested in the highest possible proportion of variance accounted for by the most parsimonious model, the final model excludes this variable. Superfluous in the same sense too, is the variable of religious denomination which in contrast to the 1950s no longer entails explanatory power for the attitude towards peace protest.

The path model optimized in this way is displayed in Figure 4. The inspection of total effects uncovers how the most important influences on support of the peace movement proceed from young age, high educational level and negative evaluation of the elites. In the ranking of importance the rejection of missile deployment follows only after these effects. In the 1950s, in contrast, it was the attitudes towards security policy and towards political parties rather than social-structural variables which were most important with respect to total effects.

Overall, the results as shown in Figure 4 evidence that peace protest in the 1980s has indeed its social bases in the same groups as the new politics. However, rather than by generalized higher esteem of increased political participation, as was assumed above, support of the peace movement seems to be furthered by a negative perception of political elites. This evaluation, on the other hand, is anchored to some

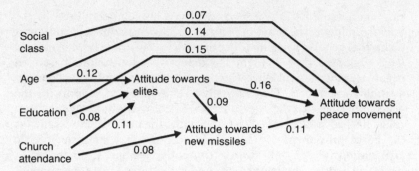

Entries are beta coefficients ($R^2 = 0.13$)

Figure 4 *Determination of support of peace protest in November 1982: a path model*

degree among the young, the higher educated and those rather distanced against the Churches. Rejection of NATO missile deployment which, according to our data, seems to be distributed in society quite unspecifically, is far from leading automatically to support for the peace movement.

Conclusion

The goal of this study has been a comparative analysis of peace protest in West Germany in the 1950s and in the 1980s regarding the extent to which ostensible historical continuity of peace protest conceals major changes in political culture. It was suggested that these changes become manifest when one considers the mobilization conditions of the various protest waves. The study has been guided by the hypothesis that contemporary peace protest can best be understood not as a renewal of an earlier tradition of peace protest in West Germany but as a manifestation of political-cultural changes which can be observed in many Western democracies. It has been suggested by some analysts that an increase in general positive evaluations of political participation is the core component of this value change from old politics to new politics.

Analyses have shown that the *contemporary peace movement* is indeed a mobilization of the same sociodemographic groups which have appeared in numerous studies as the basis for the new politics. The peace movement is evaluated most positively among the postwar generation, among the higher educated, among the new middle class, and among those with weak ties to the churches. With respect to individual party preferences and organizational ties its most distinct affiliations are with the Green party. The traditional party-political cleavage between CDU/CSU and SPD adds relatively little to the understanding of the peace movement. Contrary to our expectations it seems that general participation norms also contribute little. Analyses have suggested that it might be 'defensive' orientations based on negative evaluations of elites which could prove fruitful as explanatory attitudinal variables. The relatively weak relation of support for the peace movement to the rejection of the deployment of new medium-range nuclear weapons in West Germany, the prevention of which is the peace movement's major goal, indicates that an issue-specific explanation relying only on security-policy problems, on the other hand, also does not suffice to understand the peace movement. Furthermore, our results lead to the conclusion that the rejection of missile deployment, itself, does not belong to the syndrome of new politics.

In contrast to the peace movement of the 1980s, whose great mobilization success was not promoted by important interest organizations, the mobilization against rearmament in 1955 as well as that against nuclear armament for the West German military in 1958 were initiated by traditional intermediary organizations, namely SPD and DGB. These conditions of the protest's inception are clearly reflected in the determinants of its support. Its main potential were the partisans of the SPD. Their sympathy was instrumentally mediated by their rejection of the respective security-policy plans. To a lesser extent it was also a direct consequence of their party preference. Workers as well as those with low church attendance showed themselves clearly as social bases of peace protest in the 1950s. Also it was slightly more backed among Protestants than among Catholics. As these groups represented the traditional basis of the SPD the empirical results are in accordance with our hypothetical model of elite-induced political mobilization in the 1950s.

The differences found between the attitudinal correlates of support for peace protest in the 1950s and in the 1980s indicate changes in citizens' orientations towards the political system, that is, in the structure of political support (Easton, 1965; Gamson, 1968). Peace protest in the 1950s, to a large degree turned on and off by established party elites, was a continuation of the conflict between government and parliamentary opposition employing extra-parliamentary means. It thus reflected an intra-elite conflict and mobilized the support base of the oppositional party against the government. The contemporary peace movement, on the other hand, seems to be related to a negative sentiment towards political elites in a much more general sense. Supporters of peace protest in both periods are characterized, in Easton's terms, by distrust against political authorities. But while this in the 1950s concerned only the incumbent government and thus remained well within the framework of the model of alternating party government (Castles and Wildenmann, 1986), in the 1980s it includes both actual and possible future incumbents.[7] The conflict dimension characterizing today's protest therefore seems at least to some degree to divide the participant public from established elites in general.

One last instructive comparison between peace protest in the 1950s and in the 1980s concerns the strength of relationships found in the empirical analyses. The consistently lower levels of relationships in the 1980s compared with those in the 1950s indicate that the degree of social and political polarization with respect to peace protest has decreased in the last thirty years. The strongly marked clustering of support of peace protest in the 1950s among particular groups reflects the ' "icy blocs" between left and right which had been formed after the war' in West German society (Wildenmann, 1987: 93). Numerous conservative observers were provoked by the 'new' peace movement's appearance on the political stage to Cassandra calls forecasting an increase of intrasocietal polarization and political tension. However, contrary to these prophecies, the peace movement's roots in society, and its acceptance as a legitimate political actor are broader in absolute numbers and to a lesser degree concentrated in particular segments of society than was the case with peace protest in the 1950s, when the borders between supporters and opponents had been drawn much sharper with respect to their organizational affiliations as well as to their positions on the dimensions of social-structural conflict.

Notes

1. It should be noted that the use of the concepts old politics and new politics in the following sections of this chapter differs somewhat from the original meaning as defined above. While Baker et al. (1981) use these concepts to specify certain types of political agendas or discourses, they are used here in a broader sense as including also particular linkages of political orientations to social-structural and demographic features, as well as to political organizations.

2. American authorities conducted opinion research in West Germany constantly from 1945 to 1958. The so-called OMGUS, HICOG and EMBASSY studies lay first under the responsibility of the Office of Military Government–US, later these were carried out by the West German institute DIVO for the US High Commission for Germany and since 1955 for the US Embassy. The data sets preserved were declassified to open access for scientific research in the late 1960s. On the background of these studies, cf. Allerbeck (1976: 7ff.) and Merritt and Merritt (1980: 4ff.).

3. Data from the surveys Politische Einstellungen (January 1955), Atomare Rüstung – Form B (April 1958) and the general-election study 1983 were prepared for analysis, documented, and made accessible by the Zentralarchiv für Empirische Sozialforschung, University of Cologne (ZA No. 0447, 0436, 1276). Additional participants in the general-election study 1983 were Max Kaase, Hans-Dieter Klingemann, Manfred Küchler and Uwe Schleth. I wish to thank the Forschungsgruppe Wahlen in Mannheim for providing

me with the 'Politbarometer' studies. None of these persons or institutions bears any responsibility for analysis and interpretation of the data in this essay. All analyses have been carried out without weighting. Minor deviations to distributions of the same data published elsewhere can therefore occur.

4. Measurement of associations is based on the coefficient Phi for 2×2 tables. As this coefficient is distorted by skewed marginals – it can reach the value of 1.0 for perfect associations only if they are evenly distributed – I use the corrected coefficient Phi/Phi_{max}. This coefficient expresses the Phi value as a proportion of the value which could be reached under the given marginal distribution for a perfect association.

5. Occupational status is operationalized by the dichotomy of working class versus new middle class. Dichotomous coding is required by the method chosen. Thus the old middle class (self-employed) is excluded from analysis here. It is the traditional social basis for conservative politics and thus is constantly opposed against peace protest in the 1950s as well as in the 1980s; cf. Schmitt (1987). As to the attitudes of working class and new middle class, major changes have occurred, as the following analyses demonstrate. Thus these status groups are the more interesting for theoretical reasons.

6. Path models are based on partial least-squares estimations with the program LVPLS; cf. Lohmöller (1984).

7. The question remains open as to whether this diagnosis still holds after the CDU-FDP coalition took over government in 1982, and the SPD, now in opposition, has changed its security-policy programme position in the direction of the peace movement's positions.

Appendix: Overview of dichotomized variables

Religious denomination:
  0 Catholic
  1 Protestant
Church attendance:
  1955: How do you usually spend Sunday morning?
    0 Divine service
    1 Different; no religious denomination
  1958:
    0 Church attendance regularly
    1 Church attendance not regularly, seldom or never; no religious denomination
  1981–83:
    0 Church attendance almost every, every Sunday
    1 Church attendance now and then, once a year, less, never; no religious denomination
Occupational status of head of household:
  0 White-collar employee, civil service
  1 Blue-collar employee
  (1982, figure 4: inverse)
Trade union membership:
  0 No member
  1 Member
Age:
  0 35 years and older
  1 16 to 34 years   (in 1955 and 1958)
  1 18 to 34 years   (in 1981–83)

Level of formal education:
  0 High school graduation, university with or without degree
  1 Primary and/or secondary education
  (1982, figure 4: inverse)
Party preference:
  1955, 1958: Would you please tell me which is your preferential political party?
    0 CDU/CSU
    1 SPD
  1981–83: I have here five cards with the names of political parties in West Germany. Would you please sort these cards according to your preference order? [First position of rank order used]
    0 CDU/CSU
    1 SPD
Attitude towards participation:
  Here is a list of problems and duties which are discussed in West Germany. Please tell us for each of these problems if it is for you personally very important, important, not so important, completely unimportant: Providing citizens with more influence on decisions of the state.
    0 Not so important, unimportant, opposed
    1 Important, very important
Attitude towards elites:
  Do you believe that on the whole today in West Germany the right people are in the leading positions, or don't you believe so?
    0 Yes
    1 No
Attitude towards rearmament:
  (For question see Table 1)
    0 Very much, somewhat for rearmament
    1 Very much, somewhat against rearmament
Attitude towards nuclear armament:
  (For question see Table 1)
    0 For nuclear armament; no opinion
    1 Against nuclear armament
Attitude towards new missiles:
  (For question see Table 1)
    0 More for new missiles
    1 More against new missiles
Attitude towards antirearmament protest:
  (For question see Table 2)
    0 Against demonstrations
    1 For demonstrations
Attitude towards antinuclear armament protest:
  (For question see Table 2)
    0 Accept parliamentary decision; no opinion
    1 For referendum, for general strike
Attitude towards peace movement:
  (For question see Table 2)
    0 Peace movement is superfluous, dangerous, matter of indifference; no opinion
    1 Peace movement is necessary

References

Alber, Jens (1985) 'Modernisierung, neue Spannungslinien und die politischen Chancen der Grünen', *Politische Vierteljahresschrift*, 26: 211-27.

Albrecht, Ulrich (1980) *Die Wiederaufrüstung der Bundesrepublik*. Köln: Pahl-Rugenstein.

Allerbeck, Klaus R. (1976) *Demokratisierung und sozialer Wandel in der Bundesrepublik Deutschland: Sekundäranalysen von Umfragedaten 1953-1974*. Opladen: Westdeutscher Verlag.

Almond, Gabriel A. and Verba, Sidney (1963) *The Civic Culture: Political Attitudes and Democracy in Five Nations*. Princeton: Princeton University Press.

Almond, Gabriel A. and Verba, Sidney (eds) (1980) *The Civic Culture Revisited*. Boston: Little, Brown.

Armingeon, Klaus and Schmitt, Rüdiger (1986) 'Wie "friedensbewegt" sind die Gewerkschafter? Einstellungen von Gewerkschaftsmitgliedern zu Sicherheitspolitik und Friedensbewegung', *Politische Vierteljahresschrift*, 27: 423-36.

Baker, Kendall L., Dalton, Russell J. and Hildebrandt, Kai (1981) *Germany Transformed: Political Culture and the New Politics*. Cambridge Mass.: Harvard University Press.

Barnes, Samuel H. and Kaase, Max (eds) (1979) *Political Action: Mass Participation in Five Western Democracies*. Beverly Hills: Sage.

Bell, Daniel (1973) *The Coming of Post-Industrial Society*. New York: Basic Books.

Brand, Karl Werner (1982) *Neue soziale Bewegungen: Entstehung, Funktion und Perspektiven neuer Protestpotentiale, eine Zwischenbilanz*. Opladen: Westdeutscher Verlag.

Brand, Karl Werner (ed.) (1985) *Neue soziale Bewegungen in Westeuropa und den USA: ein internationaler Vergleich*. Frankfurt am Main: Campus.

Brand, Karl Werner, Büsser, Detlef and Rucht, Dieter (1983) *Aufbruch in eine andere Gesellschaft: neue soziale Bewegungen in der Bundesrepublik*. Frankfurt am Main: Campus.

Bürklin, Wilhelm P. (1984) *Grüne Politik: ideologische Zyklen, Wähler und Parteiensystem*. Opladen: Westdeutscher Verlag.

Buro, Andreas (1977) 'Die Entstehung der Ostermarsch-Bewegung als Beispiel für die Entfaltung von Massenlernprozessen', pp. 50-78 in *Friedensanalysen für Theorie und Praxis*. Vol. 4. Frankfurt am Main: Suhrkamp.

Buro, Andreas (1983) 'Es begann schon vor dem Ostermarsch', *Vorgänge*, 64/65: 103-10.

Castles, Francis G. and Wildenmann, Rudolf (eds) (1986) *Visions and Realities of Party Government*. Berlin: de Gruyter.

Conradt, David P. (1980) 'Changing German Political Culture', pp. 237-51 in Almond and Verba (1980).

Dietzfelbinger, Eckart (1984) *Die westdeutsche Friedensbewegung 1948 bis 1955: die Protestaktionen gegen die Remilitarisierung der Bundesrepublik*. Köln: Pahl-Rugenstein.

Easton, David (1965) *A Systems Analysis for Political Life*. New York: Wiley.

Foschepoth, Josef (ed.) (1985) *Kalter Krieg und Deutsche Frage*. Göttingen: Vandenhoeck & Ruprecht.

Gamson, William A. (1968) *Power and Discontent*. Homewood, Ill.: Dorsey Press.

Hanrieder, Wolfram F. (1967) *West German Foreign Policy 1949-1963: International Pressure and Domestic Response*. Stanford: Stanford University Press.

Hofrichter, Jürgen (1985) 'Bürger und politische Ordnung: Struktur und Wandel eines Verhältnisses', *IVS-Papers* 9. Mannheim: University of Mannheim.

Holm, Hans-Henrik and Petersen, Nikolaj (eds) (1983) *The European Missiles Crisis: Nuclear Weapons and Security Policy.* New York: St. Martin's Press.

Hütter, Joachim (1975) *SPD und nationale Sicherheit: internationale und innenpolitische Determinanten des Wandels der sozialdemokratischen Sicherheitspolitik 1959–1961.* Meisenheim: Hain.

Inglehart, Ronald (1977) *The Silent Revolution: Changing Values and Political Styles among Western Publics.* Princeton: Princeton University Press.

Inglehart, Ronald (1984) 'Generational Change and the Future of the Atlantic Alliance', *PS* (American Political Science Association), 17 (3): 525–35.

Jacobsen, Hans-Adolf (1975) 'Zur Rolle der öffentlichen Meinung bei der Debatte um die Wiederbewaffnung 1950–1955', pp. 61–117 in Militärgeschichtliches Forschungsamt (ed.), *Aspekte der deutschen Wiederbewaffnung bis 1955.* Boppard: Boldt.

Janning, Josef, Legrand, Hans-Josef and Zander, Helmut (eds) (1987) *Friedensbewegungen.* Köln: Verlag Wissenschaft und Politik.

Jenkins, J. Craig (1983) 'Resource Mobilization Theory and the Study of Social Movements', *Annual Review of Sociology*, 9: 527–53.

Kaase, Max (1984) 'The Challenge of the "Participatory Revolution" in Pluralist Democracies', *International Political Science Review*, 5: 299–318.

Kaase, Max (1989) 'Soziale Bewegungen zwischen Innovation und Antimodernismus', in Peter Flora (ed.), *Westeuropa im Wandel.* Frankfurt am Main: Campus.

Kaase, Max and Klingemann, Hans-Dieter (1979) 'Sozialstruktur, Wertorientierung und Parteiensystem: zum Problem der Interessenvermittlung in westlichen Demokratien', pp. 534–73 in Joachim Matthes (ed.), *Sozialer Wandel in Westeuropa.* Frankfurt am Main/New York: Campus.

Klingemann, Hans-Dieter (1985) 'West Germany', pp. 230–63 in Ivor Crewe and David Denner (eds), *Electoral Change in Western Democracies.* London: Croom Helm.

Krippendorff, Ekkehart (1985) *Staat und Krieg: die historische Logik politischer Unvernunft.* Frankfurt am Main: Suhrkamp.

Küchler, Manfred (1984) 'Die Friedensbewegung in der BRD – alter Pazifismus oder neue soziale Bewegung', pp. 328–37 in Jürgen W. Falter, Christian Fenner and Michael Th. Greven (eds), *Politische Willensbildung und Interessenvermittlung.* Opladen: Westdeutscher Verlag.

Küchler, Manfred (1985) 'Die Anhänger der Friedensbewegung in der BRD – Einstellungsmuster, Wertorientierungen und sozialdemographische Verankerung', pp. 213–40 in Anselm Skuhra and Hannes Wimmer (eds), *Friedensforschung und Friedensbewegung.* Wien: VWGÖ.

Leif, Thomas (1985) *Die professionelle Bewegung: Friedesbewegung von innen.* Bonn: Forum Europa-Verlag.

Lohmöller, Jan-Bernd (1984) *LVPLS 1.6 Program Manual: Latent Variables Path Analysis with Partial Least-Squares Estimation.* Köln: Zentralarchiv für Empirische Sozialforschung.

Merritt, Anna J. and Merritt, Richard L. (eds) (1980) *Public Opinion in Semisovereign Germany: the HICOG-Surveys 1949–1955.* Urbana: University of Illinois Press.

Meulemann, Heiner (1983) 'Value Change in West Germany, 1950–1980: Integrating the Empirical Evidence', *Social Science Information*, 22: 777–800.

Militärgeschichtliches Forschungsamt (1982) *Anfänge westdeutscher Sicherheitspolitik 1945–1956.* Vol. 1. München: Oldenbourg.

Mushaben, Joyce M. (1985) 'Cycles of Peace Protest in West Germany: Experiences from Three Decades', *West European Politics*, 8: 24–40.

Mushaben, Joyce M. (1986) 'Grassroots and Gewaltfreie Aktionen: a Study of Mass Mobilization Strategies in the West German Peace Movement', *Journal of Peace Research*, 23: 141–54.

Otto, Karl A. (1981) 'Der Widerstand gegen die Wiederbewaffnung der Bundesrepublik: Motivstruktur und politisch-organisatorische Ansätze', pp. 52–105 in Reiner Steinweg (ed.), *Unsere Bundeswehr?* Frankfurt am Main: Suhrkamp.

Pappi, Franz Urban and Laumann, Edward O. (1974) 'Gesellschaftliche Wertorientierungen und politisches Verhalten', *Zeitschrift für Soziologie*, 3: 157–88.

Pappi, Franz Urban and Terwey, Michael (1982) 'The German Electorate: Old Cleavages and New Political Conflicts', pp. 174–96 in Herbert Döring and Gordon Smith (eds), *Party Government and Political Culture in Western Germany*. London: Macmillan.

Raschke, Joachim (1985) *Soziale Bewegungen*. Frankfurt am Main: Campus.

Roth, Roland and Rucht, Dieter, (eds) (1987) *Neue soziale Bewegungen in der Bundesrepublik*. Frankfurt am Main: Campus.

Rupp, Hans Karl (1980) *Außerparlamentarische Opposition in der Ära Adenauer: der Kampf gegen die Atombewaffnung in den 50er Jahren*. Köln: Pahl-Rugenstein.

Schmitt, Rüdiger (1987) 'Was bewegt die Friedensbewegung? Zum sicherheitspolitischen Protest der achtziger Jahre', *Zeitschrift für Parlamentsfragen*, 18: 110–36.

Sommer, Theo (1974) 'Wiederbewaffnung und Verteidigungspolitik', pp. 580–603 in Richard Löwenthal and Hans-Peter Schwarz (eds), *Die zweite Republik*. Stuttgart: Seewald.

von Bredow, Wilfried (1982) 'Zusammensetzung und Ziele der Friedensbewegung in der Bundesrepublik Deutschland', *Aus Politik und Zeitgeschichte*, B24: 3–13.

von Bredow, Wilfried (1985) 'Sozialer Protest und Friedensbewegung in Westeuropa', *Beiträge zur Konfliktforschung*, 15 (4): 35–50.

von Kielmansegg, Peter Graf (1985) 'The Origins and Aims of the German Peace Movement', pp. 318–38 in Walter Lacqueur and Robert Hunter (eds) *European Peace Movements and the Future of the Western Alliance*. New Brunswick: Transaction Books.

von Schubert, Klaus (1970) *Wiederbewaffnung und Westintegration: die innere Auseinandersetzung um die militärische und außenpolitische Orientierung der Bundesrepublik 1950–1952*. Stuttgart: DVA.

von Schubert, Klaus (1978) *Sicherheitspolitik der Bundesrepublik Deutschland: Dokumentation 1945–1977*. Vol. 1. Köln: Verlag Wissenschaft und Politik.

Wasmuht, Ulrike C. (1987) *Friedensbewegungen der 80er Jahre*. Gießen: Focus.

Wildenmann, Rudolf (1963) *Macht und Konsens als Problem der Innen- und Außenpolitik*. Köln: Westdeutscher Verlag.

Wildenmann, Rudolf (1975) 'Towards a Sociopolitical Model of the German Federal Republic', pp. 273–301 in Rudolf Wildenmann (ed.), *Sozialwissenschaftliches Jahrbuch für Politik*. Vol. 4. München: Olzog.

Wildenmann, Rudolf (1987) 'The Party Government of the Federal Republic of Germany: Form and Experience', pp. 78–117 in Richard S. Katz (ed.), *Party Governments: European and American Experiences*. Berlin: de Gruyter.

9

From Postindustrial Society to Postmodern Politics: the Political Sociology of Daniel Bell

Bryan S. Turner

The problem of postmodernism in politics may be regarded as a new stage or new version of classical debates, namely the Hobbesian problem of order and the Weberian problem of political legitimacy. In the advanced stages of consumerism with the fragmentation of culture and the demise of the cultural establishment, a postmodern culture tears away the vestiges of a general normative legitimacy for the polity. The emergence of postmodern culture can be associated with profound changes in the class structure of so-called disorganized capitalism (Lash and Urry, 1987; Offe, 1985), the development of a narcissistic self, the growth of mass consumption and mass society, the trans-formation of the nature of work and production in contemporary society, and finally, with the general erosion of religious or quasi-religious symbolism. It is this fragmentation of cultural standards and the disjuncture between culture and other social structures which I take to be the central problem of postmodernist culture and hence of postmodern politics.

I shall discuss this issue of cultural change and politics within the framework of Daniel Bell's general social theory of capitalism, with special reference to *The Cultural Contradictions of Capitalism* (1976). The underlying argument here is that Bell largely anticipated, and to some extent worked out, many of the leading issues in current debates about modernism, postmodernism, the postindustrial society and the rise of narcissistic consumerism. Bell's whole approach to post-industrial society and modernism has, of course, been a target of much critical condemnation and devaluation (Badham, 1986; Brick, 1986; Collins, 1981). My own view of this literature is that Bell is typically misunderstood and also neglected as a contributor to the sociological analysis of the roots of postmodernism and modernism. However, while I support many of Bell's interpretations of the development of modern society and his orientation towards the explanation of such changes, I finish with a critique of his views of legitimacy, religion and the sacred, since I argue that modern society typically depends upon various forms of pragmatic acceptance of social reality rather than upon some deep or general system of legitimacy (Abercrombie et al., 1980). This evaluation of the role of legitimizing ideologies in the contemporary polity leads me finally to a critique of the historical understanding of postmodernism in the contemporary evaluation of modern cultures, in which I argue that many aspects of postmodernism were in fact anticipated in previous historical epochs and under rather different circumstances. My chapter therefore starts with an outline of Bell's political sociology of postmodernism and modernism, which leads me to an account of the social changes which lie behind a postmodern and fragmented culture, and in turn this things brings me to my conclusion which is a critical evaluation of the modern debate.

Bell's political sociology

We may associate the emergence of postmodern culture with important changes in the nature and distribution of capitalism within a world economy, that is the emergence of postmodern politics may be seen as a function of the disorganization of capitalism. Disorganized capitalism has been defined (Lash and Urry, 1987: 16) as a system of the world economy characterized by an extensive international division of ownership and production, associated with the widespread growth of capitalism throughout the world where nation-states can no longer successfully manage their own economics. This type of capitalism involves the decline of distinctive regional economies and industrial cities and the development of a service industry alongside the separation of financial and industrial capitalism (Gershuny, 1978). Finally, disorganized capitalism depends extensively on modern forms of information storage and transmission, which drastically reduces social space while also making possible greater surveillance of human populations. While Lash and Urry (1987: 13) clearly indicate the fact that many aspects of the problem of culture in disorganized capitalism were first identified by Bell in *The Cultural Contradictions of Capitalism*, I want to argue that modern theories of capitalist development in fact depend heavily, not only on Bell's views on culture, but more generally on his overall analysis of the historical growth of capitalist economies in the postwar period. In order to illustrate and justify this claim, I turn first to the influential collection of essays known as *The End of Ideology* (Bell, 1960).

In the analysis of the collapse of what he calls 'family capitalism', Bell begins by criticizing Marx for not realizing that capitalism is not only an economic system but also a social system in which power is primarily transmitted through the institutions of primogeniture and the family; therefore, the capitalist class structure has to be reproduced through the family system. Bell argues that this historical relationship between property and family has broken down in contemporary capitalism because of what has subsequently been referred to as the 'depersonalization' of ownership and control within the enterprise. With the gradual erosion of the classical, dynastic capitalist family, a new social class emerged, namely the managerial elite who ran the economic system in the United States. There were as a result two revolutionary changes in capitalism: on the one hand, the mode of access to power was no longer dependent upon family inheritance, and, on the other, technical skill and scientific knowledge rather than economic property had become the crucial feature of the political structure of contemporary capitalism. This analysis of the changing character of the American class system brought him eventually to a critique of C. Wright Mills's *The Power Elite* (1956) as a perspective on the American power system. In Bell's view, Mills's emphasis on the bureaucratization of power ignored 'the variety of interest conflicts, the growth of public responsibility, the weight of traditional freedoms (*vide* the Supreme Court, an institution that Mills fails to discuss), the role of volunteer and community groups, etc.' (Bell, 1960: 74). In short, Mills produced a theory of power but not an analysis of politics.

As a result of the decline of family-based ownership and investment, Bell perceived a change in the character of the ideological justification of capitalism away from profitability and inheritance towards productivity and performance. Alongside this changing ideological emphasis, there was a shift in the economic symbolism from property to enterprise. These comments on ideology were associated with one of Bell's most controversial positions which he stated in the epilogue with the title 'The End of Ideology in the West'. Bell argued that the ideological divisions of capitalism between 1930 and 1950 had been associated with a global economic depression and sharp class struggles, leading to the development of fascism and imperialism. In the postwar period, Bell argued that there had been a shift towards more pragmatic political practices which were not grounded in general ideological world-views. Furthermore, the new political scenario was based upon 'the acceptance of the Welfare State; the desirability of de-centralized power; a system of mixed economy and of political pluralism. In that sense, too, the ideological age has ended' (Bell, 1960: 402–3). Bell's views on ideology were criticized partly on the grounds that conflict had not so much disappeared as been suppressed, and partly on the grounds that Western capitalist societies still exhibited massive conflicts of interests which were expressed within various forms of ideological justification (Waxman, 1968).

There are two aspects of Bell's sociology which need to be considered in order to defend Bell against a number of erroneous criticisms. First, Bell did not argue that ideology as such had come to an end, but merely that the old left–right divisions of class politics had changed, bringing conflicts over the welfare state, state expenditure and public taxation to the forefront of the status-politics conflict. Secondly, Bell did not envisage the emergence of an apathetic consensus in American politics but quite the contrary predicted extensive conflicts within the 'public household'. However, these conflicts would not necessarily be of the old class-struggle variety. Bell predicted a new level of political conflict around the competition between status groups, especially within the American system where a new international role created strains on the existing political system and its cultural leadership, resulting under certain circumstances in a resurgence of extreme right-wing politics (Bell, 1964).

Bell's early work on American capitalism and politics is best regarded as a collection of brilliant but limited journalistic insights into contemporary sociopolitical processes. It was not until the publication of *The Cultural Contradictions of Capitalism* that Bell's work began to assume a more sytematic and theoretically developed position on the character of modern society. *The Cultural Contradictions* argues that we must conceive of society in terms of three primary dimensions, namely the economic, the political and the cultural aspects of a social order. The economic dimension was based on the axial principle of economizing, involving a special emphasis on efficiency and profitability. The political system, which requires significant bureaucratic coordination, is based upon the axial principles of equality, or citizenship as a bundle of entitlements. Finally, there is the cultural field which emphasizes self-expression, gratification and hedonism.

Bell argued that in capitalism these three systems were relatively autonomous and independent, requiring separate analysis. This argument was based upon a critique of the holistic view of the social system within the functionalism of Talcott Parsons. Bell's emphasis on the autonomy and differentiation of these three components was fundamental to his critique of the holistic perspective (Bell, 1982). Secondly, and possibly more importantly, Bell set out to criticize the idea of an integrated social system by arguing that the three dimensions stood in a relationship of contradiction and tension. In particular, he argued that the old values of the Protestant ethic (achievement, saving and discipline) were no longer significantly important in contemporary capitalism, which, with the development of a consumer culture, emphasized hedonistic self-gratification and enjoyment. There was, therefore a tension between the ascetic principles of production and the hedonistic principles of extended mass consumption.

These changes in consumption and production resuted in a new personality and a new sensitivity, giving rise to modernism in art and lifestyle, and producing the narcissistic self as the indulgent, hedonistic consumer of modern commodities. Bell came to see this new modernism as antipathetic to the bourgeois values of classical capitalism which had been analysed by Weber in *The Protestant Ethic and the Spirit of Capitalism* (1930). Bell thought that narcissism would cut at the very bases of advanced capitalism, because it was associated with a radical disjunction between culture and economy. Narcissistic modernism would result eventually in a major crisis of identity, a fragmentation of culture and an erosion of the values which made authority and civility possible (Hearn, 1985). Bell was quick to realize also that the new modernistic style attempted to develop an aesthetic justification for human life as a substitute for more traditional forms of religion and morality. Bell realized, partly influenced by his reading of Nietzsche, that aesthetics had become ethics. Art became the major and possibly only justification for life.

Bell, also in *The Cultural Contradictions of Capitalism*, came to identify a significant development of postmodernism in the 1960s which 'carried the logic of modernism to its farthest reaches' (1976: 51). Postmodernism, developed by the writing of Norman O. Brown, Michel Foucault and Jean Genet, took the aesthetic justification of life to a new level, by arguing that real existence could only be found in the instinctual; only hedonistic pleasure was unambiguously life-affirming and against death. Bell therefore saw postmodernism as the most significant if fashionable rejection of the rationalistic, empirical, pragmatic world-view of the bourgeois class, creating also a new challenge to the traditional avant-garde in lifestyle and art. Postmodernism broke down the divisions between art and reality, between play and realism, unleashing a new level of fantasy into general culture. Postmodernism was also associated with a new change of scale in mass culture with the development of the large cinema screen; 'this change of scale gave the culture of the 1960s its special surge, coupled with the fact that a bohemian lifestyle once limited to a tiny elite is now acted out on the giant screen of the mass media' (Bell, 1976: 54).

Postmodernism represented the final collapse of family capitalism, the political values of the small country town and puritanism, and disciplined individualism as the leading ideological doctrines of early American capitalism. Bell argued that one crucial feature of these profound changes in culture was the ready availability of the automobile to the general populace, permitting massive geographical mobility and a new secretive lifestyle, since the automobile represented a private, mobile living room. These changes in popular culture and mass society created a new sensibility which emphasized immediacy, spontaneity and sensation.

Another social aspect of this new sensibility was the growing importance of mass tourism (Urry, 1988) and the emergence of a visual culture over the culture of print. Transportation, television and tourism all produced a mobile psyche, which had no necessary or significant roots in the local culture. Tourism produced a global, if superficial, cosmopolitan culture of the immediate and the sensual. These very general changes in culture were conceptualized by Bell within the framework of Nietzsche's *The Birth of Tragedy*, namely as conflicts between the Apollonian principle of regulation and form versus the Dionysian principle of energy, sexuality and experience. The long-term implication of these changes was not only the decline of the traditional disciplined individual, but the erosion of general standards of public integration and civility, associated with the decline of rationality as the underlying standard of economic and political action. Again, Bell following Nietzsche noted that with 'the death of God' the social fabric and the social bond linking the individual to society were destroyed, again leaving merely an aesthetic impulse as the legitimizing principle of modern political systems. Bell came eventually to wonder whether the future of society and the future of civilization might in fact depend on a 'return of the sacred' which would place some limit on the development of modernism as that movement which sought to go beyond nature and beyond culture (Bell, 1980). Having sketched out the main outlines of Bell's general view of the relationship between culture, the economy and politics, we can now turn to a more specific and detailed examination of Bell's analysis of the political arena within the context of a modern capitalist culture.

Citizenship

The central issues of Bell's political sociology are the result of an integration of the theory of citizenship of T.H. Marshall (1963) and the fiscal sociology of Joseph Schumpeter (1954). The central value of modern democratic politics is equality, and political struggles are essentially about attempts to expand the rights of equality within the general framework of legal-political citizenship (Turner, 1986). Democracy requires some elementary standards of universalistic treatment of citizens and therefore the erosion of traditional, particularistic concepts of the person. Because the modern notion of equality involves an emphasis on universalism, there is a tendency for claims about entitlement to have inflationary consequences. With the revolution in rising expectations and entitlements, there is a strong tendency for the service sectors to increase because it is in this area that citizens make claims towards the development of more equitably distributed resources. In addition, the result is that the professionals who manage these service sectors have a vested interest in the continuity of citizenship entitlement (Offe, 1985). The structural consequences of these political processes are the expansion of the state as a consumer within the public household. These strong inflationary pressures within the economy threaten to undermine the position of the middle class. Where the state attempts to regulate inflation by deflationary policies, especially through the regulation of wages, there is a strong pressure on working-class standards of living. Bell therefore saw the primary conflicts within the polity in modern capitalism as a conflict between the middle class and the working class over the state budget and over the character of taxation.

Many features of Bell's analysis of the problems of modern capitalism were dependent upon an analysis of postindustrialism which he had undertaken in *The Coming of Post-Industrial Society* (1973). In that influential study he had argued that the new axial principle of postindustrial society would be the power of knowledge and technical information over property and older forms of power. These changes in the character of production were also associated as we have seen with a change in the class structure, giving rise to a new middle class of technologists and managers. In general, a postindustrial society involves a transition from the production of goods to the production of services with the emergence of a new influential tertiary area of the economy. It requires a new domination of knowledge, since postindustrial society depends on knowledge production rather than commodity production, and thereby also gives rise to a society in which the university rather than the enterprise is the leading institutional core of the system. There is also the continuing subordination of the firm to more global and concentrated economic interests. Because of the complexities and difficulties of such a society, there is also a new emphasis on social planning and social organization. Thus skills and educational certificates replace the marks of birth as the principal foundations of political power.

While Bell was generally criticized for assuming a consensual end-of-ideology position in his analysis of capitalism, it is clear that Bell in fact saw contemporary society as one characterized by major sources of instability, often associated with rising but new types of conflict and violence. Bell identified a range of conditions and circumstances which had resulted in an 'unstable America' (1976). Bell, commenting on an argument presented by S.M. Lipset (1960: 77), claims that the issue of legitimation is the critical question of all political systems. Bell claims that a variety of changes and events have destabilized the American political system, such as the disaster of the Vietnam war, the problems of youth militancy and the race conflicts of the 1950s and 1960s. There are, however, deeper issues of instability, relating to the erosion of an integrated political elite in the United States able to provide some direction and coherence to foreign policy in a context where, with the lobalization of the economy, no single government is able to control independently and autonomously the national economy, leaving the society exposed to strong international economic pressures on monetary levels and interest rates. In his more recent work, Bell (1987: 13) has noted that 'while the international economy is increasingly integrated, many polities are fragmenting'. Thus, while Bell has been persistently criticized for presenting a consensus view of modern society free of ideological conflicts, in fact the reverse is an equally plausible interpretation of Bell's analysis, namely the persistence of conflicts over the state budget, the absence of a coherent cultural legitimation of politics, the emergence of the free-floating narcissistic self, the degradation of the person through the impact of consumerism and the emergence of a postmodern irrationalism which prevents any coherent analysis of society, while also precluding any coherence for the integration of the individual and society. These are all persistent themes in Bell's analysis of contemporary society. This analysis of contemporary capitalism has often been described as neopluralist in its orientation leading to a form of 'technocratic conservatism' (Dunleavy and O'Leary, 1987: 283). Unfortunately these slogans are hardly helpful in understanding Bell's position, since rather than adopting a technocratic reductionism, Bell has clearly argued for the autonomy of various layers of society, especially the autonomy of political life in contemporary cultures. The fragmentation of values, the erosion of legitimacy and the increasing autonomy of the political order are crucial features of his theory; indeed he insists upon the separation and independence of capitalism and democracy as historically related but empirically separate realms (Bell, 1982).

It will be valuable for subsequent discussion to summarize briefly therefore the primary features of Bell's political sociology. The shift from an industrial to a postindustrial society involves the increasing dominance of consumerism and consumption over political, social and cultural life. In particular, the reflexive hedonism of contemporary consumerism produces a fragmentation of values and norms which makes the legitimation of the political impossible, or at least unstable. There is an increasing separation and autonomy of the cultural, economic and political realms. In the case of the political order, the old system of class politics has given way to status competition over the state budget, involving an inflationary rise of expectations with the growth of citizenship. Because the state is unable to satisfy these growing demands by an appropriate taxation response, there is a general dissatisfaction with democratic processes because they cannot resolve the tension between inequality and political democracy.

In order to understand Bell's position more clearly, it is interesting to examine his critical observations on the work of Jürgen Habermas. While both Bell and Habermas have concentrated on the legitimation crisis (Habermas , 1973), Bell does not share Habermas's commitment to the possibility of a social system regulated by a universalistic, democratic rationality. Bell argues that there cannot be such 'a unitary phenomenon as a set of universal, generalizable interests' (1980: 243). By contrast, Bell argues that in contemporary society there is inevitably a great plurality, multiplicity and expansion of interests which cannot be resolved by any unitary notion of, for example, the 'good society'; furthermore, these plural interests are associated with the multiplicity of commitments and identities which the modern citizen assumes. These cross-cutting and contradictory identities and interests preclude any unitary loyalties on the part of a class or status group. Modern society is necessarily a plural society. Bell argues that there can never be a 'mutual reconciliation of values' (1980: 243), because there are no common values upon which such reconciliation could be based. This view of the plurality of values in Bell's work is parallel to the argument in J.-F. Lyotard's *The Postmodern Condition*, where he suggests that the conflicting bases of legitimation produce 'noise' which rules out the discursive consensus required by Habermas's defence of enlightenment rationality (Lyotard, 1986).

While classical philosophy was often based upon the quest for the good life or the common good, the existence of postmodern pluralism precludes any such political discourse. We can consider the implications of Bell's position and the implications of postmodernism by reviewing briefly an influential book in American political debate, namely Marcus Raskin's *The Common Good* (1986). Raskin's book attempts to provide an alternative to contemporary Reaganomics and Thatcherism. Between the end of the Second World War and 1973, most industrial capitalist societies underwent profound programmes of social reconstruction which laid the basis for welfare politics in the contemporary period. In this era of welfare politics, the working class (and a variety of other subordinate social groups) achieved considerable advances in education, health and welfare, resulting in for example a significant decline in infant mortality rates, an expansion of access to higher education and an increase in life expectancy. With the oil crisis and world economic stagnation, these industrial capitalist societies have moved into a period of economic decline in which the politics of reconstruction has given way to the politics of recession and resentment. The traditional divisions between conservative, liberal and socialist politics were dismantled by a new period of neoconservatism in the form of Thatcherism. Many of the assumptions of liberal–democratic politics were challenged by laissez-faire economic theory, demanding the demolition of state-supported welfare systems, state-managed wages policies and state support for education. While diverse governments and industrial societies may be committed to political ideologies which appear to be different, there is also a remarkable convergence on neoconservative market-dominated practices. This is one aspect of disorganized capitalism.

In *The Common Good*, Raskin argues that contemporary American politics is structured around a struggle over three perceptions of the United States. These three theories or perspectives are Republicanism, Democracy and the National Security State, which are in fact three reflections upon the extent of citizenship within the polity. The concept of America as a republic was clearly outlined by Senator Robert Taft of Ohio. The republican view regards the United States as a two-class system, in which the dominant group regards itself as citizens who are property-holders, while the subordinate class is merely associate, dependent and marginal to the system. The associate classes, in fact have no real claims, since they are thought to have little to offer. Taft and his followers were against American involvement in the world political system, since they thought that military and foreign expansion would transform the republic into a welfare state, thereby destroying the market system. The democratic theory was outlined by writers like Justice William O. Douglas who believed in greater participation of all citizens within the United States. Douglas developed a view of democracy which lies at the heart of Raskin's study, namely 'democracy was not a given or finished form. It was a political process which sought the perfectability of economic, social and political relationships based upon a theory of inalienable rights which were discoverable through pain, inquiry and struggle' (Raskin, 1986: 279). The social struggles of the modern United States centre around the attempt to destroy American democracy and to replace it by a strong security state system. According to Raskin, President Reagan has 'saved the United States from democracy' (1986: 271), and has committed the population to nationalism and individualism. The rights and benefits won during the reconstruction period have been either undermined or demolished, leaving marginal or subordinate groups exposed to the hot blast of the market place. While using the slogans of democracy and republicanism, neoconservative politics in fact seek to transform the United States into a garrison, in which the haves will monopolize the rights and privileges of the system exclusively for their own personal benefit. As an alternative to this process of privatization and political authoritarianism, Raskin advocates a return to the foundation charter of the United States which conceptualized the republic as a system committed to the common good.

While Raskin is overtly conscious of the problematic character of the common good, one weakness in his argument is his failure to address the notion that there can be such a thing as 'the common good'; the book has to assume a common good which is never adequately defined, and in fact Raskin has to trade upon an implicit religious view of the commonality of goodness. He assumes that there is 'a caring instinct' (1986: 89) which is common to human beings qua human beings. In foreign policy, he associates himself with the theories of Grotius and claims that modern international relations must be based upon 'the bonds of community and natural law' (1986: 195). He also notes 'the natural right that people have as a result of their being human' (1986: 276). Finally, the rights of citizens are not artificial products of human law but 'they are natural rights and cannot be taken away' by the state or any other group (1986: 286). While the natural right tradition is a powerful argument, it is often difficult to sustain such a notion in modern philosophy and in contemporary political practice. We live in a highly fragmented, complex and diversified world in which we can no longer assume the validity of such notions as the common good, nature or natural instinct. We live necessarily in the postmodern or post-Nietzschean world in which God is dead and we are forced to come to terms with the plural values which characterize the secular political environment. Given the division of labour, the existence of social classes, the conflicts between status groups and the multiplicity of interests of various fractions of the state, it may be more appropriate to refer to the world of 'common goods' in which there is a great plurality of notions of 'goods' which cannot be resolved.

Status politics and postmodern culture

During the Second World War, in the United Kingdom the membership of the trade-union movement rose to almost eight million workers and continued to increase to its maximum of 13.4 million in 1979. In large manufacturing firms and in the large public utilities, membership increased to around 80 or 90 percent of all male workers, giving the unions a considerable political hold over industrial relations. Between the end of the war and 1973, while the British economy was weak by comparison with other industrial nations, there was full employment and expanding investment, creating an environment in which trade unions were able to negotiate relatively high pay increases. The inflationary effects of these circumstances were somewhat offset by the gradual devaluation of the pound. In this period, British political life clearly manifested sharp class divisions between an urban working class, the owners of capital and the managers of British finance; in addition the peculiarities of the British electoral system have precluded the development of a multiparty system. It also guaranteed the absence of governments of coalition (Kidron, 1970; Miliband, 1961). Partly in association with the development of North Sea oil, there was of course for a brief period some discussion of the 'breakup of Britain' (Nairn, 1978), but the overall pattern of regional voting was not in the long run significantly influenced by the development of Scottish nationalism (Hechter, 1975). This scenario of class politics in the immediate postwar period was changed fundamentally by the oil crisis of the 1970s, by changes in the structure of capitalism and by the development of a fragmented postmodern culture.

One peculiarity of the modern period is that, while unemployment has risen to unprecedented levels in the 1980s, union membership has declined from a peak of 55 percent of the labour force in 1979 to 37 percent in 1986 (Roberts, 1987). The unions have largely failed to penetrate the membership of the new high technology enterprises and, while there has been some increase in the public sector, union membership has not kept pace with the growth of the service sector (Gershuny and Miles, 1983). This erosion of union membership may be associated with a general decline in the proportion of manual workers in the labour force. For example, as a percentage of the gainfully employed population of Great Britain, manual workers have declined from around 80 percent in 1911 to 53 percent in 1971 (Abercrombie and Urry, 1983). The growth of the service sector, the expansion in white-collar employment, the new emphasis on high technology and the deskilling of the labour force as a consequence of economic change have led some writers to suggest that the industrial capitalist societies are going through a process in which the working class is disappearing (Gorz, 1982). The expansion of new white-collar employees, especially in management and supervisory roles, has in addition suggested that we are experiencing the explosion of a new middle class (Hyman and Price, 1983).

These structural changes suggest an explanation for the current dealignment between politics and class (Sarlvik and Crewe, 1983). For example, in 1959 the portion of manual workers voting Labour was 62, but this had declined to 46 in 1983. Many of the changes in class and voting behaviour in Britain may be associated with the decline of the traditional working-class community centred around a large industrial enterprise. The decline of a working-class lifestyle is also associated with the increase in home ownership and private means of trans-portation (Dunleavy, 1979). The overall effect of these changes is to make the vote in British politics far more volatile and this change may be also described simply as a decline in 'partisan alignment', since the electorate no longer consistently identifies positively with any particular party. In British politics the traditional agricultural aristocratic element within the conservative cabinets has declined, especially with the emergence of Thatcherite politics (Ross, 1983) and there has been at the same time an erosion of working-class unionized support for the British Labour party. The effect is to leave the relatively affluent, socially mobile new middle class as a significant actor within the British political scene.

Insofar as we can talk about the emergence of postmodern culture and postmodern politics, we may identify postmodern lifestyles with this new white-collar sector of the occupational system, namely with the 'yuppies' of the new middle class (Featherstone, 1987a, 1987b). Obviously the development of mass consumption and a mass society had profound implications for social differentiation in status and class terms. Mass consumption achieved some level of democratization of consumer behaviour in terms of self-image and taste. However, as privileged cultural items become increasingly available to a mass market, the avant-garde is compelled to create innovative forms of taste in order to reassert distinction and differentiation (Bourdieu, 1984). Given the speed of mass cultural production and the constant fluctuation in styles and images, changes within the cultural sphere are so rapid that it is increasingly difficult for an avant-garde to identify and defend the leading edge of cultural and artistic change. We can see the conflicts and changes within the artistic sphere as an effect of struggles between different status groups to gain some control over cultural capital. We live in a social sphere in which the signs and symbols of culture are often explosively over-produced. In a world characterized by extensive cultural pluralism and complex life-worlds, it may no longer be possible to refer to fashion but only to fashions. To this argument about the over-production of signs, we can add the theory of Bell that the cultural area has become autonomous and somewhat remote or detached from the political and economic dimensions. It is this complexity and speed of the cultural consumer world which has laid the basis for the whole idea of a postmodern order. In a postmodern world, cultural symbols become intermixed, flexible and free-ranging, precluding a clear division between high and low culture. This change has given rise to a playful and reflexive cultural world which mimics itself. With the erosion of the clear separation between high and low culture:

> We are moving towards a society without fixed status groups in which the adoption of styles of life (manifest in choice of clothes, leisure activities, consumer goods, bodily dispositions) which are fixed to specific groups have been surpassed. This apparent movement towards a post-modern consumer culture based upon a profusion of information and proliferation of images which cannot be ultimately stabilized or hierarchized into a system which correlates to fixed social divisions, would further suggest the irrelevance of social division and ultimately the end of the social as a significant reference point. (Featherstone, 1987a: 55–6)

With the development of mass consumption and mass systems of information, social styles and cultural practices become mixed into an indefinite medley of tastes and outlooks. With this fragmentation of culture there also goes a fragmentation of sensibilities, a mixing of lifestyles and the erosion of any sense of a cogent political project or coherent political programme, as the lives of individuals become increasingly merely a collection of discontinuous happenings. The development of a postmodern culture and postmodern ideology may have quite inconsistent effects in a political field. For example, Lash and Urry (1987: 299) suggest that in its negative character the postmodernism of the new middle classes may be quite compatible with Thatcherism and Reaganism, while in its more positive guise it may take an antihierarchical and populist dimension, becoming incorporated into various forms of localized democratic practices.

Towards a critique of conceptual postmodernism

My principal criticism of the notion of a postmodern culture will address the historical roots of modernism and postmodernism; in particular, I wish to argue that postmodernism cannot be associated exclusively or directly with late capitalism, since many features of postmodernism and many ideas leading into postmodernism had their origins in much earlier stages of capitalism, or indeed in much earlier socioeconomic formations. In part, this sketch is merely to point out that the cultural 'crisis' of the modern world has deep historical foundations and thus postmodernism cannot be treated as a specific effect of changes in information technology. For example, as Bell has noted, much of the philosophical groundwork for postmodernism had been established by Friedrich Nietzsche (1844–1900). Our contemporary sense of the fragmentation of culture, the fusion of aesthetics and ethics, the sense of a loss of a general value system, and the emphasis on the self as a work of art were things originally worked out in *The Birth of Tragedy* (1869–71), *Thus spake Zarathustra* (1893) and the *Anti-Christ* (1880). The core features of Nietzsche's philosophy have in recent years been the subject of considerable debate, precisely because of Nietzsche's relevance to the contemporary sense of a change in culture. Nietzsche's slogan (God is dead) neatly summarized the notion of nihilism, the erosion of conventional morality, the growing dominance of the state and its servants, the fragmentation of culture and the decline of a sense of wholeness grounded in everyday life. In fact, Nietzsche's views on power politics, professionalism, the role of ideology in society and the cultural importance of resentment were features of his philosophy which came to shape and form much of twentieth-century sociology and social theory, particularly in the work of Georg Simmel, Max Weber and Max Horkheimer (Stauth and Turner, 1986). Even in the world of practical politics, we have somewhat lost sight of the fact that Nietzsche and Wagner played a significant part in German politics in the conflicts of Austrian society, having a peculiar relationship to Austro-Marxism in the early decades of the twentieth century (McGrath, 1974).

The fact that the philosophical and aesthetic elements of post-modernism were shaped towards the end of the nineteenth century suggests immediately that any attempt to tie postmodernism directly to late capitalism must be historically problematic. We can make this point even more forcefully by noting the peculiar relationship between the themes of postmodern culture and the themes of Baroque art.

The seventeenth century produced its own culture industry, with its own mass psychology and 'kitsch' cultural frivolity. Seventeenth-century Baroque philosophers were perfectly aware of the crisis of religion, the differentiation and fragmentation of culture, the emergence of new sensibilities, the erosion of an overarching ideology, and the necessity to discover a new basis for moral order. They realized in particular that the human being is socially constructed, a made phenomenon. The Baroque mind had a fascination for artifact and for artificiality, being fascinated by clocks, mechanical devices and ruins. In short, the Baroque period saw itself as essentially a modern period, which from our perspective in fact looks like a postmodern epoch having most of the components which are typically identified with twentieth-century postmodernism (Buci-Glucksmann, 1984; Maravall, 1986).

The Baroque imagination, rather like postmodernism, represents a direct challenge to the whole idea of progress as the march of reason, the existence of linear time and the value of positivistic science as the beacon of history. Both Baroque and postmodernism appeal by contrast to fantasy and the fantastic as motifs of culture. Therefore, while I do not deny the association between postmodernism and contemporary consumer culture, I believe there are also close parallels between Baroque culture and postmodernism, and indeed that Baroque traditions are historically important in the constitution of the modern aestheticization of life.

This problem of the historical grounding of postmodernism brings me to my final criticism, namely the underlying assumption of most commentators on postmodernism that by definition the continuity of the political system depends primarily upon legitimization and its legitimization depends upon some shared values or ideology, or at least a successful claim to such a common culture. We have seen that Bell grounds his notion of political legitimacy in the tradition of Weber and more indirectly in the legacy of Nietzsche, in claiming that all political orders have to be rooted in some overarching system of legitimacy. This view of Weber and Nietzsche can be challenged (Turner, 1982).

Since Nietzsche believed that God is dead (a general system of moral values is not possible) and that the contemporary ideologies of nationalism and middle class culture are simply 'the idols of the state', it is difficult to see how an argument could be derived from Nietzsche to suggest that the state necessarily requires a unified system of values, since the state may be able to exist on a mixture of force and habit. Indeed Weber's own account of both the state and the Church as institutions depends upon his assumption that the natural law tradition is dead; it is for this reason that he defined the state as simply that institution which has a monopoly of force within a given territory, while defining the Church as that institution which has a monopoly of spiritual violence in a given terrain. Weber's sociology is a sociology of domination, not a sociology of legitimate consensus. In practice, Weber made very little appeal to the idea of legitimate authority in his actual analysis of contemporary politics, which as I have argued, he thought was dominated by the state, by power politics, by the struggle of political parties in the absence of religion, natural law or common morality and by international imperial struggles. Of course, this argument that the state could rest simply on a repressive apparatus is not entirely convincing, but it is possible to elaborate the theory without an appeal to some existing dominant ideology or common culture (Abercrombie et al., 1980). We can elaborate this statement to suggest that the social stability of modern societies depends upon the contradictory relationship between three dimensions, namely the economic, the political and the cultural (Turner, 1987).

Marx had argued in *Capital* that one crucial feature of social regulation in a capitalist society was 'the dull compulsion' of economic relations which forced people to work in order to exist. This economic cohesion has been modified by the growth of citizenship which through various welfare mechanisms has blunted the edge of dull compulsion. In addition, modern economies in the postwar period have generally provided for some increase in the standard of living of the population as a whole, making more available the consumer goods of more prosperous social groups. Consumption therefore is the positive side of the negatively coercive element of dull compulsion. While political repression in Weber's view was an important feature of social stability, again citizenship is the positive aspect of state repression, providing through political citizenship a new range of rights and duties, incorporating the mass of the population into civil society. Finally, while the Marxist tradition often puts an emphasis on cultural incorporation through a dominant ideology, it is possible to suggest that all that is required on the part of citizens is merely pragmatic acceptance (Mann, 1973) in order for the basic requirement of political order to be guaranteed. The majority of modern capitalist societies exist in the face of, or despite, major internal disruption and disorder from race riots, to urban terrorism, to workers' unrest, to the conflicts of minority groups and to the great divisions of language and culture which have persisted, particularly in Europe. These continuous and deep problems of social order have not resulted in endless political revolution, economic crisis or social collapse. Indeed the remarkable thing about industrial, whether modernist or postmodernist, society is its ability to absorb and manage very high levels of social conflict and uncertainty (Holton, 1987).

I have drawn attention to this feature of political legitimacy in order to suggest that the development of postmodernism and postmodern politics may not be the profound threat to the social order as implied by writers like Habermas and Lyotard. I have also argued that it is typically the case for social theories to put too much emphasis on political legitimacy as a necessary requirement for social and political order. Having made these criticisms of postmodernism, it can be argued that the notion of postmodernism is a very important addition to the scientific vocabulary of political science, alerting us to major and important changes in the social and political fabric of modern society which we should not and cannot ignore. In particular, this paper has attempted to make a strong connection between the disalignment, and to some extent the de-regulation, of the electoral market place and the emergence of a new middle class equipped with a postmodern culture which is a weapon against the old establishment and the institutions which made possible the continuity of high culture. Clearly this situation implies a future of considerable electoral volatility and instability, whereby the management of electoral clients will be increasingly problematic for all Western governments. Finally, this discussion has suggested that many, if not all, of these components of contemporary political theory can be seen, or at least anticipated, in the political sociology of Daniel Bell.

References

Abercrombie, N., Hill, S. and Turner, B.S. (1980) *The Dominant Ideology Thesis.* London: Allen & Unwin.

Abercrombie, N. and Urry, J. (1983) *Capital Labour and the Middle Classes.* London: Allen & Unwin.

Badham, R.J. (1986) *Theories of Industrial Society.* London/Sydney: Croom Helm.

Bell, D. (1960) *The End of Ideology: on the Exhaustion of Political Ideas in the 50s.* Glencoe, Ill.: Free Press.

Bell, D. (ed.) (1964) *The Radical Right.* Garden City, N.Y.: Anchor Books.

Bell, D. (1973) *The Coming of Post-Industrial Society*. New York: Basic Books.
Bell, D. (1976) *The Cultural Contradictions of Capitalism*. New York: Basic Books.
Bell, D. (1980) *Sociological Journeys: Essays 1960–1980*. London: Heinemann.
Bell, D. (1982) *The Social Sciences since the Second World War*. New Brunswick, NJ: Transaction Books.
Bell, D. (1987) 'The World and the United States in 2013', *Daedalus*, (Summer): 1–31.
Bourdieu, P. (1984) *Distinction: a Social Critique of the Judgement of Taste*. London: Routledge & Kegan Paul.
Brick, H. (1986) *Daniel Bell and the Decline of Intellectual Radicalism: Social Theory and Political Reconciliation in the 1940s*. Madison: University of Wisconsin Press.
Buci-Glucksmann, C. (1984) *La raison Baroque: de Baudelaire à Benjamin*. Paris: Editions Galilee.
Collins, R. (1981) *Sociology since Mid-century: Essays in Theory Cumulation*. New York: Economic Press.
Dunleavy, P. (1979) 'The Urban Basis of Political Alignment: Social Class, Domestic Property Ownership, and State Intervention in Consumption Processes', *British Journal of Political Science*, 9: 409–43.
Dunleavy, P. and O'Leary, B. (1987) *Theories of the State: the Politics of a Liberal Democracy*. London: Macmillan.
Featherstone, M. (1987a) 'Lifestyle and Consumer Culture', *Theory, Culture and Society*, 4 (1): 54–70.
Featherstone, M. (1987b) 'Postmodernism and the New Middle Class', paper for the IAPL Conference on Postmodernism, Lawrence, Kansas.
Gershuny, J. (1978) *After Industrial Society?* London: Macmillan.
Gershuny, J. and Miles, I. (1983) *The New Service Economy: Transformation of Employment in Industrial Societies*. London: Frances Pinter.
Gorz, A. (1982) *Farewell to the Working Class: an Essay on Post-Industrial Socialism*. London: Pluto.
Habermas, J. (1973) *Legitimation Crisis*. London: Heinemann.
Hearn, F. (1985) *Reason and Freedom in Sociological Thought*. London: Allen & Unwin.
Hechter, M. (1975) *Internal Colonialism: the Celtic Fringe in British National Development, 1536–1966*. London: Routledge & Kegan Paul.
Holton, R.J. (1987) 'The Idea of Crisis in Modern Society', *British Journal of Sociology*, 38: 502–20.
Hyman, R. and Price P. (eds) (1983) *The New Working Class? White-collar Workers and their Organisations*. London: Macmillan.
Kidron, M. (1970) *Western Capitalism since the War*. Harmondsworth: Penguin.
Lash, S. and Urry, J. (1987) *The End of Organized Capitalism*. Cambridge: Polity Press.
Lipset, S.M. (1960) *Political Man: the Social Basis of Politics*. Garden City, N.Y.: Doubleday.
Lyotard, J.-F. (1986) *The Postmodern Condition: a Report on Knowledge*. Manchester: Manchester University Press.
Mann, M. (1973) *Consciousness and Action among the Western Working Class*. London: Macmillan.
Maravall, J.A. (1986) *Culture of the Baroque: Analysis of a Historical Structure*. Manchester: Manchester University Ptess.
Marshall, T.H. (1963) *Sociology at the Crossroads*. London: Heinemann.
McGrath, W.J. (1974) *Dionysian Art and Populist Politics in Austria*. Newhaven: Yale University Press.
Miliband, A.R. (1961) *Parliamentary Socialism*. London: Allen & Unwin.

Mills, C.W. (1956) *The Power Elite*. New York: Simon & Schuster.

Nairn, T. (1978) *The Break-up of Britain*. London: New Left Books.

Offe, C. (1985) *Disorganized Capitalism*. Cambridge: Polity Press.

Raskin, M.G. (1986) *The Common Good: its Politics, Policies and Philosophy*. London: Routledge & Kegan Paul.

Roberts, B. (1987) *Mr Hammond's Cherry Tree: the Morphology of Union Survival*, 18th Wincott Memorial Lecture, Occasional Paper 76. London: Institute of Economic Affairs.

Ross, J. (1983) *Thatcher and Friends*. London: Pluto Press.

Sarlvik, B. and Crewe, I. (1983) *Decade of Dealignment*. Cambridge: Cambridge University Press.

Schumpeter, J. (1954) 'The Crisis of the Tax State', pp. 5–38 in *International Economic Papers*, Vol. 4. New York: Macmillan.

Stauth, G. and Turner, B.S. (1986) 'Nietzsche in Weber, oder die Geburt des modernen Genius im professionellen Menschen', *Zeitschrift für Soziologie*, 15 (2): 81–94.

Turner B.S. (1982) 'Nietzsche, Weber and the Devaluation of Politics', *Sociological Review*, 30: 367–91.

Turner B.S. (1986) *Citizenship and Capitalism: the Debate over Reformism*. London: Allen & Unwin.

Turner, B.S. (1987) 'Marx, Weber and the Coherence of Capitalism, the Problem of Ideology', pp. 169–204 in Norbert Wiley (ed.), *The Marx–Weber Debate*. Beverly Hills: Sage.

Urry, J. (1988) 'Cultural Change and Contemporary Holiday-making', *Theory, Culture and Society*, 5 (1): 35–56.

Waxman, C. (ed.) (1968) *The End of Ideology Debate*. New York: Simon & Schuster.

Weber, M. (1930) *The Protestant Ethic and the Spirit of Capitalism*. London: Allen & Unwin.

10

Nietzsche, Modernity and Politics

Ian Forbes

The possibility of political culture as the appropriate concept for understanding society, as a proper subject for research and as a substantive social phenomenon, entails at least two basic questions. Can culture be political? That is, can political theory realize itself through cultural activity, and through the medium of culture, whether it be art or a cultural movement of some kind? Second, can politics be cultural? That is, can culture in its realm yield a better demonstration of the real and possible nature of the political world, thereby leading to new forms of political understanding and practice?

Now, embedded in these question are a host of assumptions about the nature of political interpretation and of culture. Broadly speaking, culture and politics are counterposed here. They are treated as rivals in the drive to analyse, understand and express human experience and existence so to highlight the equivalences and differences, if there are any, between cultural action and political action, and the theory of knowledge attached to each of these.

Friedrich Nietzsche and the phenomenon of modernity are inseparable components of any such discussions. The problem of existence in a secular mass society is central to both, and a major preoccupation is change in society. Nietzsche's account of nihilism addresses the dominant paradoxes that confront modernity, that inspired modernism, and which underpin some postmodernist manoeuvres.[1] His rejection of traditional politics heightens dramatically the sense of the political importance of the previously non-political, namely culture as it related to mass movements and the development of mass society. But his is no simple turning away from enlightenment logocentrism and pursuit of the perfectible. Simultaneously, Nietzsche sought to import aesthetic practice into the political. That is, he was involved in two revolutions. He did not effect a compromise between politics and culture, but changed them both by demonstrating their common basis in a relativist and perspectivist view of truth and morality.[2]

Two attempts to bring about fundamental social change will illustrate these points. The first is the surrealist movement; the second is cultural feminism. I will argue that each movement is a radical heir to the paradoxes of meaning and action highlighted by Nietzsche, and that specific lessons about politics and modernity can be drawn from them. Surrealism offers up its insights as a movement of the recent past, while cultural feminism demonstrates changes in the nature of political culture with respect to one of the latest forms of political practice.

Modernity and nihilism

It is possible to characterize political culture as part of the nihilistic response to modernity indicated by Nietzsche. But concepts of culture, cultural critiques and cultural solutions can be made to do too much, and are beset by the problems of modernity. Politics too suffers from an inability to define its own boundaries, despite the growth and maturation of the Weberian/Foucauldian state. Politics is often seen as the moral organization of social power, and culture as the broader canvas of social existence. Modernity, and this is no mean achievement, incorporates what is intrinsically valuable in each of these dimensions of human existence, and attempts to combine the insights and methods of analysis found there. In the process, the underlying distinctions necessary to make such a synthetic attempt are retained, in the process confusing a sense of politics as intrusion and rationalization with a respect for culture as dynamism and novelty. Politics and power with respect to individuality and creativity become the central cultural issues.

Inevitably, political culture has become caught between and continues to reflect the tensions of these perspectives (MacIntyre, 1981; Rorty, 1979). They are problems the experience of which is their only solution. Nietzsche is the arch-theorist of these concerns, because he was deeply interested in the basis of culture for a particular community. His singular contribution may well be that he raised the questions which must continually be asked about political culture if the concept is to be able to grasp its contemporary form and enable us to grasp the nature of social change. Nietzsche signalled and helped to complete the birth of modernity, which rests particularly on his view that there has been a decisive and irretrievable break with the past – a discontinuity, as Michel Foucault would have it.

The nature of modernity, as Nietzsche saw it, was that supposed fundamental reality as well as apparent triviality were no longer stable and reliably ordered cultural commodities. Nothing could be assumed with any certainty, because the present was tainted and haunted by its association with a dead past. The world was full of words – like art, truth and morality – but there was not yet a *language* that could convey a new understanding of these aspects of existence.

It is argued here that Nietzsche provides an analysis of society in crisis. Modernity is the descriptive term for a culture which has lost its means for unification via the agency of individuals. It is the dark aspect to the achievements of Enlightenment rationalism and technology against religion and superstition, and to its glad confidence in the human governance of progress. As Jürgen Habermas (1986: 106) puts it, the Enlightenment 'designates the entry into a kind of modernity which sees itself condemned to creating its self-awareness and norms out of itself'. In Nietzsche's reading, modernity is a condition where, according to Mark Warren, 'the culture exposes the nihilism latent in its structure' (1985: 427). This theme also underpins Arthur Kroker's view of Nietzsche's nihilism as 'both antithetical to and conditional for historical emancipation' (1985: 70).

Two facets of Nietzsche's response to the crisis of society stand out. The first is the negative reaction, based on the awareness of the inadequacy of contemporary interpretations and justifications of the world. Here Nietzsche is the greatest of the masters of suspicion.[3] His announcement (1886: 108) that 'God is dead', his claim that 'there *are* no facts, only interpretations' and his assertion that 'there is no truth', find their most coherent application in his insight that 'there are no moral phenomena at all, but only a moral interpretation of phenomena'. If core values can be shown to be insubstantial and provisional, then certainty itself is suspect, so it too must be uprooted, and the world cleansed and pared down. But this entirely necessary stripping away of pre-Enlightenment accretions and the debunking of faded myths and their strident mores is not intended to rejuvenate some set of old and previously hampered truths. In *The Gay Science*, Nietzsche dispensed with the comfortable illusions offered by rationalism and perfectibilism:

> We no longer believe that truth remains truth when the veils are withdrawn; we have lived too much to believe this. Today we consider it a matter of decency not to wish to see everything naked, or to be present at everything, or to understand and 'know' everything. (1882: Preface, 4)

This is the nihilism of modernity. The implications of the loss of truth and of faith in certainty are severe, but Nietzsche did not flinch from them. 'The trust in life has gone:' he concluded, 'life itself has become a *problem*' (1882: Preface, 3). He was of necessity anti-rationalist, because rationalism preached the existence of solutions. He was antimoralist, because existing morality or mores disguised weakness as strength. He was also antipolitical, because politics had become mass politics. This set him 'against the prevailing mood', against what he saw as the 'century of the crowd', since it offered and produced a lowering and diminishing of the culturally significant in human existence.

In this respect, Nietzsche is describing what has become known as *modernism*. If modernity as nihilism is the situation of the nineteenth century, then modernism is also the nihilistic response, as reason is religiously applied in the face of irrationality. As Daniel Bell puts it, modernism becomes a cultural temper: 'the self-willed effort of a style and sensibility to remain in the forefront of "advancing consciousness" ' (1976: 46). Modernism saw uncertainty, the death of God, the provisionality of truth as a kind of challenge to be met by dynamic and stunning attempts to recreate the world, making full use of the technological wizardry which was modernity's most obvious and manipulable offering. This was a campaign of an aesthetic kind too, against intellectual, social and historical forces, in the context of the depredations of the emergent bourgeoisie and, where possible, beyond the comprehension of the general public. However, for Bell (1976: 20; see also Frisby, 1985), the power of modernism ('derived from the idolatry of the self') is now exhausted, is now 'institutionalized by the "cultural mass" '.

Modernism in crisis

In fact, Nietzsche's view of nihilism is somewhat predictive of this kind of outcome. Modernity brings on what Warren refers to as a nihilism which:

> presages an era of ideological battles between institutionalized powers, each attempting to provide post-Christian identities for those within their arena of influence. None, however, will lead individuals to self-reflectively organized power – that is, to overcome nihilism by becoming sovereign agents. (1985: 436)

But Nietzsche was not gloomy about his diagnosis. He thought that such a process would go on for at least 100 years or more. As Robert Pippin (1983: 170) claims, Nietzsche 'denies that modern scepticism, cynicism, even nihilism is the proper reaction to the news that all the old gods are dead'.[4] Modernism would continue to seek to transcend modernity, but this drive to create in such a programmatic way is the attempt to confront the problem of rationalism with reason. Modernism fails in its task; modernism becomes itself a symptom of modernity.

The second facet of Nietzsche's response to modernity was not negative but interpretative. There was a need for a 'knowledge of a kind that has never yet existed or even been desired' (1887: Preface, 6). He sought to reserve a place for the rare and the valuable in civilization and humankind, before it could be flattened and regularized by the democratic, socialist and nationalist movements. As Warren (1985: 434) notes, Nietzsche held that there was a wider realm of knowledge to be taken into account, since 'humans possess a "tacit knowledge" . . . of the Dionysian world of experience, a world that is always richer, deeper, and more chaotic'. Nietzsche paid especial attention to the kind of knowledge necessary for the transvaluation of all values, with the capability of judging, changing and justifying life, social existence and its interpretations. This was vital, since the onset of nihilism meant that human agency, life within a properly functioning collective culture, was temporarily an impossibility. Denied the old forms of social connection, and as yet unable to derive new actions from fresh interpretations, the human subject, the modern self, what Nietzsche sometimes referred to as the sovereign individual, was to all intents and purposes stillborn.

It is on this basis that Nietzsche's thought is not only sceptical but revolutionary. Effectively, he was conducting a simultaneous critique of modernity *and* the modernist response to modernity. Modernism, it must be said, was at least attempting to avoid sliding into total relativism of thought on the one hand, and complete bureaucratization of action on the other. But it was just an attempt; a response Foucault understands as only 'heroic' when it needs also to be 'ironic':

> Modernity is not a specific historical event, but a historical conjuncture that has happened several times in our history, albeit with different form and content. . . . In a modernity-crisis, a taken-for-granted understanding of reality ceases to function as a shared background in terms of which people can orient and justify their activity and the modernist response is heroically and lucidly to face up to the old order. (Dreyfus and Rabinow, 1986: 117)

Nietzsche is beyond heroism as much as he is extramoral. He wanted to deconstruct and then think beyond the real, to demonstrate the inadequacy of present understanding, and to make it necessary for a complete reconstruction of reality. It is in these respects that he inaugurates a *postmodern* element in the critique of politics and culture.

Postmodern political culture

Postmodernism is thus the latest example of a response to the crisis of modernity, even though it may also be a paradigm shift in respect of the academic attachment to modernist assumptions and practices. It is the means by which the problem of modernity is faced once more, given the absorption of modernism into mass culture. Postmodernism is a corrective to the formalism of modernism which degenerated into style or formality, losing its critical faculty. Yet the philosophical grounds of modernity – questions concerning our human, subjective place in the world – are still stable. The human *response* to the detachment from certainty and experience of ambiguity remains mobile, unsettled and volatile. There is a constant danger of yet another century of revolutions, repressions and horrors, this time all too easy to contemplate. Having gained freedom, contemporary cultural politics offers bogus freedoms, while at the same time revealing more and more about the nature of an authentic existence regularly denied us. Authenticity is no longer an ideal but a thing of our own pasts – moments of free being glimpsed and felt. Authenticity is not a promise or a future, but a matter for attention. Postmodernism is therefore a necessity, and the means to it must once more be willed, just as Nietzsche did. As Thomas Pangle puts it:

> What Nietzsche means to initiate is not a new beginning 'from scratch' but a *post*-nihilistic, *post*-democratic movement that defines and creates itself dialectically against the entire tradition of the West – and thereby presupposes and claims to possess the deepest possible understanding of that tradition. (1983: 70)

Having to dispense with all premodern assumptions and errors of interpretation, and their modernist counterparts, Nietzsche turned to the only means of analysis and understanding that had any validity. It was in his very first book (Nietzsche: 1872: xxiv) that he introduced the idea that 'this world can be justified only as an aesthetic phenomenon'. Revolution was intimately linked with the artistic, with the intrinsic power to justify our *particular* historical existence. Effectively, this establishes that the modern relationship between politics and culture is akin to the complexity of the connection between truth and life. That is, the world, like a work of art, is both determinate and ambiguous. Each has a certain amount of form, and is rich in content. Each defies a simple or single level of analysis.

At its most straightforward, Nietzsche's theory of art can be reduced to two principles. All artistic creation stems from the antitheses and antagonisms inherent in the existence of the bright Apollonian element in art and the dark Dionysian forces (see Pütz, 1978: 9). Apollo stands variously for knowledge, beauty, order, rhythm, optimism, harmony and intellectual clarity, all of which limit and simplify existence and action. Dionysus is its radical opponent. It is artistic, vital, chaotic, melodic, pessimistic, intoxicating and ecstatic; it is unconstrained by boundaries, and aspires to an all-embracing unity. The creative interaction between those nodes of aesthetics, of experience and of nature is what gives art its peculiar status in Nietzsche's thought. Art is responsive to the will to power in humans, because it is not limited by our inability to express ourselves in narrow and formal ways. For example, it is capable of creating exquisite illusions out of the most shocking and oppressive reality, and so enables us to survive and overcome that reality. Moreover, there are many such illusions that are possible. There is no one art, just as there is no one truth. A variety of *perspectives* is inevitable, each offering only what it can – a partial, unique, temporary expression of the individual's will to power. This aesthetic means of creating a part of the world highlights the central feature of Nietzsche's explanation of art. It contributes to the totality that is life, and yet stems directly from the individual's perspective on life.

Art, ultimately, is '*worth more* than truth' (Nietzsche, 1901: 853). This inversion of the existing order of rank of social values may not, of course, be an aesthetic judgement. Nietzsche's (1901: 586) aesthetic claim was that 'philosophy, religion, and morality are symptoms of decadence', and that art was the countermovement. The basis of the countermovement is not art *per se*, however, but its importance for enhancing life. Art is not the locus of realized value any more than traditional morality was. In contradistinction to their conventional interpretation and application, Nietzsche (1901: 298) was struggling to reinstate art, knowlege and morality as *means* with the aim of enhancing life. 'Art and nothing but art!' he says in the *Will to Power*: 'It is the great means of making life possible, the great seduction to life, the great stimulant of life' (Nietzsche, 1901: 853). The problem here is that art was also the means to overcome art. Put another way, art is as much a part of the reality that Nietzsche wished to transcend, just as postmodernism owes its existence to that which it seeks to overcome (modernism) and to that to which it must respond (modernity).

However, art does present particular difficulties in a critical account of politics and culture. Art (in this case high art) is so obviously a practical and public activity, concerned with change and difference, while being dependent upon both past and present. Artistic practices are not automatic or merely physical, but require a high degree of intentional and theoretical consciousness. The political analyst is thus bound to observe that the themes of appearance versus reality, theory versus practice, public versus private, and change versus conservation loom very large. Art can be seen to share some of the key characteristics and interests of politics itself. Joseph Beuys in *Art into Society, Society into Art*, for example, even goes so far as to suggest that art and its activities can actually encompass and take the place of politics: 'Only art is capable of dismantling the repressive effects of a senile social system that continues to totter along the deadline: to dismantle in order to build a social organism as a work of art' (1974: 48). It is a feature of modernity that such an argument can be made. The concerns and perspectives of politics are seen to be rather limited, only a part of a much more cogent, yet much more panoramic conception of truth that is aesthetic in form and content, and therefore related fundamentally to culture.

Fighting back as best it can, politics stakes its rival claim to universal relevance. Politics, it is argued, has permeated every aspect of human social existence in the last 200 years; it has become as ubiquitous in its influence and appearance as art.[5] If it is true that only humans have culture, then it is equally true that only humans have politics. Like art, politics has a lively preoccupation with appearance and reality and the problem of translating (political) theory into (political) practice, not to mention making sense of ordinary existence. Morover, and despite its modern grounding in scientific rationality, politics has been known to admit that it needs to explain how aspects of its domain are subject to the anarchic and the irrational. At best, it can claim to be searching for the means to understand and draw upon the irrational or non-rational dimension of human experience, because it has come to recognize in that dimension a force and a power. Power and force, it is concluded, must always be the proper concern of politics, wherever they are found. Art, therefore, is a proper concern of politics, and its truths can ultimately be administered by political discourse.

But is there any real doubt about their essential difference, their incommensurability? Art, after all, can be said to be strictly for art's sake. The same cannot be said of politics. Much more sternly, politics must always be discursive knowledge applied practically. This is certainly the view of Habermas, and that which distinguishes him as still a modernist thinker.[6] Politics presumes that it has the power of theory and the force of power. Art, however, frequently slips the markers and boundaries of political predictability. This frustrates political interpretations and their inherent desire for control, and reveals an intense jealousy of the power, the flexibility and the truthfulness of art. As Craig Owens (1983: 59) puts it, 'it is precisely at the legislative frontier between what can be represented and what cannot that the postmodernist operation is being staged'.

On the other hand, art is often implicitly regarded as a reliably stable entity which survives all merely political and social changes. Art is presumed to be about the application of skill and taste in the production of art objects, and since most of these products endure, the illusion is created that art has a unified origin and a continuous meaning and status.

Surrealism: politics or culture?

In the context of this problematic of the relationship between the real, politics and art, Surrealism takes up and explicates the Nietzschean interpretation of modernity and culture most extravagantly.[7] It is one of the few examples of politics in very close association with culture in which there is an account of radical change as well as radical affirmation. The Surrealists challenge the suggestion that art has a universal authority in itself which can confer power on those who practise, own and criticize art. They demonstrate how form comes to masquerade as real content and message in art, and 'beauty' and 'taste' become static, stagnant quantities rather than fluid and enigmatic qualities. Under the influence of Nietzsche's insistence that art has to make possible and justify this life, the Surrealists rejected all programmatic definitions of art in favour of a more open-ended view of the possibilities and functions of art.

After the First World War, the Littérature group, consisting of Louis Aragon, André Breton and Philippe Soupault, among others, were interested in the revision of certain values, the source of artistic creation and the value of the poet's human destiny. In an early Surrealist manifesto, Aragon demonstrates their response to modernity, and the prevailing cultural movements:

> No more painters, no more writers, no more musicians, no more sculptors, no more religions, no more republicans, no more royalists, no more imperialists, no more anarchists, no more socialists, no more Bolsheviks, no more politicians, no more proletarians, no more democrats, no more armies, no more police, no more nations, no more of these idiocies, no more, no more, NOTHING, NOTHING, NOTHING. Thus we hope that the novelty which will be the same thing as what we no longer want will come into being less rotten, less immediately GROTESQUE. (Nadeau, 1968: 62)

The first target, the first rejection, was the artistic community. Aragon was denying the validity of art activity as it was currently being practised. His next targets were the representatives of tradition in society at large. In this he was classically modernist, if that is possible. Third, and this is very illuminating for a 1920s document, he repudiated all the radical political responses to tradition. There are very strong echoes of Nietzsche's critique of all political movements here, and this is equally remarkable given the amount of esteem that socialist movements continued to inspire in modernists for some decades to come. This is followed by contempt for formal and informal institutions of the state, bringing to mind Zarathustra's view of the state as 'the coldest of all cold monsters'.

The Surrealists quickly became known for the daring and provocation of their Dadaist public manifestations, and they were very soon in demand from a public who wanted to see, to absorb, to annex the new aesthetics. That public was refused access; the critics denied their mediating control. Thus these nihilists of the aesthetic resisted incorporation into Bell's 'cultural mass'; they did not permit themselves to contribute to what Mike Featherstone (1985: 4) refers to as the 'aestheticisation of everyday life'. Ultimately, however, Dadaism could only replace 'the impasse of official art with the dead end of sterile agitation' (Nadeau, 1968: 63). It can be seen as the negative facet of Nietzschean nihilism – a rejection, a sweeping away of all current reality. Yet the Littérature group was soon to move toward a more sustained and creative attempt to remove the obstacles to a genuinely transfigured reality.

In about 1922, Surrealism established itself fully, with Breton (Nadeau, 1968: 76), for example, saying that 'we know now that poetry must lead somewhere'. The poetry of Lautréamont was rediscovered, as was his Nietzschean guarantee that poetry could 'satisfy the will to power in the literary realm'. Change was the goal and the means, what Nietzsche called the arrow and the longing. Apollinaire's 1917 lines were requoted not just as a description but as a task:

> O mouths, man is looking for a new language
> No grammarian can legislate. (Nadeau, 1968: 63)

Despite the negativity of Dadaism and Surrealism in their reactions to tradition and current (so-called) reality, they were nevertheless deeply connected to the most recent products of that tradition. Their focus on social change, the experience of being in a time of flux, was underpinned by visions of the natural world as fluctuation, as universal relativism, devoid of the old and comfortable causality and composed instead of the determining but unfathomable unconscious, thereby rending the traditional certainties of logic and behaviour. In terms of the established knowledge base, this rash of novelty was Dada-like. But it represented not a destructive intent, but an intensely creative drive to reformulate society in new ways.

To an extent, Surrealism became a part of that modernist enterprise. Its primary task was to destroy, because that was an integral part of any transvaluation of values. All art was tainted. Art actually prevented art. Art had to be destroyed if art was ever to become possible. But no new art was to replace old art. Surrealism was anti-art, and pro human knowledge. Human knowledge was not art, not science. It existed in the human psyche, as the unconscious, the dream, madness, altered states of consciousness – the flip side to the touchable, orderable, logical and systematized world assumed to be 'reality'.

In general, the Surrealists refused to take seriously what a reasonable society called the real. At that time, the real reflected the perspectives of a Western civilization which celebrated military victory, patriotism and the values of the old order.[8] As such, art was deeply offensive for the way that it relinquished its task vis-à-vis reality. Since there could be no sense of an alternative art, of a 'better' art, there could be no 'artistic' solution. Beauty, taste, form, style – all were bankrupted and made stale in and by art itself, and were no longer *available* to the artist. It was necessary to step right outside what art had become. Change from within was not an option.

Surrealism, therefore, had to be revolutionary; it had to conduct a total revolution on art and society, by mounting an all-out attack on its ordering of appearance and reality. But this did not mean that their own art form, poetry, was no longer possible. Poetry seemed especially open to the qualities inherent in dreams and images. As Soupault claims, they came to see poetry: 'as a liberation, as the possibility, perhaps the only one, bringing into harmony with the spirit, a freedom which we had known only in dreams; we would thereby free ourselves from all the apparatus of logic' (1964: 20). This suspicion of logic and the drive to escape it is an important theme, one which is later picked up and developed by radical feminism. In order to explore that non-logical world, and to communicate to each other 'the surreal', the Surrealists began experimenting with automatic writing, attempting to write down what the sub- or unconscious dictated. In this, they bring to mind Nietzsche's (1901: 523) view of the relationship between consciousness and action and the importance of postconscious actions. The Surrealists began to experiment with ways to alter their mental states, and produce poetry without regard to its literary merit, that is, automatic writing.

Was this art for art's sake? No. They were searching for acts of the imagination, since the imagination offered the flexibility and the openness of vision to the artist necessary to apprehend and reflect reality in image and metaphor. The imagination does not capture and regulate reality and present it as a system, as reason tries to, *even though* the imagination may grasp the whole of reality by focusing on a single droplet of water trembling on the edge of a leaf. Imagination was the means for realizing in concrete form the human knowledge that resided in each life.

Surrealism continued to challenge the existence, definition and possibility of art, showing that it is assumptions concerning the very *existence* of art which are the most crucial. For the Surrealists, art was not an autonomous activity in a compartmentalized society. Their attack on art was consequently an equally explicit attack on society. It was their view that society was a totality, each part of which was representative of that totality. On this basis, it is easy to see that the revolution they fostered in art was no local matter. A change anywhere in the structure must threaten the entire order.

Art and politics

This conception of change, the claim to be revolutionary, and the relation of the part to the whole raises the question of the overtly political nature of the Surrealist movement. The Surrealists (Nadeau, 1968: 240–1) certainly thought themselves revolutionary on a grand scale, and were clear about the political nature of their position and activity, as the following excerpts of their 1925 Manifesto show:

(1) We have nothing to do with literature;
But we are quite capable, when necessary, of making use of it like anyone else.
(2) *Surrealism* is not a new means of expression, or an easier one, nor even a metaphysic of poetry.
It is a means of total liberation of the mind *and of all that resembles it.*
(3) We are determined to make a Revolution.
. . .
(9) We say in particular to the Western World: *surrealism* exists. And what is this new ism that is fastened to us? Surrealism is not a poetic form. It is a cry of the mind turning back on itself, and it is determined to break apart its fetters, even if it must be by material hammers!

Above all, the Surrealists were concerned with liberty. This liberty was conceived in a radically new way, as a total liberation from conventional society with its ethics, religions, science and art. This was, in effet, a new ethics which rested on Desire and Love and demanded that individuals lose themselves, and thereby discover themselves, in their unconscious. Only there could one find reasons for living and loving more imaginatively, more authentically. It is an approach that finds its most explicit modern expression in the work of Herbert Marcuse, in *The Aesthetic Dimension* (1978), for example. There is a new form of politics associated with this early Surrealist position, and it has yet to be completely exhausted. Jean Schuster, Surrealism's archivist, intimates the existence of a trace, a potential, a revolutionary will:

There is a red thread of surrealism, which, given the blow of an axe, will appear anew. Who will give this blow, and when, I have no idea. I believe the future movement will relate the fundamental principles of surrealism to the needs and contingencies of its own time . . . The essential sign is a belief in the indestructible nature of the interior poetic voice . . . (1987: 22)

The contrast between this art and conventional politics, even if both claim to be revolutionary, is explicit. The one is elemental and mercurial, the other customary and calculable. As Anna Balakian argues: 'Imagination does not deceive but liberates, leads to a greater comprehension of reality. Reason leads to despair, imagination leads to exaltation and creativity' (1964: 40).

Surrealism, in other words, presents an ethical case for non-rationalist change in the world. By refusing to specify a fixed future and an official and programmatic path towards that future, and by rejecting goal-directed behaviour in favour of the open-ended activity of the creative imagination, Surrealism is able to 'prefigure, and express a new and latent order of things' (Short, 1980: 87).[9]

The culture of feminism

Radical feminism is another cultural movement of a highly political nature. In this case, the revolutionary impetus stands as a direct challenge to the notion and practice of even the most advanced notions of a participatory society, in terms of politics and culture in their broadest senses. Even that standard of feminist statements, that the personal is political, is shown by them to belong to the modernist era, along with all attempts to improve politics or to politicize areas of human existence previously taken to be natural or necessary. As it happens, radical feminism became disenchanted with the kind of political participation implicit in modernity at about the same time that modern and radical democratic political movements began to develop and expand quite dramatically the boundaries of politics.

The complete antirationalism of some recent forms of radical feminism – metaphysical feminism and cultural feminism, for example – is a uniquely revealing feature of the problem of conceptualizing a cultural whole, or, at the other extreme, of being left with no basis for cultural analysis and judgement at all. As Silvia Bovenschen asks: 'How do we speak? Is even logic a bit of vile trickery?' (1977: 136). Even more than the terrorist alternative, radical feminism is implacably opposed to the future of modernity as well as its past. It sees a political culture which cannot be improved or adjusted; it must be vacated.

Like Nietzsche, like Surrealism, radical feminism repudiates conventional politics. Power is not the province of politics; power is the essence of existence. It is to the reformulation of existence as women that radical feminists turn. If, for Nietzsche (1901: 585A), a man is a nihilist 'who judges of the world as it is that it ought *not* to be, and of the world as it ought to be that it does not exist', then, for Andrea Dworkin, a woman feels that culture:

> no longer organically reflects us, it is not our sum total, it is not the collective phenomenology of our creative possibilities – it possesses and rules us, reduces us, obstructs the flow of sexual and creative energy and activity, penetrates even into what Freud called the id, gives nightmare shape to natural desire. (1974: 157)

All the categories of political culture, particularly the false claims to universalism and bogus notions of equality and justice, are regarded with a deep suspicion borne of bitter experience. At base, the ontology and epistemology of knowledge germane to modernity are subjected to fundamental challenge. Rationality itself is patriarchal, and 'culture' exemplifies this problem of patriarchal knowledge. The feminist response exhibits a Nietzschean nihilism in the way that it first rejects the very validity of culture, and then reaffirms its necessity for existence by recreating a 'womanist' or 'wimminist' culture, characterized in this case by a total lack of identification with male categories. The outstanding example of this is to be found in the writings of Mary Daly (1984: 4), who wants to break 'the bonds/bars of phallocracy', but not in the conventional sense of bringing about political and cultural change. For her:

> The point is not to save society or to focus on escape . . . but to release the Spring of be-ing. To the inhabitants of Babel, this Spring of living speech will be unintelligible . . . So much the better for the Crone's Chorus. Left undisturbed we are free to find our own concordance, to hear our own harmony of the spheres. (Daly, 1979: 22)

A real alternative, of the kind suggested here, has by definition to be beyond the reach of current (especially malestream) understandings. The assertion of a separate realm is, however, only one of a range of responses in the cultural feminist movement; others include outright political activity and the discovery of the existing cultural contributions of women. As Brooke, one of the first to see in cultural feminism a move away from change as a political drive toward a therapy model of liberation, notes:

> Cultural feminism has evolved into spirituality and goddess-worshipping cults, disruptive 'dyketactics' groups and – more peacefully, academic cultural feminism, the main activity of which seems to be reading novels by women. (1980: 70)

One cannot but notice the similarity between 'dyketactics' and the Dadaist 'manifestations' of the early Surrealist movement. Moreover, there is a related and deliberate attempt to create an alternative world, one defined in complete isolation and separation from patriarchal culture. On the basis of an oppression that is common to women of all classes, races and cultures throughout history, political organization is replaced by an emphasis on building 'a powerful female culture with all the necessary accoutrements: music, art, poetry, films, religion, science, medicine – all female based. . . . [Cultural feminists] are often outspokenly antiauthoritarian, antileadership, and antistructure' (Valeska, 1981: 25).

There is a tension here, between the need to deconstruct a phallocentric world and the desire to create and enlarge the spaces within which women may come to be. There can be no doubt that the radical feminist attack on modernity is postmodern in its politics; in that sense, it has strong echoes of the Nietzschean influence on modernist attempts to undermine modernity. As Teresa de Lauretis points out:

> The questions of identification, self-definition, the modes of the very possibility of envisaging oneself as subject – which the male avant-garde artists and theorists have also been asking, on their part, for almost one hundred years, even as they work to subvert the dominant representations or to challenge their hegemony – are fundamental questions for feminism. (1985: 157)

This view of a feminist programme of action against the broad front of modernity generally and in terms of the cultural sphere in particular is reinforced by Gertrud Koch (1985). There is a *hope*, she says, that 'women might exorcise the demons of male technology while finding counter-images (gegenbilder) to those of the dominant male' (1985: 153). And this does represent a new, characteristically postmaterialist politics. It is reminiscent, too, of Nietzsche's turn toward the aesthetic mode for justification of his interpretation of society, and Surrealism's conviction that art can be a vehicle for making and moving toward a 'future culture'. For Koch:

> The most advanced aesthetic products represent a utopian anticipation of a yet to be fulfilled program of emancipated subjectivity: neither of a class nor of a movement or a collective, but as individuals, as concrete subjects they attempt to insist upon their authentic experience. (1985: 152)

There are two things of particular note in this search for what de Lauretis (1985: 165) calls 'a parallel universe, a time and a place elsewhere that look and feel like here and now, yet are not, just as I (and all women) live in a culture that is and is not our own'. First, the self in modernity is still a problem, but it is a new kind of subjectivity, seeking not merely to transcend unsatisfactory roles and definitions imposed by society (what Featherstone [1985: 5] refers to as the 'phallocentric order of subjectivity'), but to finding within itself the grounds and nature of its being (in Hassan's [1985: 123–4] sense of 'indetermanence').

Second, the usual, namely collectivist, solutions to the problem of modernity (existence) are rejected, much in the way that Nietzsche rejected mass movements and for some of the reasons Surrealism discovered to its cost. If the postmodern self is not yet fully possible, then any collectivity must be an oppressive one, at the very least distracting the individual from the demanding business of emancipation and the creation and construction of 'the conditions of representability of another social subject' (de Lauretis, 1985: 153). This deconstruction of the collectivity, even though it is postulated from within a universalizing (women's) movement, constitutes the most difficult challenge for any notion of politics which reaches for aggregative truths, inclusive reasoning and steady meanings. One lesson to be drawn from cultural feminism is that our human social connections, however general and however much they are experienced in common, need not be those of the group or the class as they have been theorized and made the basis for an understanding of politics.

Conclusion

In conclusion, let me make a few remarks about the questions raised at the start.

Can culture be political? Surrealism is intensely and unremittingly political in its desire and capacity to be a total revolution. Similarly, the cultural and metaphysical variants of radical feminism are pursuing a total revolution, while striving to transcend politics of the merely conventional kind. This is to make two claims about the connections between these movements, Nietzsche's thought and political culture.

First, his critique of modernity also challenges its successor, modernism. This critique cannot easily be absorbed into conventional political practice and understanding. It resists being deradicalized and made to serve the status quo. The challenge is always capable of being presented anew to modernity, and there are always new subversions to be found which can achieve this. There is no victory here of a political nature for either modernity or the new radicalism: each is locked into a conflict which ranges over the whole of social and cultural existence, highlighting how any aspect of existence can become a site for political battle of uncertain outcome, before the struggle, apparently 'won' or 'lost', re-emerges elsewhere.

Second, Nietzsche's thought offers a view that is both threatening and challenging to conventional interpretations of politics. There is the possibility that the understanding of power and hence society is better understood as a concern of aesthetics and culture, but not of politics. Those schooled in politics, then, are not the true revolutionaries, even though they may convince themselves that they are. Moreover, the schooling of the political revolutionary fosters ignorance, antagonism and superiority towards the true (cultural or aesthetic) revolutionary. Conventional politics, on this reading, is irretrievably *anti*revolutionary; it is hostile to culture and to women.

To press the claim of the aesthetic revolutionary, however, is to realize that, ultimately, the chances of any revolutionary theory realizing itself through cultural activity are slim indeed, perhaps slimmer than political and military means of bringing about change in society. This does not make the aesthetic revolution any less important, especially if a critical eye is passed over past successes of the conventionally political option.

Can politics be cultural? Politics always has been artistry in its many forms. The conflicts that I have set up between art, culture and politics are real enough, however, because the message is that politics is a subtheme of existence, *not* the organizing principle. Political interpretation is so often jealous of a domain over which it appears to preside but has never had full claim, namely human existence in all its multidimensionality and complexity.

Whether art can yield a better demonstration of the real and possible nature of the expressly political world is open to question still. Postmodern art, for example, seems much more unsettling and exploratory than postmodern architecture. Nevertheless, both represent a rekindling of the Surrealist spirit, a wakefulness and willingness that may, of course, be traduced and absorbed once more. Radical feminism, however, is especially alive to the propensity of patriarchy to render invisible women and their achievements, and constructs its culture, self-understanding and herstory accordingly.

At least in the West, the politics/art split, or the creation of an alternate culture, or a separate discourse, may be local peculiarities, products of false dichotomization imposed upon us by our habit of indulging in either/or thinking. On the other hand (and this is an example of that habit), there is no doubt that such questions are real and that the battle is still being fought between those who think that politics is capable of being quite narrowly defined and is or must be instrumental, and those who, like me (Forbes and Street, 1986), lament the exclusion of the apparently non-political and incline towards a more expressive politics. It is difficult, then, to share Hassan's (1985: 128) confidence that the conditions for a more open political culture already exist and are manifest in these very discussions, or that 'we live in one human universe and astonish each other with our assents'. These reflections do not amount to a conclusion at all, it must be observed, because they imply a demand for 'a new ethical form of life which foregrounds imagination, lucidity, humour, disciplined thought and practical wisdom' (Dreyfus and Rabinow, 1986: 121). This would constitute a political culture worthy of the name. Until that time, Surrealism and its successors, as well as present and future feminist struggles will go on challenging and subverting the political culture of modernity, since both movements acknowledge the importance of and explore the realities of otherness.

Notes

Thanks to John Gibbins for his encouragement.

1. The claim that Nietzsche is postmodernist as well as modernist is supported by Ihab Hassan's (1985: 121) observation that: 'Modernism and postmodernism are not separated by an Iron Curtain or Chinese Wall; history is a palimpsest, and culture is permeable to time past, time present, and time future.'

2. The impact of this approach is indicated by the number of terms now available to the cultural critic, from 'the decentred subject and the accentuation of difference' to 'the metaphysics of presence' and 'dispersal' and 'antinarrative'. See Featherstone (1985: passim).

3. 'A philosopher – is a human being who constantly experiences, sees, hears, suspects, hopes, and dreams extraordinary things; who is struck by his own thoughts as if from outside, as from above and below, as by *his* type of experiences and lightning bolts; who is perhaps himself a storm pregnant with new lightnings, a fatal human being around whom there are constant rumblings and growlings, crevices, and uncanny doings. A philosopher – alas, a being that often runs away from itself, often is afraid of itself – but too inquisitive not to "come to" again – always back to himself.' (Nietzsche, 1886: 292)

4. Pippin's use of the term modernism corresponds to my understanding of modernity.

5. This process is usually deemed to have begun with Rousseau's *Confessions*, and 'The Creed of the Savoyard Priest' in *Emile* (see Berman, 1971).

6. 'For Habermas, then, the problem of modernity, a unique historical problem, consists in preserving the primacy of reason . . . while facing up to the loss of metaphysical ground of our substantive beliefs.' (Dreyfus and Rabinow, 1986: 111)

7. As Robert Short remarks, Surrealism proceeds 'in the footsteps of Nietzsche' (1980: 135).

8. 'The military, the bourgeois industrialists, even the leaders of the Communist Party in France, tightening their power over the daily life of the population, had put up barricades against art and poetry, and therefore needed to be swept away.' (Carre, 1964: 78)

9. Of course, some may want to argue that this is a very reasoned attempt to discover the rational kernel beneath a discordant and confused but nevertheless superficial reality.

References

Balakian, Anna (1964) 'André Breton as Philosopher', *Yale French Studies*, 31.
Bell, Daniel (1976) *The Crucial Contradictions of Capitalism*. London: Heinemann.
Berman, Marshall (1971) *The Politics of Authenticity*. London: Allen & Unwin.
Beuys, Joseph (1974) *Art into Society, Society into Art*. Catalogue. London: Institute of Contemporary Arts.
Bovenschen, Silvia (1977) 'Is there a Feminist Aesthetic?' tr. B. Weckmueller, *New German Critique*, 10 (Winter).
Brooke (1980) 'The Chador of Women's Liberation: Cultural Feminism and the Movement Press', *Heresies* 3 (1), Issue 9.
Carre, Marie-Rose (1964) 'René Crevel: Surrealism and the Individual', *Yale French Studies*, 31.
Daly, Mary (1979) *Gyn/Ecology*. London: Women's Press.
Daly, Mary (1984) *Pure Lust*. London: Women's Press.
Dreyfus, Hubert and Rabinow, Paul (1986) 'What is Maturity? Habermas and Foucault

on "What is Enlightenment?"', in David Couzens Hoy (ed.), *Foucault: a Critical Reader*. Oxford: Blackwell.

Dworkin, Andrea (1974) *Woman Hating*. New York: Dutton.

Featherstone, Mike (1985) 'The Fate of Modernity: an Introduction', *Theory, Culture and Society*, 2 (3).

Forbes, Ian and Street, John (1986) 'Individual Transitions to Socialism', *Theory, Culture and Society*. 3 (1).

Frisby, David (1985) 'Georg Simmel, First Sociologist of Modernity', *Theory, Culture and Society*, 2 (3).

Habermas, Jürgen (1986) 'Taking Aim at the Heart of the Present', in David Couzens Hoy (ed.), *Foucault: a Critical Reader*. Oxford: Blackwell.

Hassan, Ihab (1985) 'The Culture of Postmodernism', *Theory, Culture and Society*, 2 (3).

Koch, Gertrude (1985) 'Ex-Changing the Gaze: Re-Visioning Feminist Film Theory', *New German Critique*, 34 (Winter).

Kroker, Arthur (1985) 'Baudrillard's Marx', *Theory, Culture and Society*, 2 (3).

Lauretis, Teresa de (1985) 'Aesthetic and Feminist Theory: Rethinking Women's Cinema', *New German Critique*, 34 (Winter).

MacIntyre, Alisdair (1981) *After Virtue*. Notre Dame: University of Notre Dame Press.

Marcuse, Herbert (1978) *The Aesthetic Dimension*. Boston: Beacon Press.

Nadeau, Maurice (1968) *The History of Surrealism*, tr. R. Howard. London: Cape.

Nietzsche, Friedrich (1872) *The Birth of Tragedy*, in *The Birth of Tragedy and the Genealogy of Morals*, tr. F. Golffing. New York: Doubleday Anchor, 1956.

Nietzsche, Friedrich (1882) *The Gay Science*, in *The Basic Writings of Nietzsche*, tr. and ed. W. Kaufmann. New York: Modern Library, 1966.

Nietzsche, Friedrich (1886) *Beyond Good and Evil*, in *The Basic Writings of Nietzsche*, tr. and ed. W. Kaufmann. New York: Modern Library, 1966.

Nietzsche, Friedrich (1887) *Genealogy of Morals*, in *Birth of Tragedy and the Genealogy of Morals*, tr. F. Golffing. New York: Doubleday Anchor, 1956.

Nietzsche, Friedrich (1901) *The Will to Power*, tr. W. Kaufmann and R. Hollingdale, ed. W. Kaufmann. New York: Vintage, 1968.

Owens, Craig (1983) 'The Discourse of Others: Feminists and Post-Modernism', in H. Foster (ed.), *The Anti-Aesthetic*. Washington.

Pangle, Thomas (1983) 'The Roots of Contemporary Nihilism and its Political Consequences according to Nietzsche', *The Review of Politics*, 45 (1).

Pippin, Ronert (1983) 'Nietzsche and the Origin of the Idea of Modernism', *Inquiry*, 26.

Putz, Peter (1978) 'Nietzsche: Art and Intellectual Inquiry', in M. Pasley (ed.), *Nietzsche: Imagery and Thought*. London: Methuen.

Rorty, Richard (1979) *Philosophy and the Mirror of Nature*. Princeton: Princeton University Press.

Schuster, Jean (1987) 'Specialists in Revolt', interviewed by Paul Hammond, *New Statesman*, 4 Dec.

Soupault, Philippe (1964) ' "Traces which Last" in Surrealism', *Yale French Studies*, 31: 9–22.

Short, Robert (1980) *Dada and Surrealism*. London: Book Club Associates.

Valeska, Lucia (1981) 'The Future of Female Separatism', in Quest Staff (eds), *Building Feminist Theory: Essays from Quest*. New York: Longman.

Warren, Mark (1985) 'The Politics of Nietzsche's Philosophy: Nihilism, Culture and Power', *Political Studies*, 33.

11

Incommensurability, International Theory and the Fragmentation of Western Political Culture

N.J. Rengger

At the end of his essay 'International Relations Theory 1919–69' the late Hedley Bull posed a question which reveals the tip of a conceptual iceberg for students of international relations, one which still remains largely uncharted. If, he wrote, available theories of how state and other agents in world politics do and should behave are 'almost exclusively Western in origin and perspective, can they convey an adequate understanding of a world political system that is predominantly non-Western?' (Bull, 1972: 55).

Now the locus of this question is clearly the view that the set of theoretical understandings developed by international relations scholars is no longer fully adequate to comprehend the changed and changing nature of the contemporary international order. Bull amplified his point in a later essay:

> It cannot be denied that the role of the Europeans in shaping an international society of worldwide dimension has been a special one . . . it was their conception of juridically equally sovereign states that came to be accepted by independent political communities everywhere as the basis of their relationships . . . by seeking a place in this society [the non-European or non-Western states] have given their consent to its basic rules and institutions. (1984: 123–4)

They are 'naturally and properly', of course, modifying it to their own especial interests and concerns (Bull, 1984: 124–6).

It is with the possibility and implications of this modification that I shall be chiefly concerned in this chapter, but before I begin I want to sketch in the character of the problem a little more fully. If it is granted that the prevailing assumptions of the international order are still predominantly Western (in inspiration at least) then the assertion that the conceptual foundations of these assumptions are now irredeemably fissured and that, consequently, the assumptions themselves are fatally compromised, is an extraordinarily serious one, and not just for the West. It is precisely this claim, however, which is

made by an increasingly large and influential group of thinkers drawn
from an astonishingly wide variety of backgrounds and disciplinary
perspectives.[1]

It is more worrying still for international relations theory when it is
remembered that the modes of understanding chiefly operative within
it come precisely from those areas most heavily under siege. One recent
survey of both Western and non-Western theory suggests three
conceptual underpinnings for contemporary international theory:

> Nineteenth century rationalism – the view that all things may be
> encompassed by reason; positivism – the argument that the aim of
> knowledge is the exact determination and exploration of facts; and
> pragmatism – the position that theories are valuable because of their
> practical application. (Beal and Misra, 1980: 1)

Now it is true that contemporary International Theory is very far
from being monolithic. A number of scholars have identified three
distinct 'paradigms' within it, and there is arguably a fourth; nonetheless the epistemological base for all these different approaches is, I
submit, at least one of the three sketched above. Identified variably as
the realist (or neorealist), structuralist and pluralist approaches, (with
a parvenu called critical international theory), the scope of possible
approaches in international theory is greater than at any time in the
development of international relations as a discrete subject of study,
and I for one am unambiguously supportive of such a development.
However, none of these various approaches has yet, I think, fully come
to terms with the problems that lie behind Bull's question, problems
which take us far beyond simply the question of the diversity of
cultural practices. I shall argue, in this chapter, that one of the keys to
unlocking this question is some version of what I shall choose to call
radical value incommensurability, predicated on a series of assumptions about the crisis of contemporary European culture. It is,
therefore, important to discuss the essentials, at least for international
theory, of the culture that is said to be so inwardly riven.

Western culture and international theory

Joseph Margolis has identified the generic sense of the term 'culture' as
identifying 'the space proper to persons, artworks, language, history,
institutions, civilizations, states, ideologies, myths and deeds' and they
have in common that:

> They obtain only in contexts formed by related phenomena. Artworks, for
> example, are produced by persons; persons are whatever they are not
> without some aggregative sharing of language; and the histories of states are
> projections of some kind that depend on the deeds of ideologically linked
> individuals. (1986: 653)

Margolis might have added that both conceptions of and perceptions about the relations between states are also a part of this phenomenon. As Lucien Pye has said, a political culture expresses 'attitudes, beliefs and sentiments that give order and meaning to the political process and provide the underlying assumptions and rules that govern behaviour' (Pye, 1966: 104–5).

In an influential essay, Martin Wight has attempted to distil a core of 'Western values' in international relations theory, meaning here 'the highest common factor of the range of beliefs by which Western men live' (1966a: 89) and by means of which they orientate themselves and their place in the world. This 'highest common factor', what Wight later calls a 'coherent pattern of ideas', is discernible in the history of Western culture and revolves around four key notions: (a) the idea of an International Society; (b) the maintenance of order within that society; (c) the idea of Intervention; (d) the assumption that there is an International Morality.

According to Wight one aspect of international relations related peculiarly to Western values is the cultivation of a 'moral middle ground':

Political morality is different from personal morality, as the moral duties of a trustee are different from those of one who acts on his own behalf . . . [there is] a permissible accommodation between moral necessity and practical demands. (1966a: 128)

There are writers in the Western tradition who hold a more absolute position (either one way or another) but even a cursory glance at the history of Western reflection on 'ethics in international politics' illustrates that Wight clearly has a point,[2] and that Grotius's assertion that 'a remedy must be found for those that believe that in war nothing is lawful, and for those for whom all things are lawful in war' (Butterfield and Wight, 1966: 9) echoes a very powerful tone in Western political thought, perhaps even a predominant one.

Let me pause for a moment and relate this discussion of Wight's to the notions of culture I mentioned briefly earlier on. Challenging the physicalism of Donald Davidson (1980), amongst others, Margolis points out that a homonomic explanation of the physical world cannot be sustained if it is the case that (for example) artworks and persons enter into causally efficacious relations, not reducible solely to physical properties and laws (Margolis, 1986: 659). As a backdrop to this discussion, a distinction explored by Charles Taylor between two concepts of a person active in the history of Western thought (roughly from the seventeenth century onward) is useful. Two views 'which . . . underpin a host of different positions and attitudes evident in modern culture' (Taylor, 1985a: 97–8). On the first view, what is essential to the peculiarly human powers of evaluating and choosing is the clarity and complexity of the computation '. . . what makes an agent a person, a fully human respondent, is [the] power to plan' (Taylor, 1985a: 104). On the second:

> The essence of evaluation no longer consists of assessment in the light of fixed goals, but also and even more in the sensitivity to certain standards, those involved in the peculiarly human goals. The sense of self is the sense of where one stands in relation to these standards . . . [personal agency] is no longer the power to plan but the openness to certain matters of significance. (Taylor, 1985a: 105)

For Taylor both these views are present in modern culture and are usually combined in an uneasy and tense alliance. The second perspective, which Taylor calls the 'significance' view, is tentative and exploratory whereas 'those who hunger for certainty will only find it in the first perspective' (1985a: 114). Now it is clear, I think, that in essentials Margolis is an advocate of the significance view and that (in a rather different way) so is Wight. Wight's via media, wherein he finds the pattern of ideas peculiar to Western culture in international relations, is essentially one, as he says, of a 'juste milieu between definable extremes' (1966: 91), the extremes being largely absolute certainty on the one hand and realist scepticism on the other. The language in which this is expressed is, as Wight says, necessarily full of qualifications and imprecision, and it is expressed in a memorable paragraph by Suarez:

> The human race, though divided into no matter how many different peoples and nations, has for all that a certain unity, a unity not merely physical, but also in a sense political and moral. This is shown by the natural precept of mutual love and mercy, which extends to all men . . . wherefore any state . . . be in itself a perfect community and constant in its members, nevertheless each of the states is also a member, in a certain manner, of the world. (Cited in Wight, 1966: 94–7)

If this is the core of Western political culture as far as international relations are concerned, Wight does not deny the existence of contrary views, with Hobbes and the realist school being the most prominent. Perhaps the most influential twentieth-century realist, Hans Morgenthau said that the key aspects of the realist interpretation of international politics were power, rationality and the balance of power (Morgenthau, 1948); most contemporary realist theorists would follow him in this, in form if not always in content. The most interesting and sophisticated adaptation of realist ideas in recent international theory, Kenneth Waltz's Theory of International Politics, is methodologically vastly superior to Morgenthau but is still arguing broadly the same case. His real originality, as Robert Keohane and others have perceptively pointed out, has been to attempt to wed the realist case to a powerful, rigorous systemic theory of international politics (Waltz, 1979; Keohane, 1984).

In Waltz, the first of Taylor's concepts of a person is clearly on view, partly in the assumed rationality that guides Waltz's enquiry and partly through the necessary belief in at least a degree of 'certainty' in the conclusions Waltz reaches. 'Our ends are seen as set by nature', Taylor says of his first perspective, 'and thus discoverable by objective scrutiny . . . [it is] beyond the ambiguous field of interpretation of the peculiarly human significances' (Taylor, 1985a: 113). Compare this with Waltz's criticism of Stanley Hoffman and Richard Rosecrance that:

> In order to turn a systems approach into a theory, one has to move from the usual vague identification of systematic forces and effects to their more precise specification, to say what units the system comprises, to indicate the comparative weights of systemic and subsystemic causes, and to show how forces and effects change from one system to another. (Waltz, 1979: 40-1)

Waltz clearly lays claim to the methodology of the natural sciences (though not in any manner of simplistic equivalence) when he adopts, as his definition of a theory, that 'theories explain Laws'.

Other structuralist theories also seem to rely on this. For example, world systems analysis argues that there is a single integrated world system with a logic and a structure of its own that we can perceive and accurately interpret (Wallerstein, 1976, 1980, 1982; Skocpol, 1977). Now while this method may not be positivistic it is certainly rationalistic, in the sense implied by Beal and Misra, and that some claims for certainty, for objectivity, are being made.

With pluralism, although the eclecticism of pluralistic approaches often obscures the fact, much the same applies. Although there are elements in, for example, Burton's world society approach (Burton, 1972; Banks, 1984) that look close to the significance view (especially his development of the idea of human needs), there is still the rationalistic claim that this is the truth for all, and that as a result, action *x* should be attempted, action *y* refrained from. The tension created in this approach is, I suspect, partly the result of attempting to work with both concepts of the human agent at once.

The problems inherent in this situation become clearer, I think, when the multicultural context of Bull's question is remembered. In a long, diffuse and characteristically stimulating paper, Adda Bozeman has drawn attention (1984) to the obvious and significant differences between European culture, and Indian, Chinese and African cultures. In particular, she argues, there is a crucial uniqueness in the European idea of individuation:

'This principle, rooted in the linguistic and intellectual heritage of Greece and Rome, was to remain the guiding force in Western approaches to the arts, sciences and letters as well as to religion, ethics, politics and law. The primary concern in each of these contexts was not the age set, the family, an economic class or caste . . . but the individual human being viewed here as the exclusive source of thought and the carrier of rights as well as obligations. (Bozeman, 1984: 390)

In the course of an extended rumination on the significance of this feature of European thought, and on its absence from other cultures, Bozeman comes to the conclusion that:

The majority of non-Western and non-communist states . . . have not accepted certain crucial European norms. The most important of these relate to . . . the whole complex of ideas that sustain the cause of self-determination and development and that makes it mandatory to think of the individual as an autonomous person and a citizen, endowed with rights as well as responsibilities . . . the post–1945 framework for the conduct of relations between states has come to rest precisely on these embattled norms. Thus we do not have . . . a globally meaningful system because the world society consists today, as it did before the nineteenth century, of a plurality of diverse political systems, each an outgrowth of culture specific concepts. (1984: 404)

The problem is more complex still, however, principally because these two views, both the rationalism and search for objectivity of much contemporary international theory and the thesis that there is a privileged and crucial uniqueness to European culture, are themselves under heavy, and potentially fatal, internal attack, and it is to this I now turn.

The challenge of radical incommensurability

The armies conducting this attack are, it must be admitted, in a decidedly unholy alliance (if, indeed, they are in any sort of alliance). They include the vanguard of continental postmodernism (Featherstone, 1985; Foucault, 1981), some luminaries of the now fragmented Frankfurt school (not, it should be emphasized, its most distinguished contemporary representative, Habermas), refugees from the once all-conquering analytic philosophy movement (Rorty, 1979; MacIntyre, 1981) and even some of the contemporary allies of analytic philosophy (Williams and Montefiore, 1981; Williams, 1985; Dunn, 1985).

Naturally enough so large a group of thinkers do not agree even amongst themselves about a good deal, but they are all agreed that the characteristic stances of modern European culture no longer cohere. In order to make clear what I take to be the implications of this view for contemporary international theory I shall concentrate on the aspect of my discussion to date that has been a thread linking otherwise very different accounts, that notion called by Bozeman 'individuation'. I shall take this to mean notions of personality and moral agency distinctive of modern Western culture in the sense discussed above, and shall address myself to the implications of what we can (without imprecision) refer to as the critique of modernity theories for this topic and its relation to international theory.

Of all the theorists I refer to above, perhaps the most disconcerting for our present question is Foucault. Habermas has called him a 'Stoic' (1986: 103) and the reason is clearly that Foucault's position, while very difficult to pigeonhole, seems to be an explicitly Nietzschean one of neutrality between all-competing value systems, frames of reference and validating criteria:

> Each society has its regime of truth, its general politics of truth; that is the type of discourse which it accepts and makes function as true; the mechanisms and instances which enable one to distinguish true and false statements, the means by which each is sanctioned; the techniques and procedures accorded value in the acquisition of truth; the status of those who are charged with saying what is true. (Foucault, 1981: 131)

We are trapped in notions of truth forced on us by our regime of power, the two together helping to establish the 'grid' within which we have our being. According to Ian Hacking: 'Foucault propounds an extreme nominalism: nothing, not even the ways I can describe myself, is either this or that but history [and, Foucault would probably add, contingency] made it so' (1986: 37).

Now the true significance of this for my concern in this paper is that, if Foucault is right, Bozeman's portrayal of the existing international order portrays not something that has happened just because certain societies do not accept Western norms but is something that is intrinsic to all notions of power, system, truth, understanding, explanation or justification. The fact of broad agreement (in, for example, the nineteenth century) is purely a contingent matter, one which will inevitably break down with the emergence of new, challenging regimes of power. In particular, those notions intrinsic, even unique in the Western approach to international theory, predicated as they are on certain equally unique notions of personality, agency and individuation, are in no sense true or right outside the characteristic stances of the grid for which they form part of the conceptual warrant. As John Dunn has argued:

> The claim to know better . . . can be vindicated only within identities . . . the only authority which it can possess is a human authority, an authority for human beings not an external domination over them . . . what it is to be modern is simply to face up to this knowledge. (1985: 153)

This claim is utterly destructive not only of specific parts of the Western approach to international theory (theories of international society discussed by Wight, for example, or the aspiration to explanatory certainty made by Waltz); it is destructive of the whole project of a rationalistic international political theory.

Interestingly, the point is present, at least in embryonic form, in Wight's own reflections. 'Is the capacity for detached self-scrutiny itself a Western quality', he asks at one point, 'the fruit of a "Western value"?' (1966a: 89). Elsewhere he goes even further:

> Theorizing has to be done in the language of political theory and of law . . .
> the language appropriate to man's control of his social life . . . the traditional
> effort of international lawyers to define the right of devastation and pillage
> in war: the long diplomatic debate in the nineteenth century about the right
> of intervention in aid of oppressed nationalities . . . all this is the stuff of
> international theory, and is constantly bursting the bounds of the language
> in which we try to handle it. (Wight, 1966b: 33)

Now, I am not, of course, attempting to assert any kind of equivalence between two scholars as dissimilar in outlook and interests as Foucault and Wight, but what to Wight is a troublesome question has, in Foucault, become the sword that can completely cut the Gordian knot which has been the constant effort of most Western international theorists, of whatever stamp, to produce: that there is, in some way, to some degree, a level of theorizing about international relations which can produce a non-culturally relative interpretation of, or mode of understanding for, the international order.

It is the general position adopted by Foucault, and others, that I call radical incommensurability: incommensurability because the claim is made that gradations of power, knowledge, truth and value are, and can only be, susceptible of internal definition and location;[3] radical because the claim is that all such gradations or criteria are so ordered, and that there is no way out. This affects 'scientific' approaches to theory as completely as it does Wight's or Bull's more diffuse, historical one, for, of course, as studies such as those of Rorty (1979) and Kuhn (1962) have ably demonstrated, science is as vulnerable to this kind of hermeneutic reductionism as history or ethics. Waltz, of course, is fully aware of the Kuhnian account of the nature of scientific theories, indeed he uses it to bolster his own approach, but he fails to take on board the fact that if Kuhn's views are extended beyond the boundaries of science (as Rorty has done [1979]), then the possibility of using science (which would naturally be part of a 'regime of power', part of a particular conceptual 'grid') to attempt to understand systems, structures and meanings non-congruent with that grid is doomed to conceptual incoherence from the start.

If this kind of argument is correct, 'Western values in international relations' will remain not only stubbornly Western, but such values cannot be meaningful outside the grid which originally gave them meaning, nor will any attempt to understand the complex natural and systemic pattern of the contemporary order on principles or methods themselves intrinsic to a particular cultural grid, be possible.

International theory in a fragmented world

What, then, are the implications of all this, and is there a way out? An interesting place to start is Ernest Gellner's essay 'Relativism and Universals' (1985); a spectre, he says, haunts human thought: relativism. 'If truth has many faces', he has this spectre assert, 'not one of them deserves trust or respect' (1985: 83). The problem of relativism, Gellner thinks, dissolves into two problems: 'but those two problems are absolutely fundamental: is there but one kind of man or are there many? Is there but one world, or are there many? These two questions are not identical but they are not unconnected either' (1985: 83). Gellner concedes that it is perfectly plausible to conceive of a plurality of worlds and truths, but he points out that:

> Such relativism is perfectly compatible with the existence of any number of, so to speak, de facto or contingent human universals. In a world unbounded by any unique truth, it might still be the case, by accident, that all human languages had a certain grammatical structure, that chromatic perception was identical in all cultures, that all societies proscribed certain relations as incestuous. (1985: 85)

Of course the reverse might be the case, 'it is possible that relativism may be false, and yet no universals obtain (or only trivial ones)' (Gellner, 1985: 86).

Gellner's conclusion is that the two questions are not the same because:

> The problem of relativism is . . . whether all the divergent visions of reality can in the end be shown (leaving out cases when they are simply mistaken) to be diverse aspects of one and the same objective world, whose diversity can itself be explained in terms of the properties or laws of that world. (1985: 87)

This is not the same question as whether or not man is one and unique, and not only are the questions distinct. Gellner thinks that the widely assumed view that a positive answer to the first depends upon a positive answer to the second is seriously incorrect. Indeed he argues that the reverse obtains:

> The positive answer to the first hinges on a negative answer to the second. The uniqueness of the world hinges on the diversity, the non-universality of man. There is one world only, there are many men; and just because there are many kinds of men, there is one world. For the unique world is the achievement of some men only. (1985: 87)

This one world is, of course, that of Western science and its assumptions. It is a world both public and symmetrical: 'symmetrical in that it contains within itself no privileged places, times, individuals or groups, which would be allowed to exempt cognitive claims from testing or scrutiny' (Gellner, 1985: 88). Gellner suggests that there are a number of non-question begging ways of supporting this position and discusses two of them in detail; the epistemological and the sociological. In the former an initial assumption is that anything may be true:

> We ask, how can we pick out the correct option of belief, seeing that we have no prior indication of what it may be? The answer is contained in the epistemological tradition which has accompanied the rise of modern science . . . if cumulative and communicable knowledge is to be possible at all, then the principle of orderliness must also apply to it . . . the inherently idiosyncratic has no place in a corpus of knowledge. (Gellner, 1985: 90)

The sociological level of support, on the other hand, argues that:

> The world contains many communities, but they are seen to inhabit the same world and compete within it. Some are cognitively stagnant, and a few are even regressive; some on the other hand, possess enormous, and indeed growing cognitive wealth, which is, so to speak, validated by works as well as faith; its implementation leads to very powerful technology . . . those who do not possess such knowledge and technology endeavour to emulate and acquire it. (Gellner, 1985: 91)

This approach is revealing for my concerns in this paper for two related reasons. Consider first the epistemological prop to his thesis. I submit that while it might put a spoke in the wheels of (at least some) relativities, it fails even to dent the armour of the conceptual tank surrounding the proponents of what I have called radical incommensurability. For Rorty, for example, the history of the rise of 'epistemology', far from being a confirmation of the uniqueness of the Western world view, is a triumphant assertion of the role of contingency in the history of thought (Rorty, 1979: 330–1); on Rorty's account of this history, 'to proclaim our loyalty to (Western) distinctions is not to say that there are objective and rational standards for adopting them'. For Rorty himself, of course, these distinctions are simply all part of the seamless 'conversation of the West' and of the West's 'conversation' with other cultures. However, such a view would destroy Gellner's 'one world' thesis comprehensively, because for him there must be rational reasons for the adoption of Western norms and for their adoption outside the West, at least under certain circumstances.

Neither, though, can he take refuge in his sociological explanation. While it is certainly the case that those who do not adopt the kind of knowledge and technology possessed by the West, broadly speaking, attempt to emulate it, this gives at best circumstantial support to the 'one world' hypothesis, certainly not enough to prove much of a problem to the hydra of incommensurability. As Ronald Dore has suggested in his perceptive essay on 'Unity and Diversity in World Culture': 'when one says that, other things being equal, an increasing density of communication should ensure an increasing basis for fellow feeling between the nations . . . one has to acknowledge that some of the things that may not be equal can be very important indeed' (1984: 423). For the advocates of incommensurability one of the things that would most certainly not be equal would be what would count as relevant perceptions of the required reality, and, consequently, what would count as an increase in fellow feeling. The putative history of the 'increase of fellow feeling' could never take place if, as Foucault argues, we must 'record the singularity of events outside of any monotonous finality; [we] must seek them in the most unpromising places . . . to isolate the different scenes where they engaged in different roles' and that the only role for 'the historical sense' (for Foucault) is to give 'the kind of disassociating view . . . capable of shattering the unity of man's being through which it was thought he could extend his sovereignty to the events of the past' (Foucault, 1977: 139–40).

In other words, an argument like Gellner's could never undercut radical incommensurability theses that would do away with all the familiar conceptual signposts that the analysis rests on (such as 'epistemology' as, in a sense, foundational). Foucault's reference to history, however, gives us a clue at least to a glimmer of light, perhaps the faintest trace of light at the end of the tunnel. Charles Taylor, in an acute critical essay on Foucault again points the way. Simply that:

> We have become certain things in Western civilization, our humanitarianism, our notions of freedom . . . have helped to define a political identity we share and one which is deeply rooted in our more basic understandings . . . of course these elements of identity are contested . . . but they all count for us. (1985b: 181)

We have, in short, already become something, we have a history: we are 'not just self enclosed in the present, but essentially related to a past which has helped define our identity, and a future which puts it again in question' (Taylor, 1985b: 182).

I want to elaborate on this by assuming that Taylor is correct in conceiving the history of Western thought about the person and its agency as a divided one. Given this it is likely, as Taylor himself suggests, that our practices will also be held in an analogous tension and that therefore any attempt at understanding either the practices or their conceptual alter egos must take this into account. If the analysis of Western international thought offered by Wight, Bull, Bozeman, Dore and others is even partially correct – and elsewhere I have offered reasons for suggesting that it is, at least in a modified form (Rengger, 1988b) – then such notions hold the key to an adequate understanding of the Western tradition of international thought; what we have become, as Taylor says.

This form of international theory, involving as it does what Rorty (1984) would call the creation of 'thick' geistesgesichte as well as detailed intellectual history is largely immune to the problems posed by radical incommensurability that I have outlined above. International theory conducted in this way is not immune from normative questions, because these are the stuff of any living tradition of thought, but they will take the form of 'conversations' within and between the representatives of the Western tradition and as such the extreme form of incommensurability adopted by Foucault, for example, falls at the fence erected by Charles Taylor.

However, Western political culture is not only internally fragmented, its paradigmatic status in the international system that grew out of it is increasingly under strain, if it has not already collapsed. The modifications of the tradition being attempted by non-Western societies, added to the disputes within the tradition itself, make it impossible to see the world society through one perspective any longer. Thus any theory which depends so heavily on the rationalist assumptions common to much contemporary international theory (as Waltz's does, for example) fails in the sense that it cannot convey the extent to which the paradigm that gives it meaning is now a thoroughly fragmented one, and in failing to do this it fails to convey a fundamental component of contemporary international relations and of our attempts to understand it.

Conclusion

The implications of this seem to me to leave us with both a regret and an opportunity. The regret is that the kind of large-scale, holistic, explanatory and normative theory that many contemporary international theorists aspire to will never be a sound conceptual bet until the thesis of radical incommensurability has been adequately overcome and that is some time away I suspect, to say the least. The opportunity, however, is to recognize that international theory is not a distinct body of enquiry but is part of the wider debates and discussions that are increasingly coming to characterize contemporary political and social theory; that it is an eclectic enquiry and that, particularly in the present circumstances, it should be prepared to experiment as it has not, perhaps, since the late Renaissance. If the world system is undergoing significant change (and practically everyone agrees about that, at least), then innovation and novelty in method may bring unexpected benefits. As Guicciardini presciently remarked four and a half centuries ago: 'Since the affairs of the world are subject to chance and to a thousand and one different accidents, there are many ways in which the passage of time may bring unexpected help to those who persevere in their obstinacy' (1965: 39).

Notes

1. See, for example, Rorty, 1979; MacIntyre, 1981; Foucault, 1981. The literature on this is vast so I do not propose to do more than scratch the surface here.
2. Wight has in mind, of course, the realists as well as thinkers such as Hobbes, Bodin, and Machiavelli.
3. I take the notion of incommensurability from discussions originally in the philosophy of science, though it has been applied elsewhere.

References

Banks, Michael (ed.) (1984) *Conflict in World Society*. Brighton: Wheatsheaf.
Beal, R.S. and Misra, K.P. (eds) (1980) *International Relations Theory: Western and Non-Western Perspectives*. New Delhi: Vikas.
Bozeman, Adda (1984) 'The International Order in a Multi-Cultural World', in Bull and Watson (1984).
Bull, Hedley (1972) 'International Relations Theory 1919-69', in Porter (1972).
Bull, Hedley (1977) *The Anarchical Society*. London: Macmillan.
Bull, Hedley (1984) 'The Emergence of a Universal International Society', in Bull and Watson (1984).
Bull, Hedley and Watson, Adam (eds) (1984) *The Expansion of International Society*. Oxford: Clarendon Press.
Burton, John W. (1972) *World Society*. Cambridge: Cambridge University Press.
Butterfield, Herbert and Wight, Martin (eds) (1966) *Diplomatic Investigations*. London: Allen & Unwin.
Cox, Robert W. (1981) 'Social Forces, States and World Orders: Beyond International Relations Theory', *Millennium: Journal of International Studies*, 10.
Davidson, Donald (1980) *Essays on Action and Events*. Oxford: Clarendon Press.
Dore, Ronald (1984) 'Unity and Diversity in World Culture', in Hedly Bull and Adam Watson (eds), *The Expansion of International Society*. Oxford: Clarendon Press.
Dunn, John (1985) *Rethinking Modern Political Theories*. Cambridge: Cambridge University Press.
Featherstone, Mike (1985) 'The Fate of Modernity: an Introduction', *Theory, Culture and Society*, 2 (3).
Foucault, Michel (1977) *Language, Counter-Memory Practice: Selected Essays and Interviews*, ed. D.F. Bouchard. New York: Cornell University Press.
Foucault, Michel (1981) *Power/Knowledge*. New York: Pantheon.
Gellner, Ernest (1985) *Relativism and Universals*. Cambridge: Cambridge University Press.

250   *Contemporary Political Culture*

Guicciardini, Francesco (1965) *Maxims and Reflections of a Renaissance Statesman*, tr. Mario Donnard. New York: Harper Torch Books.
Habermas, Jürgen (1986) 'Taking Aim at the Heart of the Present', in Hoy (1986).
Hacking, Ian (1986) 'The Archeology of Foucault', in Hoy (1986).
Hoy, D.C. (ed.) (1986) *Foucault: a Critical Reader*. Oxford: Blackwell.
Keohane, Robert (ed.) (1984) *Neo-Realism and Its Critics*. New York: Columbia University Press.
Kuhn, Thomas (1962) *The Structure of Scientific Revolutions*. Chicago: University of Chicago Press.
MacIntyre, Alasdair (1981) *After Virtue*. London: Duckworth.
Margolis, Joseph (1986) 'Constraints on the Metaphysics of Culture', *Review of Metaphysics*, 39.
Morgenthau, Hans J. (1948) *Politics among Nations: the Struggle for Power and Peace*. New York: A.A. Knopf.
Porter, B. (ed.) (1972) *The Aberystwyth Papers: International Politics, 1919-1969*. London: Oxford University Press.
Pye, Lucien (1966) *Aspects of Political Development*. Boston, Mass.: Little, Brown.
Rengger, N.J. (1988a) 'Going Critical? A Response to Hoffman', *Millennium: Journal of International Studies*, 17 (2).
Rengger, N.J. (1988b) 'Serpents and Doves in Classical International Theory', *Millennium: Journal of International Studies*, 17 (3).
Rorty, Richard (1979) *Philosophy and the Mirror of Nature*. Princeton: Princeton University Press.
Skocpol, Theda (1977) 'Wallerstein's World Capitalist Systems: a Critique', *American Journal of Sociology*, 82.
Taylor, Charles (1985a) *Human Agency and Language*, Collected Philosophical Papers, Vol. 1. Cambridge: Cambridge University Press.
Taylor, Charles (1985b) *Philosophy and the Human Sciences*, Collected Philosophical Papers, Vol. 2. Cambridge: Cambridge University Press.
Wallerstein, Immanuel (1976) *The Modern World System*, Vol. 1. London: Sage.
Wallerstein, Immanuel (1980) *The Modern World System*, Vol. 2. London: Sage.
Wallerstein, Immanuel (1982) *World Systems Analysis*. London: Sage.
Waltz, Kenneth (1979) *Theory of International Politics*. Reading, Mass.: Addison Wesley.
Wight, Martin (1966a) 'Western Values in International Relations', in Butterfield and Wight (1966).
Wight, Martin (1966b) 'Why is There No International Theory?' in Butterfield and Wight (1966).
Williams, Bernard and Montefiore, Alan (eds) (1981) *British Analytic Philosophy*. London: Routledge & Kegan Paul.
Williams, Bernard (1985) *Ethics and the Limits of Philosophy*. London: Collins.

12

Observations on Cultural Change and Postmodernism

Ronald Inglehart

In his thought-provoking essay in this book, Bo Reimer argues that the orientations of young people are too diverse to be contained inside a materialist/postmaterialist value conception. On this point he is clearly correct. The materialist/postmaterialist construct was conceived and operationalized to measure one precisely defined component of a human world-view that is manifestly multidimensional (Inglehart, 1977, 1988). It focuses on one dimension of what people seek in life, without attempting to encompass everything.

The concept of postmodernism, by contrast, is amorphous. Defined as 'a space where diverse social and intellectual tendencies converge and clash', almost anything, including postmaterialism, could fit into this diffuse concept. Indeed, postmaterialism fits particularly well because one of its characteristics is the fact that it has raised new issues and a new axis of conflict. Less than a generation ago, a materialist consensus reigned. Both left and right, both Marxists and capitalists agreed that economic growth was a good thing – they simply disagreed on how its fruits should be distributed. Today, with the rise of postmaterialism, the value of economic growth itself has been called into question – together with traditional views on work, authority, traditional religion, sexual and social norms (Inglehart, 1989).

Because it has introduced a major axis of social and political polarization, the emergence of a sizeable and articulate postmaterialist minority has made Western culture even more heterogeneous than it was two or three decades ago. Though the materialistic/post-materialistic dimension does *not* encompass any culture as a whole, it seems to be an important factor contributing to the evolution of the postmodernist culture much discussed in this volume.

Though I would agree with the first of Reimer's points, he advances a second argument that I find untenable. He argues that West European youth is no longer postmaterialist – and presents Swedish data that seem to demonstrate the point. They indicate that, as of 1986, age was uncorrelated with materialistic/postmaterialistic values. Here Reimer seems to be mistaken for (as Table 1 shows) survey evidence from a number of West European societies demonstrate that as recently as 1986–87, materialist/postmaterialist values were very strongly related to age: in all twelve member-countries of the European

Table 1   *Distribution of materialist (M) and postmaterialist (PM)*
value types by age cohort in eleven Western nations (1986–7)

Age range in 1986	Netherlands M	PM	West Germany M	PM	Denmark M	PM	United Kingdom M	PM
15–20	8	36	7	32	16	19	12	19
21–30	12	33	11	36	13	30	18	19
31–40	13	27	13	31	17	24	22	16
41–50	18	23	18	22	21	18	18	15
51–60	24	16	24	15	26	9	23	11
61–70	24	13	24	14	29	8	29	9
71–80	30	7	31	10	36	7	34	11
Total	17	25	17	24	21	18	22	15

Age range in 1986	France M	PM	Belgium M	PM	Italy M	PM	Ireland M	PM
15–20	24	15	27	20	25	15	20	19
21–30	27	21	30	18	25	16	31	9
31–40	31	18	32	17	29	13	37	8
41–50	34	14	38	16	40	9	41	7
51–60	38	8	45	10	42	7	42	6
61–70	42	7	48	10	52	4	55	3
71–80	50	4	59	9	44	4	47	6
Total	33	14	38	15	35	11	37	9

Age range in 1986	Spain M	PM	Greece M	PM	Portugal M	PM	European Community M	PM
15–20	20	24	26	16	37	12	18	21
21–30	25	21	34	14	44	8	23	22
31–40	37	14	44	8	49	6	27	18
41–50	51	7	53	5	52	6	32	13
51–60	62	3	53	4	59	5	36	9
61–70	58	3	60	4	68	3	38	9
71–80	69	1	68	1	75	1	44	6
Total	43	12	46	8	52	6	30	15

Number of cases for each country are: Netherlands, 2,919; West Germany, 2,820; Denmark 2,848; United Kingdom, 2,930; France, 2,850; Belgium, 2,828; Italy, 3,116; Ireland, 2,921; Spain, 2,702; Greece, 2,726; Portugal, 2,768.
Figures for the European Community are weighted according to the population of each country.

Source: Combined results from *Euro-Barometer* surveys 25, 26 and 27 (carried out in Spring 1986, Fall 1986 and Spring 1987, respectively)

Community, the young were far more apt to have postmaterialist value priorities than were their elders.

Let us examine the evidence in Table 1. For each of eleven nations, it shows the distribution of the materialist and postmaterialist value types among seven birth cohorts, ranging from a youngest group that was 15–20 years old in 1986, to an oldest cohort that was from 71 to 80 years old. To save space in a complex table, the mixed types are not shown, but they constitute roughly half the population in each country. The countries are ordered according to the ratio of materialists to postmaterialists in the population as a whole, starting with the Netherlands, West Germany and Denmark (where there are about as many postmaterialists as materialists); to Spain, Greece and Portugal (where the materialists vastly outnumber the postmaterialists). In keeping with our theory, postmaterialists are more numerous in the richer countries than in the poorer ones.

For the European Community as a whole, we find that materialists were still about twice as numerous as postmaterialists in 1986–7. This reflects a substantial increase in the relative proportion of post-materialists, since 1970 (Abramson and Inglehart, 1987). And the change is largely due to intergenerational population replacement. As Table 1 demonstrates, the distribution of the two pure value types change dramatically, as we move from oldest to youngest cohort. The combined European Community results (shown in the lower right-hand corner of the table) reveal that, among the oldest cohort, materialists outnumber postmaterialists by a ratio of more than 7 to 1, with nearly half the cohorts falling into the pure materialist category, and only 6 percent being postmaterialists. The ratio of postmaterialists to materialists rises steadily as we move from older to younger cohorts, until we reach the 21–30 year old group, where the two types are almost evenly balanced; and when we move to the youngest cohort, post-materialists actually outnumber the materialists.

The same basic pattern occurs in every one of the eleven nations from which we have data (it occurs also in the twelfth European Community member, Luxembourg: but because our samples from that country are smaller and less reliable than the other samples, we do not show these results here). In every case, without exception, the young are much more likely to have postmaterialist value priorities than are the old.

Though this basic pattern is constant, the actual distribution of values varies a good deal cross-nationally. Thus in the Netherlands, among the oldest cohort, materialists outnumber postmaterialists by more than 4 to 1, but among all of the groups less than 50 years of age, postmaterialists outnumber the materialists – and among the very youngest cohort, they outnumber them overwhelmingly, by more than

4 to 1. In Portugal, by contrast, among the oldest cohort, materialists outnumber postmaterialists by a ratio of 75:1, with postmaterialists being virtually non-existent. And even among the youngest cohort, materialists still outnumber postmaterialists by better than 3:1. The process of value change has moved farther in the more prosperous countries than in the poorer ones; but in all twelve countries, the young are far more likely to be postmaterialists than are the old.

The contrast between Reimer's findings and our own is truly striking. How can we explain this contradiction? One possible explanation would lie in the fact that Reimer's evidence comes from Sweden, while my own comes from eleven other West European societies. Could it be that Sweden is, for some reason completely different from the rest of Europe in the way its culture has been evolving? I doubt that this is the case, but there are some plausible reasons why one might expect to find smaller differences between the values of younger and older generations in Sweden than elsewhere.

Our theory of value change hypothesizes that intergenerational value differences reflect differences in the degree of economic and physical security that prevailed during the formative years of the respective cohorts. The older generation, who were shaped by the violence and hunger of the Great Depression and the Second World War, would be more likely to give top priority to materialist goals such as maintaining order and economic stability, while the younger cohorts, raised in the relative security and prosperity of the postwar era, would be likelier to give top priority to such postmaterialist goals as belonging and self-expression.

Sweden constitutes something of a deviant case in two respects. First, it has for many decades been one of the world's leading welfare states. As such, even older Swedes were relatively sheltered from the economic insecurity that shaped their counterparts in other countries: consequently, they might be less materialistic in their values and more similar to the younger generation in their country.

Sweden constitutes a deviant case in another respect also: she remained neutral during the Second World War, and was spared the devastation and turmoil that afflicted nearly all of her neighbours during that era. This too implies that in Sweden the formative experience of the older generation differed less from that of their younger compatriots than is true in most other West European countries.

These arguments seem plausible, but the empirical evidence provides little support for an interpretation based on Swedish uniqueness. For one thing both Denmark and the Netherlands also rank among the world's most advanced welfare states, providing high levels of security against economic deprivation. Though this is a relatively recent development in the Dutch case, it has held true of Denmark for almost as long as Sweden. If Sweden were a deviant case because of her advanced social welfare legislation, we might expect to find a similar pattern of weak intergroup differences in Denmark and the Netherlands as well. But in fact the age-related differences are almost as large in Denmark and the Netherlands as anywhere else.

Another possible reason why Sweden might be a deviant case is the fact that she did not take part in the Second World War. But both Ireland and Portugal were also neutrals – and we find relatively strong evidence of intergenerational value differences in both cases (Spain, of course, was also neutral during the Second World War, but the Spanish Civil War caused devastation and loss of life comparable to that of the Second World War). It is still possible to argue that age-related value differences are absent only if a society has been spared *both* the physical upheaval of war *and* has the sense of economic security provided by advanced social legislation – but this begins to seem like bending over backwards to save the hypothesis. Perhaps Sweden is *not* really a deviant case: perhaps its different pattern is an artefact.

This possibility exists, and it could explain the apparent contrast between the pattern Reimer found in Sweden, and the one we found everywhere else we have looked. For Reimer's survey used a technique to measure materialist/postmaterialist values that differs from the one that has been used everywhere else. The change that was introduced in Sweden may seem slight – at first glance seemingly too insignificant to affect the results in any decisive fashion. But in fact the change was crucial: for the Swedish survey did *not* actually measure one's value *priorities*; instead, it simply asks the respondent to rate the importance of a list of items that include both materialist and postmaterialist goals.

This technique is much easier and faster than forcing the respondent to weigh one goal against the other, choosing which one should be given priority over others. With the rating approach, one can simply race through the list, giving high ratings to all or nearly all of the goals. Reimer argues that this is actually an *advantage* of his method, for it enables one to give top ratings to *both* the materialist and post-materialist items. But this is precisely the problem. We are not seeking to identify those respondents who give high ratings to all items, and those who give low ratings to everything. The tendency to do so – also known as response set – may be interesting methodologically, but our theory focuses on something else: we are interested in people's *priorities*.

In Western society, almost everyone is in favour of free speech *and* of order; of economic growth *and* protecting the environment. But in politics it is sometimes necessary to choose *between* competing goals,

256   *Contemporary Political Culture*

both of which are desirable. Quite often, the most crucial and significant political decisions are of this nature: in a given situation one must decide whether to give priority to liberty over order; or decide whether to build a highway, even at the cost of cutting down trees. It is easier to pretend that difficult choices such as these do not exist. Thus, we have politicians who promise to balance the budget without raising taxes, *and* to spend more on defence and social services. When they get into office, reality strikes back: choices must be made.

The forced choice format that is used, in the standard way of measuring materialist/postmaterialist values, reflects this reality. Almost everyone is in favour of free speech – but *not* everyone is willing to give it priority over maintaining order. In fact, in advanced Western societies, we find massive differences between the priorities of older and younger generations. I suspect that such differences would emerge in Sweden, as well, if the respondent's *priorities* were measured rather simply by their tendency to give high or low ratings to a series of goals.

Until the relevant data are available, I retain an open mind on the subject. It may be that Sweden actually *is* a striking deviant case – and, if so, it behoves us to probe further into determining why it is. In any event, we are indebted to Reimer for providing a stimulating contribution on this subject. The process of cultural change has far-reaching implications. It merits serious investigation from a variety of perspectives.

References

Abramson, Paul and Inglehart, Ronald (1987) 'The Future of Postmaterialist Values: Population Replacement Effects, 1970–1985 and 1985–2000', *Journal of Politics*, 49 (Feb.): 231–41.

Inglehart, Ronald (1976) 'Changing Values and Attitudes toward Military Service among the American Public', pp. 255–80 in Nancy Goldman and David Segal (eds), *The Social Psychology of Military Service*. Beverly Hills: Sage.

Inglehart, Ronald (1977) *The Silent Revolution: Changing Values and Political Styles among Western Publics*. Princeton: Princeton University Press.

Inglehart, Ronald (1981) 'Post-Materialism in an Environment of Insecurity', *American Political Science Review*, 75 (4): 880–900.

Inglehart, Ronald (1982) 'Changing Values in Japan and the West', *Comparative Political Studies*, 14 (4): 445–80.

Inglehart, Ronald (1985) 'New Perspectives on Value Change: Responses to Lafferty and Knutsen, Savage, Böltken and Jagodzinski', *Comparative Political Studies*, 17 (4): 485–532.

Inglehart, Ronald (1986) 'Aggregate Stability and Individual-Level Change in Mass Belief Systems: the Level of Analysis Paradox', *American Political Science Review*, 79 (1): 97–117.

Inglehart, Ronald (1989) *Culture Shift in Advanced Industrial Society*. Princeton: Princeton University Press.

13

Constructing Value Orientations:
Reply to Ronald Inglehart

Bo Reimer

The generous and stimulating response by Ronald Inglehart to my chapter 'Postmodern Structures of Feeling' deals primarily with my statement that Western European youth is no longer postmaterialist. Focusing on the empirical part of my chapter, Inglehart discusses the possible reasons for my (to the postmaterialist hypothesis) contradictory findings concerning Swedish youth. One reason, he argues, might be substantial (Swedish youth differs in its value orientations from youth in other Western European countries), another reason might be methodological (a rating technique gives different results from a ranking technique when measuring people's values). Inglehart finds the second reason to be the more plausible, retaining an open mind on my statement until Swedish data collected with the 'proper' techniques are available.

I agree with Inglehart that my contradictory findings are probably not due to any substantial differences in value orientations between Swedish and, say, Danish youth. And, if we were to accept the proposed distinction between substantial and methodological reasons, then the differences in results would seem to be purely methodological. This is not the only possible interpretation, however.

It is obvious that the technique used to measure theoretical constructs matters. Presumably a ranking technique would in Sweden give results similar to those gathered in other countries. The use of the small four-item scale in another Swedish survey seems to suggest this (Reimer, 1988). In the same way, results gathered with the help of a rating technique in other Western European countries would probably not be unlike the results presented here.

Nevertheless, my point is that these techniques are based on different theoretical conceptions – and that the choice between them therefore has to be justified theoretically. The 'correct' technique cannot be decided on the basis of data. The choice of measurement technique cannot be made outside substantial and theoretical considerations. It belongs *inside* theory (Reimer, 1985). The Swedish data were used in what I believe to be the only way possible in this context; to demonstrate and add strength to my hypothesis, not to verify it.

For obvious reasons, there is no space here to justify in detail why I believe the rating technique to be the most appropriate. Briefly, it is based on the belief that it may more accurately mirror the way value conflicts are solved in daily life. Very seldom is one in the position to invoke just the one, supreme value. Rather, in concrete day-to-day situations one has to take into account different, sometimes contradictory, values, having to make compromises between them. Inside a framework that I would like to denote *the whole formation of values*, the importance assigned to each value is determined in its relations to *other* values. The forced either/or distinction created by a ranking technique may make for ideal types but may not be equally valid for living beings in historically specific settings.

These tentative remarks should be treated precisely as such; as remarks in an ongoing discussion, not as definitive statements. No doubt one of the strengths of Professor Inglehart's postmaterialist hypothesis is that, after almost twenty years, there is still room for theorizing. For this we are truly grateful.

References

Reimer, Bo (1985) 'Values and the Choice of Measurement Technique: the Rating and Ranking of Postmaterialism', Working Paper 8, Unit of Mass Communication, University of Gothenburg, Sweden.

Reimer Bo (1988) 'No Values – New Values? Youth and Postmaterialism', *Scandinavian Political Studies*, 11: 347–59.

Index

260 Contemporary Political Culture

'Fight Nuclear Death', 174, 178, 180–2, *183*,
  184–8, *188*, 190, 192
1980s, 174, 178–9, *179*, 182–4, *183*, 186–7,
  189, 189–93, *191*
Pekonen, Kyösti, 19, 127–42
Phillips, Howard, 89
philosophy, analytic, 242
Pippin, Robert, 221
pluralism
  of feelings, 111
  in international theory, 241–2
  in political culture, 23, 123, 201, 207, 209,
    211
  in research, 13
politics
  abstraction, 136–8
  and art, 224–5, 229–30, 232, 234
  in culture, 127–9, 133–4
  as culture, 129–32
  new, 1, 9, 16, 24, 82, 95–7, 99–100, 103, 131–
    2, 141, 174, 176–8, 184, 188–9, 191–2; and
    trade unions, 154, 156, 158–9, 161, 163–6,
    168; USA, 44–5
  old, 88–95, 155, 156–8, 165, 176, 177–8, 191,
    193n
  parliamentary, 137–9, 141
  personalization, 19, 127, 132, 138–41
  and values, 131
populism, 23, 45, 57, 75n, 81, 89, 91, 212
Portugal, value conflicts, 22–3
postindustrialism, 12, 15, 81, 83, 87, 147, 185,
  199–200, 205–6
postmaterialism, 7, 8–11, 16–17, 21, 24, 43, 69–
  70, 82–3, 110
  and neoconservatism, 85–90, 95–8, 102–3
  and peace protest, 189
  and postmodernism, 16–17, 112–13, 251
  theory and method, 111–12
  and trade unions, 158–9, 166
  and young people, 85–6, 103, 113–17, *115*,
    123
postmodernism
  criticism of, 212–15
  definition, 14–16, 110–11, 146–7, 251
  earlier roots, 200, 203, 212–15, 218–34
  and politics, 2, 14–20, 23–4, 110, 199, 207,
    222–5
  and status politics, 202, 206, 209–12
power, bureaucratization, 201
protest potential, 10, 56, 61, 62, 69, 73, 75n
Pye, Lucien, 239

race, and neoconservatism, 98, 99, 100
Raskin, Marcus, 207–9
rational choice theory, 59
rationality
  functional, 149–51
  instrumental, 8, 21, 67, 167
  technical, 18
rationalization, 129–31
Reagan, Ronald, 45, 47, 81, 139, 208, 212
realism, and international theory, 238, 240–1
reductionism, technocratic, 206
referenda, 38–9, 150, 152, 154, 166–7, 180–2
Reimer, Bo, 11, 17–18, 110–24, 251–6,
  257–8
relativism, 245–6

religion
  and conflict, 40
  and identity, 35, 36, 37–9
  and new right, 89, 98, 99, 100–2
  and peace protest, 184–5, 188–92, 194
Rengger, Nick, 19–20, 237–49
Republican party (US), 47
  and conservatism, 95–7
  and neoconservatism, 92, 97, 100–1
Republicanism, 208
revolution, 36, 49
  participatory, 174, 176–7
  and Surrealism, 229, 233
right, new, 10, 20–1, 23–4, 35, 45–7, 74, 81,
  88–91
rights, natural, 209
risk society, 147
Robertson, R. and Lechner, F., 20
Rokeach, Milton, 11, 17, 116
role, as unit of political system, 54, 65–8, 137
Roman Catholic Church, Ireland, 31–2, 37–9
Rorty, Richard, 19, 244, 246, 248
Rose, Richard, 4–5, 41, 52, 57, 58–9
Rosecrance, Richard, 241
Rousseau, Jean-Jacques, 235n
Rustow, D.A., 34, 40
Ryan, Michael, 24

Sabel, C.F., 156
Sahlins, Marshall, 128
Scheuch, E.K., 53
Schmitt, Rüdiger, 6, 21, 174–95
Schumann, Hans-Gerd, 86
Schumpeter, Joseph, 204
Schuster, Jean, 229
secularization, 177, 184–5, 189, 191–2
self, and modernism, 203, 206
service sector, and postmaterialism, 83, 150,
  158, 167, 204–5, 210–11
Shils, E., 54, 68, 76n
Short, Robert, 230, 235n
signs, discourse of, 19, 113, 140–1
Simmel, Georg, 213
Singapore, cultural change, 23
slogans, party political, 138–9
Social Democrat party (Sweden), 150, 152–4
Social Democratic party (SPD, Germany),
  153–4
socialism, and postmaterialism, 21, 22
socialization, 113, 123, 132, 177
  group-specific, 9, 85, 184, 186
  theory, 111
sociology
  of Bell, 200–4, 213–14, 215
  fiscal, 204
  and political culture, 3, 4, 199
  of Weber, 213–14
Sorsa, Kalevi, 142n
Soupault, Philippe, 226, 228
space, social, 117–19, 121, 123, 217
speech, 132–4, 135, 137
stability, political, 4, 36, 40, 47–214
  and civic culture, 32–4, 43, 53–5, 66, 68, 69,
    75n
state
  and economy, 12, 44–5, 84, 88, 205
  national security, 208

Index compiled by Meg Davies (Society of Indexers)

Notes on Contributors

Ian Forbes lectures in Politics at the University of Southampton. He studies Nietzsche, Marx, culture and human nature (*Politics and Human Nature*, edited with S. Smith, Frances Pinter, 1983; 'People or Processes? Freud and Einstein on the Causes of War', *Politics*, 1985), and convened the Socialist Philosophy Group ('Market Socialism: Whose Choice?' (ed.), *Fabian Tract*, 1986). Other interests are feminist theory and Foucault, ethics and power in international society (*International Relations, Political Theory and the Ethics of Intervention*, edited with M. Hoffman, Macmillan, forthcoming) and equal opportunity.

John R. Gibbins studied politics at the universities of London, Durham and Newcastle and now lecturers at Teesside Polytechnic and for the Open University. He is co-founder and has been a reviews editor for the journal, *Theory, Culture and Society* since 1982, and has special interests in the fields of political culture, social policy and modern political theory. Having recently completed a doctoral thesis on 'John Grote, Cambridge University and the Development of Victorian Ideas', he has written an essay on 'Mill, Liberalism, and Progress' for a book on *Victorian Liberalism*, edited by R. Bellamy (Methuen, forthcoming).

Brian Girvin lectures in Modern History and Politics at University College, Cork. His current research interests include a study of conservative politics in liberal democratic societies since 1890, economic nationalism and development, and political culture. He is the editor of *The Transformation of Contemporary Conservatism* (Sage and the European Consortium for Political Research, 1988). His most recent book is *Between Two Worlds: Politics and Economy in Independent Ireland* (Gill and Macmillan, 1989).

Ronald Inglehart is the Professor of Politics and Program Director in the Centre for Political Studies, and Institute for Social Research at the University of Michigan. His book *The Silent Revolution* has directed the contemporary debate on political cultural change and his thesis has been elaborated and defended in numerous subsequent publications. His latest book, *Culture Shift in Advanced Industrial Society* (Princeton University Press) is forthcoming in summer 1989.

Detlef Jahn studied sociology, history and political science at the universities of Duisburg, Edinburgh, and Bielefeld, where he received his Diploma in Sociology (MA) in 1985. Until recently he was a researcher at the European University Institute (Florence). There he was working on 'Trade Unions and Interest Diversity: Challenge and Response of the Swedish and West German Unions in the Debate on Nuclear Energy'. He now lectures in sociology at the University of Paderborn. He is at present also a Guest Researcher in the Department of Political Science at the University of Gothenburg, Sweden.

Michael Minkenberg received his MA in government from Georgetown University, Washington DC, in 1984. He has studied political science at the universities of Heidelberg, Freiburg, Bonn and Cologne before leaving for Georgetown University with a Fulbright scholarship. He is a doctoral candidate at Heidelberg University writing on 'Neoconservatism in the USA: New Conservative Currents in the Content of Social and Cultural Change'. His research interests include political culture, political parties, classical and modern political theory.

Kyösti Pekonen is Associate Professor of Political Science at the University of Jyvaskyla in Finland. He is the chief editor of the journal *Politiikka* published by the Finnish Political Science Association. His research interests are in the fields of modern politics, political symbols and imagery, and political culture.

Bo Reimer is a Research Associate at the Unit of Mass Communication, University of Gothenburg, Sweden. He is currently working on a doctoral thesis on lifestyles and the media. His research interests include popular culture and the sociology of communication and culture.

N.J. Rengger lectures in Politics at the University of Bristol. Until recently he was Research Fellow in the Department of International Politics at the University College of Wales at Aberystwyth. He completed a doctorate in 1987 at the University of Durham on postmodern political theory and has published articles on various aspects of political theory, international theory and international relations. He is currently writing a book on international relations theory with Mark Huffman.

Rüdiger Schmitt is a lecturer in Politics at the University of Heidelberg. His research and teaching interests are in the fields of new social movements, foreign-policy attitudes and electoral studies.

Richard Topf is Senior Lecturer in Politics at the City of London Polytechnic, and Member of Nuffield College, Oxford. His research interests include political culture and participation, policy analysis, and theories of the state. He is a regular contributor to the *British Social Attitudes* series, and currently co-ordinating a comparative study of Britain and West Germany.

Bryan S. Turner is currently Professor of Social Transformation at the State University of Utrecht. Until recently he was a visiting Professor in the Faculty of Sociology at the University of Bielefeld after leaving the Chair of Sociology at the Flinders University, South Australia. His research interests cover a wide field from sociological theory to cultural studies, and philosophy to history. His recent publications include *Equality* (Tavistock), with N. Abercrombie and S. Hill, *Sovereign Individuals of Capitalism* (Allen & Unwin), with R.J. Holton, *Talcott Parsons on Economy and Society* (Routledge & Kegan Paul), *Citizenship and Capitalism* (Sage).